THE OUTSIDER

THE OUTSIDER

A MEMOIR FOR MISFITS

VIR DAS

SIMON ELEMENT
New York   Amsterdam/Antwerp   London
Toronto   Sydney/Melbourne   New Delhi

SIMON ELEMENT

An Imprint of Simon & Schuster, LLC
1230 Avenue of the Americas
New York, NY 10020

Some names and identifying characteristics have been changed. Some dialogue has been re-created.

For more than 100 years, Simon & Schuster has championed authors and the stories they create. By respecting the copyright of an author's intellectual property, you enable Simon & Schuster and the author to continue publishing exceptional books for years to come. We thank you for supporting the author's copyright by purchasing an authorized edition of this book.

No amount of this book may be reproduced or stored in any format, nor may it be uploaded to any website, database, language-learning model, or other repository, retrieval, or artificial intelligence system without express permission. All rights reserved. Inquiries may be directed to Simon & Schuster, 1230 Avenue of the Americas, New York, NY 10020 or permissions@simonandschuster.com.

Copyright © 2025 by Vir Das

All rights reserved, including the right to reproduce this book or portions thereof in any form whatsoever. For information, address Simon Element Subsidiary Rights Department, 1230 Avenue of the Americas, New York, NY 10020.

First Simon Element hardcover edition November 2025

SIMON ELEMENT is a trademark of Simon & Schuster, LLC

Simon & Schuster strongly believes in freedom of expression and stands against censorship in all its forms. For more information, visit BooksBelong.com.

For information about special discounts for bulk purchases, please contact Simon & Schuster Special Sales at 1-866-506-1949 or business@simonandschuster.com.

The Simon & Schuster Speakers Bureau can bring authors to your live event. For more information or to book an event, contact the Simon & Schuster Speakers Bureau at 1-866-248-3049 or visit our website at www.simonspeakers.com.

Interior design by Hope Herr-Cardillo

Manufactured in the United States of America

1 3 5 7 9 10 8 6 4 2

Library of Congress Control Number: 2025939427

ISBN 978-1-6680-6632-4
ISBN 978-1-6680-6633-1 (ebook)

Listen...

I'm not sure you should be reading this book. The only reason to do it is if you're not sure... about ANYTHING.

This is not a success story, it's a search. There isn't a hero in this book, just a fool. All you will find in this book is someone who is lost. It doesn't go in the right order, it's full of distractions, and most of it is random. What I've learned is that life is also full of distractions. This book is about someone in the middle of their life with no answers, just more questions.

If you're a winner, this may not be your book. Just to make sure, after every chapter I have included a story of failure. Call it a short dose of grounding. I hate an arrogant memoir.

This book is for fellow wanderers, complete vagabonds, utter idiots, committed clowns, and lonely people looking to belong. Always looking, never knowing.

If that's you, this book belongs to you.

Here's looking at you.

For my parents, Ranu and Madhur.

See? I FINALLY did some homework.

All of my love.

CONTENTS

INTRODUCTION:	Fuck This Ship	xi
CHAPTER ONE:	Committing to the Bit	1
CHAPTER TWO:	AFRICA: A Montage	23
CHAPTER THREE:	A Teenager Living with Two Saints	39
CHAPTER FOUR:	Fool for Love	55
CHAPTER FIVE:	Go West	79
CHAPTER SIX:	The Mecca of the Midwest	93
CHAPTER SEVEN:	Alabama Detour	111
CHAPTER EIGHT:	Only in Mumbai	133
CHAPTER NINE:	Bollywood Antihero	159
CHAPTER TEN:	The Devil Hands You a Microphone	179
CHAPTER ELEVEN:	A Tale of Two Passports	205
CHAPTER TWELVE:	B.W.D.	221
CHAPTER THIRTEEN:	I NEED YOU TO KNOW ONE MORE THING	241
EPILOGUE		245
ACKNOWLEDGMENTS		253

INTRODUCTION

FUCK THIS SHIP

Vir as a child on vacation in Italy.

Picture, if you will, the most beautiful sunset you have ever seen. Each shade is perfect. It's fading, but it hasn't quite disappeared yet, this blurry ball of orange in the sky that ripples into pink and purple shimmers. Imagine golden clouds over an ocean with water so still it's like god's mirror. There are no Instagram influencers taking selfies, no TikTok trends compelling you to stay glued to your phone. Zero distractions.

The scene is accompanied by tinny dance music blaring from unseen speakers, which is slowly drowned out by the sound of the waves. A luxury ship sails away into the distance, taking the music with it. A lone lifeguard scans the coast. A Mexican man sits at a tiny plastic desk on a pier, checking passports and visas as tourists enter and exit the next ship coming to port. Beside him on the pier, watching all of this, is a young Indian man. He's laughing, thinking: Fuck this sunset. Fuck this beach. Fuck Carnival Cruise Line. Instagram influencers didn't even exist yet, but if they had, he would have said fuck them too, on principle.

That young Indian man is—surprise!—me. I sit on the pier and let the warm water wash over my feet as I sob with laughter. I am looking at the most beautiful thing I have ever seen (the sunset, not the cruise ship), yet I feel completely broken. The tragedy of the situation is so deep, it becomes hilarious. I am bankrupt, hungover, dumped, lost, fired, I have sand in my trousers, and I just want to go home. It is both humorous and sad.

The ship that was supposed to take me home is sailing away, getting smaller with each wave that crashes into its hull. Somehow, despite the fact that I'm stranded in a foreign country, I know that it is going to be okay. If it wasn't, I wouldn't be laughing, right?

If this logic makes zero sense to you, then *your* logic would be correct.

In case you're getting excited that you're about to dive into the pages of a riveting tale about a mysterious ship and the handsome Indian man who's supposed to be on it—chill. Just so we are clear, this book is not *The Da Vinci Code*. There is no murder, no historical saga, very few chase scenes (unless you count multiple instances of me running from malicious boarding school teachers), and no discovery of god. Okay fine, there is *one* discovery of god.

But back to that young man who is laugh-crying/cry-laughing on the beach.

I am in Cozumel, Mexico, one of the most beautiful places in the world, listening to a six-star luxury ship blow its horn as it heads back to the United States with a thousand drunk Indians on board. Sadly, I am not one of those drunk Indians, even though I am supposed to be on the ship.

I am the ship comedian. Or, I *was* the ship comedian.

During the forty-eight whole hours I spent on the ship, it felt weirdly ironic to be part of a group of a thousand Indians planning to invade a Mexican island to blare Hindi music while having a dandiya dance party for six hours dressed head to toe in heavy Indian clothing. I've never seen white, mostly naked tourists look as confused as when they saw an army of naked local brown people dancing next to overly dressed foreign brown people, on the same beach. It was like the global extremities of brown had collided and the Indians had won for a night . . . but then retreated. The retreat makes sense because we're not historically known for our colonizing abilities.

This dance party happens once a year, thanks to a few rich Indians from Texas who rent out a luxury Carnival Cruise Line ship. They change the menu, the staff (to Indian chefs who make legit Indian food), the music, the entertainment—pretty much everything but the captain and the design of the ship. Then they go on a three-day "family" retreat, where old people mingle, matchmake, and pretend that their kids aren't doing drugs and having sex in every corner of the ship that has low lighting.

For the amusement of the young people, this "family" took a punt and decided to hire a young comedian who had just graduated from a small Midwestern college. I had done stand-up comedy exactly *once* before the trip. I said yes not for money but for the alleged "exposure." Of all the "red flag words" a freelancer can hear, "exposure" is the biggest one. NOTHING good comes after that word. The logic is that because Indians are so well networked, if you perform for one group for next to nothing it will lead to word-of-mouth publicity, and therefore more offers to entertain the next group. What they don't tell you is that the word of mouth mentions that you perform for next to nothing. As if performing for a bunch of cruise ship guests would land me an Emmy. I took the ship gig to see something new. To feel something new.

I needed a change because I had spent the last four years hopelessly in love with someone who I'd recently found out was cheating on me. Making a roomful of captive rich people laugh (or really, failing to make them laugh) barely dulled the pain. Nor did bingeing on kulfi at the buffet or dancing with an Indian cougar mom who was struggling to not spill piña colada all over herself.

Unfortunately, I was only becoming more miserable by the day. When we had gotten off the ship for the "Cozumel excursion," I had called my bank from a pay phone (yes, a pay phone) to learn that I was two thousand dollars overdrawn. Now imagine me—scared, heartbroken, and at a loss, literally. My two shows for the one thousand Indians had mostly gone disastrously, with old people scoffing and young people too scared to laugh in front of the uptight elders. I had had sex with a stranger on the ship, and it had NOT gone well. I'd spent my last dollar trying to contact my family, and I couldn't reach them. And then, as I'd attempted to get on the ship to depart, the tiny Mexican man at the desk on the pier had informed me that my I-20 student visa was expiring and because I had technically left American waters, he couldn't let me back on.

I was stuck on an island in Mexico that was the size of a public park in New Delhi. Not one of the hundreds of Indians on the ship tried to save me. Thanks, guys.

I asked the man at immigration what I was supposed to do, and he said, "I don't know, but you have to stay here, outside."

I was twenty-two years old, exactly half my life ago. I was told I had to stay outside the boat, the country, everything.

As I write this, I am forty-four, and I am still outside.

We live in the future, so we all know I eventually made it back to India. But I'll get to that later.

You can probably guess that, aside from *not* being an action-mystery-thriller full of chase scenes, this isn't a story about a man who started a comedy scene in Cozumel and grew to be the most beloved (and only) comedian on the island, his humor being the perfect intersection of local and foreign brown.

Rather, it's about being a perpetual outsider, and finding hope and humor in my alienation and through my failures, which is the story of my life. I've lived between countries and continents; I've played roles that never really fit but always gave me a clue about the cultural mores of each place I was in. I'm a citizen of everywhere and nowhere all at once.

I'm going to tell you about being an Indian child growing up in cultural confusion, in Lagos, Nigeria, and feeling about as African as I did Indian. And later being a kid from Africa, enrolled in an Indian boarding school (slash ex–military academy) where, let's just say, "individuality" was not a high priority. And then being thrown out of said boarding school and making my way to a public school in Noida, in the northern state of Uttar Pradesh, where I was the "English speaker."

My childhood was one of constant transition, relocation, and cultural adaptation. When we left my childhood home in Lagos, I moved from a big, privileged African house to a tiny Indian one, with aging Buddhist grandparents. Later I left Delhi University to go to Knox College in Galesburg, Illinois—the Mecca of civilization, if you've never left the city limits of Galesburg. I had the honor of being their first-ever Indian theater major.

Later, when I helped build the continental Indian comedy scene from scratch (with the help of thousands of handmade flyers), I was the guy from the U.S. in Mumbai. Or was I the guy from Mumbai in the U.S.? The guy from a Western drama school working in Bollywood? Or the guy from Bollywood in Hollywood?

I was all of those things at one point: the Western guy for Indian audiences, the Indian guy for Western audiences. The guy outside.

In these pages, you can follow a line zigzagging across the globe and experience my life of cultural confusion firsthand. We will be bullied, we will fall in love, we will fail (and fail hard), we will fuck up, we will fuck around, we will sell out, we will struggle and get famous, we will get rich and declare bankruptcy, we will get charged up, we will be charged with sedition, and we will be celebrated and canceled and reborn. Thrice. At the end of the chapters, you'll hear about the times I screwed up, said the wrong thing, humiliated myself, and generally did *not* succeed. Sure, I've had successes in my life, and I'm fucking grateful for all of it. But between those successes, there have been many moments that have grounded me and reminded me that I still do not have my shit together. But I'm trying.

Maybe you're reading this book because you know who I am and want to find out more. Maybe you have no clue who I am, and my face looked funny or mildly appealing as you were glancing at the books in the airport. I'm in the middle of my life, on a journey that has no logical end point. I'm not writing as an eighty-year-old who's learned all the life lessons, but as a guy who has done some great things, had some wild experiences, and is always striving to find his place. I'm not writing from a place of glory; I'm writing because I know you can relate.

Let me tell you why you should stick around. The comedian in me knows the first five minutes of the show are the promise, and the rest of it is the prestige. So, I tend to come out onstage and just get honest with the audience about what the show is, and then they can decide whether I lived up to it.

I have spent my entire life feeling like I do not belong. I am still searching for a feeling of home, and I do not have all or really any of the answers yet. Maybe I have a few answers. One or two.

Actually, I've come to the conclusion that the outside IS my home. If you're reading this, maybe it's yours too.

This book is for us, the outsiders.

If you know nothing about me or my story, just know this: Through all of it, I have felt like a boy sitting on a pier, watching a ship he is supposed to be on sail away, with all the dancing cougar moms and horny teenagers in tow. And somehow, I have always managed to notice something beautiful and laugh.

Laughter truly has saved my life.

So let the warm water wash over your feet as you look at the orange sun setting in the sky.

And all together now, let's say: *Fuck this ship*. It's not where we belong.

CHAPTER ONE

COMMITTING TO THE BIT

Vir in The Lawrence School, Sanawar.

When you're a kid, you're supposed to be climbing trees, riding bikes, playing cricket (or baseball, if that's your poison) in the streets, and getting tucked into bed each night by your family. This is what commercials for everything, from Tide to Disneyland, sell us—one big blissful childhood jumping through sprinklers and riding roller coasters. You're not supposed to be sitting on a pile of laundry, alone, two continents away from your parents, crying over a beating you received with a hockey stick, which made a perfectly formed Nike sign on each of your ass cheeks. That image of childhood would not sell a lot of detergent.

Why was I sitting on a pile of laundry, you might wonder. It was the only thing soft enough to sit on, given the state of my rear end after the beating. Let me be clear, this is not a ploy for self-pity. It is too early in the book for that. I can promise you, any pity I earn will be purely unintentional. One of the big things I've learned along the way is that pity carries zero currency unless you're trying to do anything but get laid, and that's usually a one-time thing. No one bangs the person they feel sorry for *a second time*. I don't think there is a single Indian reader who will feel bad for me having a sore ass. For most Indians, ass whoopings are a big part of our childhoods. Americans kneel down to eye level and sternly (but gently) tell a child to "make better choices." Indian parents do a surprise full-body assault with a rubber slipper, so the child stays alert until they are eighty-five years old. My grandfather once legendarily tied my father to a tree and beat him; he then took a break from beating my father to go drink some water. Who hydrates mid–child abuse?

Many Indian kids from my generation had two states of being: high-alert ninja . . . and dead. My parents, however, never hit me, not once. They hired someone else to do it for them.

Welcome to boarding school, where for the past hundred years, young, impressionable Indian children have been thoughtfully molded into raging adult assholes. Perhaps some kids do thrive in this environment (and by "thrive," I mean develop military-level discipline, graduate with top honors, and make millions as deeply repressed surgeons, engineers, or politicians). As a child who enjoyed scaring the hell out of my mother by walking along balconies and railings four stories high, I probably would have benefited from acquiring *some* sense of discipline. I am not condemning *all* boarding schools. They produce many great leaders and successful people who win awards, run countries, and harbor serious anger issues, having internalized the idea that a B+ will equal sudden death. In essence, my theory is that boarding schools produce two types of people: happy conformists and miserable misfits.

If you're reading his book, you already know which one the author is.

My boarding school was called The Lawrence School, Sanawar. To this day, it's beautiful in structure and location, with historic brick buildings covered in lush ivy and surrounded by forests of towering pine and other conifer trees. The school is nestled in the gorgeous Kasauli hills in northern India and spreads over more than one hundred acres. It's probably the most stunning campus you will ever see in your life, a lovely place where, in my time, children were beaten up regularly. It is technically one of the oldest private boarding schools in the world, an ex–military academy founded by Sir Henry Lawrence and his wife, Honoria, more than 175 years ago, back when women were sucked into corsets and a French astronomer named Urbain Le Verrier told everyone there was a planet named Vulcan hanging out next to Mercury (there's not).

The campus includes about thirty grand buildings that look just like *Harry Potter*'s Hogwarts, complete with British architecture and pointy roofs and turrets. There are sweeping views and painstakingly detailed staircases everywhere you look. There are five hockey fields, two swimming pools, tennis courts, soccer fields, and a chapel with stained glass windows.

It was a place for the privileged, the one percenters. My mother attended the school, as did all her siblings and relatives going back several generations, which is why my parents sent my sister, Trisha, and me there when I was only nine years old. We elite children would wake up to the sound of a bugle at 5:30 in the morning, do our physical exercises, march to breakfast, and attend class in the most pristine colonial building you've ever seen. After class, we'd march, literally, military-style, to lunch. We'd have sports in the afternoon, "enjoy" supper and tea in the communal rooms, and be marched back to our architecturally superior dormitories by 7:00 p.m.

The dormitories were basically long hallways. Each was a room that was fifty feet wide and four hundred feet long, with rows of beds on either side along the longer walls, and next to each bed was a tiny locker that held all your belongings. So, at any given time you were surrounded by about fifty boys. If you cried, they could hear you. If you were homesick, they could hear you. If you wet the bed, they would know. I sometimes think back to my first year at that school and remember how many young boys I could hear quietly sobbing because they missed their moms. It also makes you realize crying is kind of contagious. You'd wake up in the middle of the night because someone else's crying woke you up, and then you'd miss your mom too. Plus it'd be dark and kind of cold. Now you're crying in a chorus of eight other boys. God forbid one of you should make the walk over and console even one of the others. You just lie there in the dark, kind of comforted by the fact that at least you're not alone. Some of those scared little boys would go on to become brave little soldiers who marched in lockstep through the campus to breakfast, lunch, and dinner. Some of them, like me, would be thrown out of boarding school by the time they were thirteen.

I'm told Sanawar has recently gotten its act together and is now a safe place for kids to study. Violence is way down! But when I was there, it seemed to me that corporal punishment was considered as vital as oxygen to the success of the school. The rules were simple: It was all about hierarchy. In my mind, it seemed like the teachers and senior students could beat you whenever they wanted to, so that when *you* were a senior student, you could pass on the legacy of violence. It made zero sense to me, even then. I've never wanted to beat someone because I was beaten; it would just remind me of how much I had suffered. I wanted to forget that shit, not explore every angle of it.

I must have had a masochistic streak, because the harder the teachers and seniors hit me, the more I talked back. I still cannot tell you why. I was the kid who wouldn't shut up during a beating. "Does this make you feel better? You feel like a big man?" I'd taunt as they twisted my arm or whipped me with a cane. "Did you skip lunch? That last swing was weak." I think my strategy was to annoy my assailant enough that they realized the beating itself had marginal utility. "What does this even accomplish?" I'd argue as they chased me around the room. My friends would beg me, "If you just shut your mouth, they will leave you alone." Who knew these scared kids were fortune-tellers? I once had a prefect beg me to shut up because even he was exhausted. Until then, I never knew beatings were hard on the beater. I didn't imagine that when my grandfather took that water break while beating my dad he was actually *suffering*. You learn something new every day.

I don't want to lionize my childhood, so here is the truth: I was a bit of a punk, too young and too spoiled for boarding school. Rule following was not in my nature.

When my parents plunked me there at age nine, I resisted it from the very start. I knew from the moment I walked into the dormitory that I needed to escape that place like Indiana Jones needed to escape those craven Indians who ate monkey brains for dinner (for the eight-hundredth time, the only Indians eating monkey brains are serial killers). It just took me five years, a massive lie, and an organ removal to make my escape.

If you can be privileged as a nine-year-old, then yes, I was privileged. If I am being totally honest, given a choice, I would beat up the younger version of me. Happily. I wouldn't even hydrate in the middle. I was a pretty insufferable kid in retrospect. I'd grown up in the expat community in Lagos, a guarded, golden, prosperous little bubble where we were pretty much given everything and appreciated nothing. Trisha was four years older than me, and both of us were pretty hard to impress. I remember we went on a childhood vacation with our parents to Italy, where we flew on Alitalia and ate caviar and drank vodka onboard. We saw the Sistine Chapel and went to Venice, but the whole time we were like, "This is so fucking boring, this sucks. We want to go stay with our grandparents in Delhi . . ." We literally threw a tantrum at the Pope's residence. Once our parents realized priceless artworks were wasted on us, we were sent to Delhi, unaccompanied, on Alitalia first class. We requested extra warm towelettes, of course.

My parents sent my sister to Sanawar when she was thirteen years old. I guess they figured it would be good for us to stick together, which is why I was sent there too, even though I was still young enough to wet the bed, and not because I was drunk. I wet the bed because I was TOO YOUNG TO BE AT BOARDING SCHOOL.

The Lawrence School was like a fancy British academy/bourgeois fantasy sequence, the kind of school every Indian parent dreams of for their child's school-going years. These hopes and dreams rested on the rickety theory that boarding school would toughen us up, teach us community, and induct us into a life of privilege, wealth, and decorum.

I walked into that all-Indian school as the weak, skinny kid with the strange accent who had been living in Africa with his expat family. My dad was working at a trading company in Nigeria, so my cultural whiplash started early in childhood. I was a kid who'd never been in a fight, who spoke more English than Hindi, and who wore baggy plaid button-up shirts matched with a perfect short haircut, all of which made me an outsider. It set the tone for my entire life.

I don't remember much from before I was nine, but I distinctly remember my parents dropping me off at the boarding school dormitory. It was one of the most frightening days of my life. It was late afternoon when the car pulled up to two huge iron gates with a crest reading *Never Give In*. The sun was starting to set over the hills, just like you'd imagine a boarding school looking in the movies. I walked from the parking lot to my dormitory and found my locker and immediately felt resentment. I was too young to even know what that emotion was or how complex an effect it can have on you. I felt supremely pissed about the life that had been taken away from me, instead of feeling lucky or excited about the one that lay ahead.

I remember sitting on the dorm bed when a kid who was from Kolkata walked up and asked me where my shoes were from. They were Reebok Pumps. The 1990s kind where you inflated the sole. I showed him how the pump worked, and he looked at me as if I were this alien thing that was never going to survive here because I was so spoiled, like a lot of other kids at school. But it didn't matter because the next morning we all transformed by having to wear standard boarding school uniforms. Blue cardigan, sky-blue shirt, gray shorts, black Bata leather shoes, knee-high gray woolen socks. One of the few boarding school practices I condone is the fairness that comes with a standard uniform that everyone is forced to wear. It takes away what your dad does, how well connected you are, all your entitlement. The Reebok Pumps just stay in your soul.

I was a dramatic kid. I'm also a dramatic man. Some kids have an imaginary friend. My constant companion was martyrdom. I rarely ever saw my sister on campus, since I was in the younger school made up of grades four and five and she was in the senior school. Each school was on its own hilltop, separated by nearly two miles. When Trisha and I traveled home to our parents for four months each summer, I cried nonstop and told my mom and dad they didn't love me and that they had abandoned me. In one of my finer performances, I sent them a note written in red ink that said, "This is written in my blood because you don't love me." Never mind that my "blood" was clearly manufactured by the Chelpark ink company.

Since I was young, I've loved running away. It was my premier hobby at boarding school. My equally naughty friends, Nikhil and Damandeep, also enjoyed it when I ran away. I had only two friends at boarding school, which tells you all you need to know about my status. Damandeep was a theater kid with an overactive imagination. Nikhil was the smallest kid in our class by a foot. Still one of my six best friends to date, he is now way taller than me. Unlike me, Nikhil never got into trouble. His M.O. was keep your head down and do as they say, but he *always* stood by me when I fucked up. He currently lives in San Jose, California, with his childhood sweetheart whom he married, has the perfect suburban home, and two adorable kids. Sheer goodness in a human being. He's always mildly amused by his crazy, spoiled comedian friend.

Everyone loves an impossible mission, so Nikhil and Damandeep cheered me on every time I escaped, dropping me at the gates, sometimes even slipping me five bucks for the journey. Always with the parting words, "I hope you make it, man!" I tried to run away from the school about three times that first year. My strategies didn't include a way to get from northern India to western Africa, so the escapes never worked out. I guess I wasn't fully committed to the plan. Once I got as far as Kasauli, which was five kilometers (3.1 miles to some of you) away. At that age, it felt as far as Africa. But as usual, I was caught by a teacher and escorted back to school. My only real outlets were my notes home, each little guilt trip a plea for my parents to come and get me. The teachers would give international students envelopes into which we were supposed to place our letters, and we would seal them ourselves before they were sent off. My parents wrote to me occasionally, and we spoke every ten days, but they never acknowledged my desperate "written-in-blood" pleas. Their response was classic for Indian parents at the time: Let's pretend this is not happening. If we show him he's breaking our hearts, he's gonna feel even worse than he does now.

It's sad that it takes some people thirty years or more to realize how tough sending a kid to boarding school can be on the parents, or that they might be barely able to afford the school, but they want a better education for you than they ever had. Or that they don't want you to turn into some Lagos douchebag, since all the signs are showing up pretty early. Or that while you are homesick, they might be kid-sick, meaning, they might miss you. In your mind they are sick of their kid. Which is why they decided to make you miserable.

I WAS miserable. And the thing is, that's normal. You're supposed to be miserable when you get to boarding school. EVERYONE is going through the same thing, even kids with more courage than you. But it's assumed that you will grow out of your misery and integrate, toughen up, learn to obey. What you are not supposed to do is launch a years-long, full-scale revolution.

One of the greatest favors in my boarding school life was done for me by one of my sister's friends. Now, thirteen isn't too old to be homesick either. I'd meet Trisha once a week, on Sundays, and she would give me half her pocket money—ten rupees of her twenty—to ensure I was okay. We wouldn't really talk about what I was going through because there wasn't enough time. Also, I thought the world knew because I had written it all in red Chelpark ink to my parents in glaring literary detail. I remember, one week, I wrote to my parents that I would jump off a cliff if they didn't come get me. Keep in mind, this is a legitimate threat because Sanawar had at least fifty-three great cliffs to offer for prospective suicide. And all of this drama kind of monopolized the conversation in my family to the point where no one was talking about how tough boarding school was for Trisha. My whole life, her struggle has taken a back seat to my drama, causing me to feel terrible guilt. She possesses a kind of quiet grace I admire. She must have spoken about it to her friend, because one Sunday, said friend caught me by the arm in front of my sister and dragged me to the edge of a cliff and said, "You keep fucking telling people you're gonna jump, right? Jump."

Now to recap, this is an eleven-year-old and a fifteen-year-old standing in front of a fifty-foot drop. Not suicide height, but definitely "good for a few broken bones" height. She said it again, "Come on, JUMP!" My sister cried in the background. This utter badass of a friend knew to call my bluff and call out my cowardice. I never threatened to jump again. But as an adult, all I think about is how fucking hilarious it would have been HAD I jumped. The conversation afterward, where she would turn to my sister and say, "Yep. Wasn't bluffing. Respect." It would have been comedy gold.

Despite my suffering, I was blessed with the ever-dependable, quietly hilarious brother from another mother, Nikhil. The guy who now lives in San Jose. He's the strongest, most silent friend I have. Not a big talker, just the possessor of a huge heart. We've bunked class in boarding school, bunked class in college, ridden bikes like maniacs all over Delhi, and gotten our asses whooped together for the better part of three decades. Let's return to that moment of me sitting on that pile of laundry and crying at boarding school. That's the moment we met. We were eleven years old. I had just taken twelve hockey sticks to each ass cheek. Let me explain.

We were now in senior school, which is where you live with kids from grades six to twelve. Here, it was kind of open season on beatings. Prep school is grade four to six. Because it's on a different hill, you're only ever getting into fights with people who are, at most, two years older than you. But in senior school, you meet the big boys. Getting hit on the ass with a hockey stick wasn't something that was alien to any of us. At the time, elders didn't really need a reason for a beatdown. Think about how tiny an eleven-year-old really is, and how much damage a full swing from a seventeen-year-old kid does. It's something we saw every single day: The little kid gets hit, he cries, everyone moves on.

There was one prefect—let's call him Vishal Patel. One day he starts out giving me one, then two, then four, then five smacks. The dormitory gathers around us. I start to make eye contact with Vishal while I cry, and then the word "pussy" comes out of my mouth. I don't know if the guy can even fully hear it through my sobs. I was eleven, so what the hell did I know about pussy? But friends who were there tell me I said it. Vishal hits me with the hockey stick eight, nine times. There are now forty kids watching, and everyone knows this has crossed over into something very wrong. Even the guy holding the hockey stick knows it. I'm actually bleeding through my shorts. Hot blood is streaming onto my gray woolen socks. Vishal can't seem to make eye contact with me. Twelve level-12 hockey lashes. Now about sixty boys are looking on. I finally collapse on the floor and watch him walk away, and some boys immediately pick me up and carry me to my bed, where I black out. We don't go to the hospital because that constitutes tattling. Being a tattler is the quickest way to lose friends in boarding school. Getting the shit kicked out of you is a pretty good way to make one.

Later, Nikhil helped me fold the laundry, listened to me cry, and eventually took me to the on-campus hospital. I remember him looking at me in confusion. "Why wouldn't you just shut the hell up?" Today I see him three times a year in San Jose. He still looks at me with the same confusion. "Vir, why are you still talking?" But to this day, he still listens to me rant. Nikhil's wife, Vidhi, is also one of my closest friends. I have six close friends, which may seem like a lot to some, but they are scattered across the globe. It's friendships like this that help me feel like maybe I belong a tiny bit. Not at boarding school, but just, like, on the planet.

Some pretty horrible things, of various natures, happened to me in boarding school. But that's life. They weren't happening to everyone, and they shouldn't happen to anyone. But I did learn some lessons. Hockey sticks taught me to look a bully in the eye. There comes a point where you and the bully both accept the fact that the beating is going to happen. There is no getting out of this. At that moment, if you can, somehow look the ass whooping in the eye, and proceed to have your ass royally whooped. Perhaps then, the eye contact is more memorable than the whooping. Like a little battle you won for yourself. Solace, if you will.

That was the 1990s, and a few older kids inflicted terrible, frequent, brutal, and scheduled beatings upon us that year. Perhaps another lesson is: Don't make a seventeen-year-old live in a dorm with eleven-year-olds, and then give him complete power. It's going to go bad. And it did go bad. At one point, Vishal beat a kid called Jasbir to the point where his eyes wouldn't open properly in class because they were swollen shut. That night, ten boys who were seventeen years old came into our dorm. They lined us up, especially the four of us who took Vishal's worst beatings. Then Vishal's own classmates beat him in front of the kids he was elected prefect for. The entire dorm, maybe sixty of us, watched in silence as our older prefect was cut down to size by his own peers.

It was kind of a confirmation that goodness and justice exist in the world. Goodness and justice, though, do not feel half as good as revenge. Four of us who took the worst of the beatings all year watched and waited until the night before Vishal graduated school. As he slept, we snuck into his room, put a pillowcase over his head, and beat him until the pillowcase bled. A kid from Africa, a kid from Delhi, two kids from Punjab, beating a young man. It was perhaps the only club I really felt part of in that school. The pillowcase was pistachio colored, and the blood took to it like some weird Rorschach test. I know now that revenge makes you become the thing you hate the most. On that night, I vowed I'd never become a vengeful person.

I have a few good memories from boarding school, like the time I stole food from a teacher's home. It wasn't a long, planned con. It was a spur-of-the-moment thing. As I casually walked past the house of this teacher—yet another guy who had beaten the hell out of us multiple times—I spotted a plate of potato-stuffed parathas. Who the hell leaves parathas on a windowsill? This dude was ASKING to be robbed. This wasn't America in the 1950s with blueberry pies cooling on every windowsill (every single American family did that back then, right?). It wasn't even India in the 1990s. Sanawar was the British empire in the 1860s—lock up your food! Because I am clearly not a strategic thinker, I had no plan for swiping his meal except to break in through a window, grab the parathas, and run as fast as I could. I was in so much trouble all the time at school, I figured I had nothing to lose. What were they going to do, throw me out? I wish! Plus swiping the parathas seemed like a sweet way to get revenge on this guy.

After I ran off, I found some friends, showed them the parathas inside my coat, and we hid in the Khad (basically a hillside full of trees and pine cones) and ate our feast. It was by far my best moment in boarding school. Have you ever eaten food you stole from people you despise? It tastes fucking DELICIOUS.

The teachers at the school were a mixed bag. Perhaps the biggest influence in my early life was a gentleman called Mr. Samuels, an English teacher whose words were so perfectly pronounced, somehow perfectly aged and impeccably English accented, that his speech sounded like Dumbledore fucked Shakespeare. He was an eloquent asshole, and one good thing he did was encourage me to enter the What's the Good Word tournament, which is basically a competitive vocabulary game you perform in front of the whole school. Made sense to place the kid who couldn't shut up on the stage where he never had to shut up. Nicely done, Mr. Samuels.

This is going to sound arrogant (and you know I dislike arrogant memoirs), but if you're looking for humility, maybe there are better books for you out there. The second I walked onto that stage, I knew how to be myself. My only previous stage experience was being a tree in the school play at the Indian Language School in Lagos. I had waved from side to side and silently judged the leads in the play for being average. Sure, school theater productions are usually ninety-minute torture sessions for parents, in which teachers take revenge and make the parents watch the brain rot they have to deal with for six hours a day. But can we at least make good casting choices?

I was pretty good at this game, just like I was good at debating (lots of talking), so finally I found something where I felt like I fit, at least some of the time. That tiny, poorly lit stage became my refuge, the only place where the one thing that caused me so much trouble—my big fat mouth—felt like a superpower. Those moments were magic.

Off the stage, I am socially awkward. I hate a party, and have zero skills when it comes to small talk. I have anxiety most of each day. But put me on a stage and give me a mic? Zero fear. I'm home. That comes from Mr. Samuels and the lessons he taught me. Rehearsing, practicing, performing . . . escaping.

Mr. Samuels was a very good man when he was coaching you, but a very bad man when he was drunk, which was usually every day by 8:00 p.m. We were too young to understand it at the time, but we had a real love-hate thing with the man. He was a good teacher, but if we missed a vocabulary word, we got caned. Lost a debate? Caned. Looked at him funny? Caned. You HAD to get out of his house before the first whiskey, or the cane would find you. The beatings were tough enough, but this man managed to beat you with his words too. I'm still not sure which was scarier.

I'll break your bones and parcel them to your father!
I'll skin your backside and feed you to the wolves!

Yup. The cane was nothing. Words win. When it came to Mr. Samuels, I was operating completely out of fear. The goal was: Don't get caned (which didn't always work, clearly). If I got the words right, he'd be pleased, and my ass would be spared. I could have left debating, but two things made me stick with it: I loved it, and I did not want Mr. Samuels's cane to win.

I heard about one student who graduated, and years later came back specifically to beat the shit out of Mr. Samuels. I understand that kid completely, and if you're reading this, thanks, man.

Once I did flip out after a beating. I guess I'd had enough. Earlier that day, I'd lost a debate and been beaten by a prefect, and now Mr. Samuels was coming after me. I couldn't figure out why, in such a scenic landscape, my backside was such a popular goddamn destination. I was DONE. So on that day, something inside me drove me to grab Mr. Samuels's cane just as he was about to beat my ass. He was as surprised as I was. I had never seen Dumblespeare look so shocked. As soon as I did it, he backed off, which was good, but there was a problem. I quickly realized that the minute I let go of the cane I would be properly, completely, undeniably screwed. So I held on. Wherever Mr. Samuels went, I followed, like a dog chasing his tail. We ran around in circles like this until *he* let go of the cane and proceeded to beat the crap out of me with his hands. Eventually, I dropped the cane and left his house with a limp. This behavior would get a teacher sent straight to prison in America, but I assure you, at my school, it was totally, utterly, legal. It probably led to tenure.

The day of Mr. Samuels's ass whooping was brutal, but it's not what got me kicked out. I didn't hit back, after all; I just tormented him a little bit. At this school, if you got three Headmaster's Cards, you were gone. I got my first card when I was caught in the girls' dormitory talking to Meeta, a beautiful co-ed with whom I was hopelessly in love. Being the purple-assed loser that I was, I had no shot with this girl. She was dating a dude called Aman Jolly. How do you compete with a guy named Jolly? His last name means "happy and cheerful." My last name, Das, means "servant." That didn't stop me from talking to her, though. I was in the girls' dorm delivering a senior's card when I spotted Meeta and her friend Simran. I was talking so quickly and was so focused on my nonexistent game that I didn't even notice that Simran was wearing a bathrobe and holding a shower basket full of shampoo and soap. A bell rang out, signaling that it was bath time in the girls' dorm. Legions of girls in bathrobes flooded the corridor. I was not a girl, nor was I in a robe. A dorm matron spotted me, scolded me, and pulled me by my ear all the way to the headmaster's office, which was about a kilometer and a half away (nearly a mile!), on a totally different hillside. Being dragged up and down steep slopes by your ear is not a vibe.

I got in trouble yet another time because one night, as I smuggled cigarettes and booze across campus, a teacher spotted me and found my contraband, which led to my second Headmaster's Card. The cigarettes were mine, the booze was for a senior. And the third card? The third was probably my finest performance to date, and this coming from the guy who costarred in *Delhi Belly* many years later.

Once a year, Sanawar did hikes and camps. The higher-ups figured, "Maybe the kids who walk six kilometers a day on a hill eighteen hundred meters above sea level need a little more walking and steeper slopes." We'd gone on a two-week hiking trip with some teachers, and during that trip one of my close friends got appendicitis and had to be rushed into surgery. I didn't know what appendicitis was, and I am dyslexic, so I still can't even fully spell it. This kid got to sit in the hospital eating ice cream and reading comics for a week. Seemed like a pretty good deal. He didn't tell me too much about his surgery, so I blame my friend's lack of detail and storytelling prowess for what happened next. When he came back to school after recovering, he lifted up his shirt like a grizzled cowboy in an old Western to show me where they operated. I was like, "Got it, lower right abdomen, cool scar. Cool . . . scar."

A fleeting thought whizzed through my brain: Maybe everyone would stop hitting me if I had a cool scar? Maybe Meeta would talk to me if I had a cool scar? Maybe my parents would take me back to Africa and the good life if I had a cool scar?

And then that fleeting thought got real. One day—I still cannot for the life of me tell you why—I marched into the campus hospital, lifted my shirt, and pointed to the exact spot on my body where my friend had pointed on his.

"My appendix hurts," I told the nurse.

I had no plan, other than knowing that I wanted ice cream and a comic book.

"You're sure it's your appendix?" the nurse asked.

"Totally sure," I said, sounding way too confident for someone who had learned where an appendix was located just a few days earlier.

They took me at my word for some reason, and I stayed in the infirmary for a few days eating ice cream because they either felt sorry for me or thought that vanilla ice cream would settle my stomach. Either they were being overcautious and keeping a watch because the kid who had his appendix ruptured during hikes and camps was under serious threat for a hot minute and they'd got him to the hospital just in time, or they just didn't trust me. I mean, I wouldn't trust me. I guess they didn't rush me to surgery because they wanted to make sure I was truly sick, so I kept complaining of stomach pains, and I kept reading comic books and eating ice cream. My plan was working out?! Apparently, appendicitis is hard to detect, especially in young kids, so they were probably praying I'd hop out of the infirmary cot one day and go back to class. Also, you're up in the bloody mountains in the nineties. This "hospital" is set up for injuries, fevers, colds, and chicken pox at best.

I could have just ended the routine on my own terms, but I didn't. Every day, they would check on me.

"Does it still hurt, Das?"

"Yep. Still hurts."

"Where?"

"Lower right abdomen?"

They'd push down on it. I'd squeal. I'd wince. I'd shift around. Zero training at this point, and I killed that role. I was the De Niro of Sanawar.

I wasn't going to class, I wasn't getting caned. I didn't know if I could keep this up forever, but I was damn well going to try.

"Das? Is it still hurting?"

"Yep. Still hurts."

They'd push down. I'd act like I couldn't breathe. My future as a performer was set.

Dr. Natasha was head of the hospital. Truly one of the sweetest women you could ever meet. Just warm and kind and caring, like a mother to eight hundred kids. I don't remember her face, but I remember a gentle voice and soft hands. I especially remember that voice and those hands on my forehead, waking me up in the middle of the night.

"Vir. Get up."

She called me Vir, not Das. That felt good. But why was she even there? She was never there. Nurses were always there. Something was up.

"Vir, we're taking you to Chandigarh."

Chandigarh was the nearest big city. Where the nearest big hospital was. Unlike De Niro, who would have remained in character to the bitter end, I hesitated.

"You're sure it still hurts, right?"

This is the moment that most kids would probably throw their hands up and yell, "Just kidding!"

I nodded vigorously.

"Yep. Still hurts."

I got out of bed and followed the nice doctor into the dark night. I got into an ambulance with Dr. Natasha at 2:00 a.m., and it was a three-hour drive to Chandigarh. I think she had just wound down for the day dealing with all the fevers and scratches, and got in a car to make sure the Das kid was all right. *Maybe she called Africa? Fuck, did she call Africa?* I had 180 whole minutes to come clean, but instead I just moaned and groaned in fake pain. I had my head on her shoulder, really working the sympathy angle. Also, I missed my mom.

The doctor looked at me and told me I was going to be okay.

After the three-hour ride along bumpy roads ("Ow! My appendix!"), we went into the hospital. I followed the doctor's and nurses' instructions and wound up on an operating table in Santokh Singh Nursing Home in Chandigarh. Two doctors in turbans and masks, which I didn't see again until Covid, peered down at me. Everyone was wearing blue, which was weird because no one was playing cricket (Team India!). As soon as I noticed that Dr. Natasha was not in the room, I started feeling VERY homesick. Whose shoulder could I cry on? In the midst of my panic, I heard the hiss of a gas cylinder being opened. Sort of a *sssssssssssssssssss*, like a snake going to sleep.

"Are you sure it still hurts?" asked the anesthesiologist.

"Yep . . . still hurts."

They put a mask on me, and one of the turbaned doctors said, "Vir, why don't you count to ten."

Sure. Counting to ten is easy. You should see me when I play What's the Good Word.

"One . . . two . . . three . . . four . . . five . . . six . . . seven . . . eight . . . nine . . . ten?"

". . . You're still awake?"

"Yep."

The doctors looked confused. The other turbaned doctor goes, "Okay, count *backwards* from ten."

He was a sly one.

"Ten . . . nine . . . eight . . . seven . . . six . . . five . . . four . . . three . . . two . . . one?"

Both doctors looked very confused.

"Vir, why don't you, um, sing the national anthem?"

So, half-naked on an operating table at Santokh Singh Nursing Home at 5:20 a.m., I started singing the Indian national anthem and passed out halfway through. The anesthesiologist later told me that even though I was flat on my back, I still clenched my fists, straightened my legs, and lay down at full attention before I passed out. For any police or authorities reading this: See, I AM a patriot. Why the doctors actually operated on me even though I had no fever or any other signs of something being wrong is still a mystery to me. Maybe they figured no child would be insane enough to allow someone to cut them open if they weren't actually in excruciating pain. They had never encountered *me* though.

Remember how my parents were far away in Africa, which is why I couldn't ever run away successfully? Turns out it's not that far from

India after all, because when I woke up, my mother, who had flown in from Africa, was sitting in the room, scowling at me. You know the movies where people wake up from surgery and someone cries because the person woke up safe? Yup. Not that movie. She was pissed. Next to her stood Dr. Natasha. Also pissed. One of the surgeons was there too. Yep. Pissed.

Someone *had* called Africa.

"Your appendix wasn't hurting, was it?" my mom asked me.

My lip quivered, and I broke character completely.

"Noooooo!" I started crying, and then my mother started crying. When my dad came to the hospital a day later from Africa, he started crying. It's the only time in my life I've ever seen him cry.

Despite my mom and every doctor and nurse at the hospital being pissed at me, I got a lot of ice cream and comic books, but with a sort of "You're a seriously deranged kid, but you're in pain, so eat up" look.

Another doctor came into the room at one point and showed me my appendix in a jar. He pointed to the slimy, wormlike organ floating around inside.

"Your appendix was fine," said the doctor. And then, just like my mom, he asked, "You lied, didn't you?"

"Yes!"

What else are you gonna say? "Hey, Doc, I'm pretty sure word has gotten around the hospital, I'm pretty sure everyone in the next sector knows I lied. Shit, people in Africa know I lied, so maybe don't let everyone come in here to get their own personalized confession. I faked appendicitis, I'm not on OnlyFans!" Of course, OnlyFans hadn't been invented yet, and in that room I had zero fans.

I cried some more.

All right, let's pause. I know this shit's gotten dark, and I want to give you a silver lining here, which will hopefully erase the disgusting image of my appendix in a jar from your mind.

I was a chronic nail-biter. I'm talking skip lunch, go straight to fingers, all day. When I came out of surgery, I was so weak they had to put IV drips in both of my arms for three days. Since I couldn't really move my fingers to my mouth to chew them, the IVs cured me. I never bit my nails ever again. See? All the lying and manipulating, and even the price of my parents' plane tickets from Africa, were totally worth it.

After I recovered from surgery and from my nail-biting habit, my parents met with the headmaster.

"Mr. and Mrs. Das? We don't think your son is very happy here, and we are thinking maybe he shouldn't come back?"

Thanks, Captain Obvious. This whole thing would've been easier and could've been avoided if we all just believed human blood was red and made by Chelpark. I wasn't kicked out per se, but I was politely asked to never come back. The boarding school version of "It's not you, it's me."

It sounds strange, but I'm grateful I went to boarding school, in *some* ways. It is deeply ironic that someone who tried so desperately to get home because he never fit in has spent the bulk of his life far away from home, not fitting in. I am a stage performer because of Mr. Samuels's cane. Grabbing a mic is a little like grabbing that cane. It's a way to use my voice and fight against whatever society (or whatever drunk teacher) is trying to shut me up. Sanawar taught me that sometimes wonderful places are just imaginary, and that my imagination could be a wonderful place to escape to. It taught me that when you beat my ass, you do not beat me (I mean that metaphorically, because it did hurt like hell). And in a weird, twisted, fucked-up way, it taught me that two people who I'd imagined had abandoned me really did love me and wanted what was best for me.

It also taught me that I could act. If three nurses, Dr. Natasha, two surgeons, and an anesthesiologist bought my act, maybe everyone else would too. It was the culmination of a problem with fibbing, casual lies, that I had. And for the first time it had real-world consequences for my family, and my body. It would take me a long, long time to drop the habit. Ironically, stand-up, which is all about embellishment and fictionalizing the factual, made me a lot more honest than life. But that's for later.

I went to Delhi with my parents to recover, and while I was there I felt horrible, but it was still better than boarding school. About four weeks after my surgery, my dad traveled back to gather the things I'd left at school. Everyone in my dorm had heard I "may not be coming back." When my dad returned, he told me that my locker had been raided, and all my running amounted to a dirty pile on the floor.

"That wasn't the right place for you, Vir."

That was the first time I'd ever heard my dad say what I had known to be true all along. Instead of making me angry, it made me love him more. (I was also so weak from surgery and typhoid fever that I didn't have the energy to be angry.) It also made me realize something extremely important that has followed me throughout my entire life: how important it is to commit to the fucking bit.

A SHORT DOSE OF GROUNDING

Just once, I went onstage at the Comedy Cellar with no underwear on and sat on my own junk. It turns out that high stools, going commando, and performing comedy are not a great combo. I was dizzy and on the verge of passing out, but I got through a fifteen-minute spot with pins and needles in my testicles and static in my eyes. It was actually a good set. Then I walked from the Cellar to the Soho Grand Hotel and iced my nuts.

CHAPTER TWO

AFRICA: A MONTAGE

LEFT: *Vir and his sister, Trisha, in Nigeria.*
RIGHT: *The Das family in Lagos.*

There's a phenomenon in theater called the "second show slump." It's where the first show has gone well, and you're feeling comfortable and loose, and because of this the second show will suck, or at the very least take a dip. That's when you really find out if your shit is any good. Because the second show is where weird shit begins to happen; flaws begin to rise to the surface. I would really like to avoid the infamous slump with this chapter, but I find myself in a bit of a predicament. This chapter is about my childhood.

That being said, let's dive into the slump.

I cannot remember most of my early childhood. I have almost no memories before the age of nine. I have found out with age that this is not normal at all. Most people have wonderful recollections of the first time they were held, the light in the room next to their cot, the song their mother sang them to sleep with, and the exact tone of her soprano voice. I remember very little about who I was, or how I felt, before the age of nine. My family moved to Africa when I was about ten months old. I stayed there full-time till I was nine, the year I went to boarding school. For the first nine years of my life, I retained about nine memories. Some of those memories are in this chapter. Now, in my defense, who gives a fuck about my childhood? You're waiting for the good shit, the fun stories, the crazy gossip from a life spent traveling the world. You don't want to hear about my stuffed toys and afternoon naps, right? Or maybe you do.

If you spoke to my therapist (which you shouldn't, since she's terribly expensive), she would tell you that horrible things began to happen to me after the age of nine. When they began to happen, something in my brain blocked out the earlier version of my life, where I felt safe. This way my new normal didn't seem abnormal. And I am so at peace with the fact that my childhood seems like something alien that I wasn't part of, I write dick jokes, and make an ass of myself trying to give *you* a core memory. That seems like a better use of my time than trying to dig up more of mine.

So here are nine memories. Think of them as that first-act montage in the rom-com you and I are in where we talk about our past. It's great to get to know one another, but we've got two acts to go. We haven't even hooked up yet.

I REMEMBER WHO MY PARENTS WERE.

Gorgeous, young outcasts, full of promise, and desperately in love. You should see photos of them in college together. It's the perfect image of a true love story. My dad, the long-haired lead singer in a rock band who wore plastic pants and smoked weed. The son of a foreign service diplomat. My mother, the beautiful, well-behaved daughter of a railway family, the youngest of four, severely protected, earner of good grades, bright future. She falls for the slacker. Dad went from St. Stephen's College, Delhi (basically India's Oxford), to Talegaon, a small town in Maharashtra, where he worked on a poultry farm. My sister was born there. Then they moved to Dehradun, where I was born. And then they were given an offer to go abroad. Africa is where they were truly free, and away from their families.

It's common for Indian parents to brag about the things they've endured. It's not just common, it's a goddamn birthright. Your birthright? Listening to their hardships (or supposed hardships) is the gateway to their love, and to your inheritance. "We had one room and we all slept on the floor and had no money for fun or utensils or oxygen!" Or, "We only had two pots and one fork for a family of ten!" These stories are even more frustrating when they're true.

When my sister and I were kids, our parents moved to Lagos, Nigeria, having never been abroad. There were jobs there, so Indians were moving to Nigeria to work in food processing or at trading companies, and anything linked to the oil industry. We were complete outsiders, living in a gated community full of other expat families. At first, my parents moved into a one-room house that was paid for by the company that had hired my father, and in that house they did actually sleep on the floor with me and my sister. The bedroom, kitchen, and living room were the same room. When our dad started making money, we had more space *and* we could afford luxuries like beds and a cook and—most important to me—Reebok Pumps.

My parents are the definition of a "started from the bottom, now we're here" success story. When I was a kid, this tale of perseverance didn't resonate the way it does now that I'm a grown man who respects my dad's hard work. I can't imagine what it was like for my parents to take that chance with two kids to move to a new country where they didn't speak the language or understand the culture. What did it mean for my parents, at twenty, to go, "Fuck this scene. There's a place where we can make a better life. We're out." Looking back at it now, I admire them for it. Maybe it even taught me to have the guts to create a better reality when the one you are living isn't cutting it. There have been many times in my life, as you'll learn, where I've been forced to start over, reinvent, figure it out, and make something happen out of thin air. In many ways, watching my parents do this in Africa set the tone for my future.

They'd made it. If you look at their photos from the eighties, you'll see my dad wearing loose, baggy jeans, with a full beard and massive shades. He was always—smoking. My mother got into bright dresses, tried short hair for the first time. She taught at the Indian Language School in Lagos for the first few years they were there, before she went back to college in her late thirties. You can see that they let loose when they were away from India. My mother is the pragmatist, kind of the central rock that holds our extended family together. My father is an ambitious dreamer born for entrepreneurship. His biggest shortcoming is that he is incapable of thinking small.

When I think about my early years in Nigeria, once my father started making money, I think of two words: Casual Privilege. Suddenly they went from sleeping on the floor to being foreigners who lived in a gated compound. Indians in 1980s Africa had cash to burn. They lived large. It was the perfect privileged expat community: trusted by white people and tolerated by Black people, or at least hated *less* than white people by Black locals. My parents and their peers were not old enough to own the businesses, but they were young enough to be directly employed by the guy who did. My dad worked hard to provide for us, and when he wasn't working he and my mother partied their asses off. This was a tiny community of rich, successful, thirty- to forty-something Indians who had escaped their conservative families and found freedom in a place that was too far for the family to visit regularly.

The compound was full of two-car households, with two to three staff members per house, even for just a family of three or four. No one had much to complain about, unless their driver or private cook dropped dead. Looking back, it was a strange existence. Being outsiders, trying to fit in, but staying isolated from the wider world surrounding you. We Indians have this concept called "nazar." It means the evil eye, and because of this belief, we're psychologically programmed to hide our happiness and not act like everything is *too* good at any given moment. The mantra we are taught is "Hide your happiness or you will attract nazar." This sort of famine mindset is a hangover from colonialism. Underplay your joy, hide your pain, pretend to be slightly unhappy your entire life. Enjoy it when no one is watching. Nigeria was the perfect place to be happy and have NO ONE find out about it. Africa is nazar-proof.

We built, we grew, we bonded, and we missed home. My father was in Nigeria for seventeen years, and he woke up every single morning saying he missed home, and that India was the future. He couldn't have been more right. I remember judging him at the time, because to me India represented a boarding school/boxing ring. But it's crazy how that has basically wound up becoming my life too. Traveling across the world, waking up in the morning, going, "Man, I miss home. It's the future."

I REMEMBER ENJOYING THE ESCAPE.

At the very peak of my father's Africa earnings we moved to a party of a town called Ikoyi. This is where the middle class in Lagos lived. We actually had white expat neighbors. And while we couldn't afford to live on the same street as them, we lived in a tiny gated community behind their fancy street called Karamo Close. Karamo Close consisted of four houses and a guard with an AK-47 at the gate because, well, Lagos is unsafe.

In Lagos, we were told that expat kids were valuable collateral for kidnappers lurking outside our gates. Nigeria extricated itself from the British in 1960, so when we were there the country was still figuring itself out. This kind of slow transition is something India went through as well. You go through 250 years of being taught that every rule was created by a white ruler to oppress you, so you have to hustle and find ways to buck the system without getting killed. And then suddenly you're freed and being told that the rules are made by you? That's a big shift, and it takes some getting used to. And until that happens, it's anarchy. So when we lived in Nigeria, we were always taught that we were in danger. Inside our gates it was safe, outside it was anarchy. Our parents felt a hint of fear everywhere we went, which kept us from being able to actually integrate into the community there, which, looking back, may have been by design.

I remember an Indian uncle once telling me, "Don't shake hands with a stranger!" So I said, "Because they might grab me?"

"No," he said. "Some thieves hide razor blades taped to their index fingers. They will hold your hand and threaten to slit your vein if you don't empty your pockets." I was five. The only things I had in my pockets were boogers and lint. Sure enough, though, the next week a newspaper reported that two tourists in a market had their wrists cut. So we were raised with these rules: Never go anywhere without a nanny or a driver, never talk to strangers, and never, ever, ever leave the compound on our own. So I immediately knew I *had* to leave the compound. This instinct would become my M.O. for the rest of my life. Feeling trapped and stifled? TRAVEL! BREAK A BARRIER! GO OUTSIDE YOUR COMFORT ZONE! Even if scary men with razors were (supposedly) lurking.

In the tiny compound with four houses, there was another Indian family, a British businessman who was never there, and one house that kept changing tenants. In our house there were three bedrooms, three bathrooms, a kitchen, and a massive backyard. Or, it felt massive to me as a child. We had a full-time cook named Adamu, who learned to make every Indian dish under the sun; a driver named Anthony; and a butler named Peace. Peace's sister, our nanny, was named Comfort. Yup, I was literally raised in peace and comfort *by* Peace and Comfort. The parents put a basketball hoop in the front parking area, and we had a table tennis setup. Our only friends were the neighbors' kids or the kids at school.

Once in a while we went into Lagos proper, which had crowded markets and a hustle and bustle that I have yet to see another city rival. Do you know what a traffic jam is called in Nigeria? It's called a "Go-Slow," and it's basically like moving through a giant outdoor mall. Everyone has their windows down, and you can buy anything from vegetables to shower curtain rings to DVDs to weed. You can probably buy bitcoin now. Everyone is chatting, music is playing, sellers are walking around in bright colors, there's dancing. Strangely, very little seems to be bought or sold. Nigerians are the only people who can rival Indians when it comes to bargaining. If you ever saw these two nationalities get into a haggling match, your goddamn head would explode. At some point it's not even about the product, it's just pride, and then spite sends you home with a plaster statue of a dolphin you didn't need but wanted to buy at a price that pissed them off.

Nigerians and Indians shared a strange relationship. We prospered, they worked. We both resented the white man equally, and Indians oscillated between having Nigerians' hardworking spirit and exercising white men's dominance. Lagos is one of those strange dichotomies where there are successful people and the people who serve those successful people living very close together. Kind of like Mumbai. Mumbai, however, has the "haves" and the "have-nots." Nigeria has haves, have-nots, have-somes, get-mores, and take-yours. India is not for beginners; Nigeria is for cutthroat professionals. You could feel palpable resentment of your progress from Nigerians and white people alike. It was this ticking time bomb that you couldn't hear within the gates of your AK-47–guarded safe zone.

We spent most of the day in classes for tae kwon do, sitar, tabla, math, Hindi, singing, and other skill sets that every single six-year-old needs to have in case you are ever attacked by classical music vigilantes who want you to solve an equation. And every so often, in the middle of a party, the Indian parents would decide it was time for their kids to perform. Mortified children from various families would do kicks, sing songs, and recite poetry for proud parents. It turned some of us into performers, and some of us went in the complete opposite direction. I still believe my sister could have been a better actor and singer than me, but she went inward and became a writer. She's published three bestselling books now, and she's going to read this one, so I'm terrified.

Some afternoons, when no one was watching, not even the guard with his semiautomatic rifle, I would throw my bike over the boundary wall and crawl under the gate. I'd ride off to a beautiful road called Queens Drive, where white people lived right off a lagoon. Some of their houses had boats and tiny private jetties going out into the water. I knew I had one hour to escape, because everyone who worked for us (and my mom) took an afternoon nap. I'd walk on the jetty and look at the afternoon water as golden light shimmered on the surface. The day was still bright and not yet sullied with the melancholy of evening, and I'd dive into the lagoon. Afternoon is still my favorite time of day. It's the only time of day when, for some reason, I feel like anything is possible. I still do not know how no one, kidnappers or rich folks, noticed a brown boy swimming alone in the lagoon, but it tees up why my parents started thinking about boarding school for me in India once they discovered that I did things like sneak out to the lagoon. Their kid (me!) was breaking rules and possibly setting himself up to get kidnapped for ransom.

> Years later, at the age of thirty-five, I changed my email password. I realized that my password had long been *Queensdrive*. A street I had never lived on, in a country I hadn't seen in more than twenty-three years. It was all because of a few good swims that allowed me to feel free.

I REMEMBER FIGHTING (AND BONDING) WITH TRISHA.

My sister was my closest companion during our time in Africa, but that doesn't mean we always got along. She has been my worst bully and my primary protector in a beautiful way for the majority of my life. She's the voice in my head. She can crumple me with feedback. Her words may have pierced the hardest of any words ever said to me (even more than those of my future boarding school teachers), and yet she's always stepped up to care for me. She's the insider who knew I was on the outside, and because of that, she's always fought for me.

When she wasn't protecting me, I would throw darts at her (once causing the AC unit to explode), and she would behead my G.I. Joes. I burnt her Barbies, and she retaliated by deflating my basketball. But once one of us was under threat, a shift happened. One day when I was maybe six and Trisha was ten, we were standing at the school gate, and I found out that she'd been scratched up by a much bigger girl.

"Which one?" I asked, like a forty-five-pound, unarmed John Wick. "That one?" I pointed to a thirteen-year-old girl who was glaring at my sister. She was the obvious culprit. All Trisha had to do was nod her head, and there I went. I launched myself into the air like a superhero (or so it felt), and I pummeled this much bigger girl. Other kids dragged me off, telling me that I wasn't allowed to hit girls.

"But she hit my sister! Only I can hit my sister!"

Our parents sent us to boarding school because my mom and her whole family went to the school, but also possibly because they sensed something was wrong with their kids. Maybe it was that trip to Italy, where Trisha and I complained about seeing too many historic chapels, and bitched about all the boring water in Venice. Now let's be clear, six and ten are not the ideal ages to take people to Venice. To us at that time, it was a bunch of dirty water and ceilings with paintings of unhappy people. Everything was so old!

Besides being spoiled, another reason we needed to leave Africa while our parents stayed was that we were turning violent. Maybe because we felt cooped up, or maybe because being separated from the people outside our gates was turning us into monsters. I don't know any other way to say it. We had to change nannies every six months because we were such terrors. I'm not proud of this, and Trisha, please forgive me for telling this shameful story from our past, but one day we convinced our driver to play "cops and robbers." We told him it would be a good idea for the robbers (us) to catch the policeman (him) and tie him to a chair. The guy underestimated how good we might be at tying knots. Again, I am older, wiser, and more empathetic now, so I AM NOT proud of this. We tied him up in the chair and threw ice cubes at him. Not a single cube—cubes. We took our time. We watched him look shocked at the first cube, then get really upset, then really struggle to get out of the chair at full force, and then just sit there in disbelief as we still kept throwing cubes.

We weren't playing this "game" because we felt superior to him, or because we hated him. I was a little kid, so at that time, I was a robber and he was a cop. I was way too young to understand class divisions or cultural tensions. I could understand cruelty, but to me, it was as if I were playing with any friend or family member. If anything, I blame my sister. She was older and she should have known better! Truly, we both should have known better. Hierarchies are not healthy, and even though we thought of this man as a playmate (albeit one we were pelting with ice), the structures in place when it came to expats in Africa were obviously not teaching us to be compassionate. The driver was not playing along for fun like we were. He actually looked like he might kill us. If we were not so great at knots, there would've been a murder. He ended up quitting instead of killing us, and I don't blame him at all. If you're reading this, sir, I deeply, deeply apologize. I had not yet learned that all humans are equal and deserve respect.

I REMEMBER A SATELLITE DISH.

It took up half our goddamn yard. Dad had it installed maybe when I was seven or eight, and this meant that we were limited to a local Nigerian station called BOP TV, from Bophuthatswana. For the first time, I saw comedy. Specifically, Black comedy.

I loved *The Cosby Show*, *Sanford and Son*, and *The Fresh Prince of Bel-Air*. Richard Pryor was a favorite of mine even then. It's messed up that a bunch of spoiled Indian expat kids in Africa with their Nigerian staff were watching Will Smith play a Black kid from a rough Philly neighborhood who goes to live with his privileged relatives in Beverly Hills. We grew up knowing about the west, in a preserved time capsule of the east, by parents who had run away. It's this strange set of contradictions that can lead you down a path of either desperately wanting to fit in or realizing you never will. I ended up taking the latter path.

The Cosby Show inspired me to seek out all of Bill Cosby's albums when I got older. Much like the rest of the world, I was devastated to hear about the shithouse fuckbag he wound up being. In my youth, I identified with almost every kid on that show. Then BOP TV would do reruns of Eddie Murphy's *Raw* and *Delirious* and Pryor's specials on the Sunset Strip. These guys were my first exposure to comedy, and it stayed with me.

I didn't know it then, but we were about to lose everything we had. I would never encounter this kind of privilege ever again and was in for some very hard times, and I like to think my early comedy influences prepped me to have a sense of humor about it.

I REMEMBER A *PENTHOUSE*.

A magazine, not an actual penthouse. If you are under twenty-five and reading this, maybe you've never held a magazine in your Gen-Z hands. There was a time when porn was 2-D. It was static on the page and you had to memorize the picture and make the movement happen in your mind.

I vividly remember finding my first porn magazine in my dad's study. Samantha Fox was on the cover. Yes, that Samantha Fox. The gorgeous British pop singer from the 1980s whose songs had names like "Touch Me (I Want Your Body)."

Her picture on the cover of *Penthouse* rocked my insular, gilded cage of a world. I didn't want to lose this precious gift, and I knew I couldn't take it back to school with me, so after I "read" it several times, I carefully wrapped it in layers of plastic, tied it up, and hid it in a drain on the roof of our house.

Keep in mind, this was Africa, where there are monsoons that could easily blow a porno magazine out of the drain and into the lagoon down the street in five seconds flat. I left it in that spot for months, and lucky for me, it was still there, and still dry, when I came back home from boarding school. Also lucky for me, my dad didn't even notice it was gone.

You know how sailors out at sea have to remind themselves in the middle of a storm that a shoreline exists? That somewhere wait sunshine and a drink and the comfort of someone's arms? It gets them through the North Sea or a treacherous storm. Samantha Fox got me through a semester in boarding school. Just the thought that somewhere in a gutter 8,086 kilometers (5,000 miles) away was a porn star in polythene, waiting for me! That *Penthouse* was my North Star.

I REMEMBER SUYA.

Suya is a magical spice that you only find in Nigeria. They put it on skewered beef that you can get at the beach or on the street. If you're ever in Africa, just try it. It will definitely destroy your intestines, but no meat or beef will ever taste as good. Ever. Five years ago I was in Dubai, and I was taken to the high-end steak house Nusr-Et, belonging to the famous chef Salt Bae. We ordered their very best steak, and all I remember thinking is "Bitch, you ain't suya."

I REMEMBER LELE.

Lele is a chicken we made friends with as kids. Lele lived on our father's farm in Ibadan when he was working for a company called Primlaks. We loved vacationing in that area. We'd get to swim in a stream, and there were armadillos and porcupines. In Africa, it felt like every single tree, fruit, vegetable, stream, or flower was triple the size of those same things anywhere else in the world. Do me a favor. If you're ever in Africa, ask someone for a pineapple. You'll see for yourself that it is bigger than most watermelons. African mosquitoes look like they would fuck up any large spider anywhere else on the planet. But back to Lele.

Trisha and I made friends with this massive African chicken on the farm and fed her for a week. The staff thought this was all very amusing. They'd smile and laugh as we ran after Lele in the hot sun, tossing her birdseed. Then on our last day, we were out in the afternoon running around with Lele, and one of the watchmen casually called her over. "Lele, come." That angel of a chicken complied, and he snapped her neck right in front of us. That night at dinner, the farm served Lele while two Indian kids bawled and sulked. I'm not gonna lie, Lele smelled *good*. I wonder if it's bad form to eat a fallen comrade, or if it's like you're honoring them by taking a piece of them with you forever? Preferably a leg.

I REMEMBER LONELINESS.

I didn't return to Lagos again until I was thirty-nine years old. I was there for a corporate show, and I went back to that old compound to see what it looked like all these years later. To me as a kid, it felt massive. I remembered gardens and basketball courts, huge homes and luxury. To me as an adult, it looked fucking tiny. I peered through the gates and wondered how I had made this an entire world in my mind. To me as a thirty-nine-year-old man, it looked . . . quaint. Have you ever taken a walk down memory lane and remembered how lonely you were at a certain moment in time? How out of place you felt there? That's how returning to Lagos, a place where I barely had friends and spent the majority of my time alone, made me feel. It all just felt so far away when I was an adult. This tiny compound in a country across the world where a few Indian families had holed up with all their hopes and dreams. I looked at the roof I used to climb every afternoon, which featured the gutter that had held my first love, Samantha Fox. I visited Queens Drive and parked by the lagoon in front of a fancy house. I took a selfie, and one of the guards from the house came out and talked to my security person, who was a local. The security guy must have said something like "This emotional Indian I've never heard of is having some sort of existential crisis." I was told a Nigerian businessman lived in the house by the lagoon, and that maybe I shouldn't be having an emotional breakdown on his property.

As I watched them have a conversation that I couldn't understand, I remember thinking, "I wonder what would happen if I just broke the rules and dove in?" Instead, I pulled myself together. I finally understood that Lagos will forever be a place that shaped me, even if I didn't truly belong there.

I REMEMBER RUNNING.

For us as Indians in Africa, it felt like we were getting away with something. Prosperity and oppression were close cousins. The country went through the political changes that come with any country trying to reclaim their economy and identity. And then we had to leave. I never felt like we belonged there, but abruptly fleeing a life you've (sort of) gotten used to can be a shock. I know it was a shock for our parents.

Long story short: A Nigerian dictator got shot, a general was instated, and the powers that be decided their country had been exploited for too long. They made life very, very difficult for foreign business owners who wanted to set up shop. My dad had just gone out on his own with his own money, giving up the cushy job working for the big trading company and starting his own little food-processing company. He had put his own money in, all of it. Which is exactly how much he lost. So, we needed to leave.

It's one thing for that to be a purely political sentiment, but the reaction of the public showed us something we had all been missing while being lost in the party. They felt it too, and I get it now. They were probably like, "Get the fuck out. You're making all this money and we're doing all the work!" It felt inherently and systemically unreal and wrong and racist. Looking back, I think me becoming aware of social structures and bias and bullshit in the world started during this period. At the time, I was a cop throwing ice at a robber. As an adult, though, I think about what that guy must have been thinking, and I am ashamed.

For many years, I took our privilege for granted and didn't appreciate how hard my father worked. In a way, Africa felt like a dream sequence, and India was reality. Back to India we went. My parents had six months to get out, so they packed all of their belongings into a twenty-foot container and shipped their lives back to India. Karmically, Indians had it coming in Africa, but it still hurt. The outsiders were cast out, back where they belonged.

I hadn't been back in Africa for a few years when my parents left, since I was studying in Delhi after getting kicked out of boarding school. I remember being in Delhi and taking a long bus ride out to a truck yard full of massive shipping containers. It was about 110 degrees Fahrenheit (about 43 degrees Celcius) outside. One of them held our entire lives. There stood a tiny little container containing seventeen years of my parents' work, sweat, and tears. I still remember the smell when they opened the doors. The scent of packaging meets the smells of Lagos.

It cannot have been easy. To have played every single card right, to have saved, succeeded, uplifted the income level of your family, made your parents proud, and then to have had it all yanked away because you were the wrong person in the wrong nation where you felt right as rain just the week before? I've since been forced to shut down a business I built with my bare hands (coming up later), so I know how devastating losing his business and having to leave must have been for my father, but I've never seen him talk about it without a smile on his face. He never showed how broken he felt. It's one of the things I admire most about him. Losing it all at forty-five, yet determined to survive and start again.

A SHORT DOSE OF GROUNDING

I once went to a meeting with two producers who were casting me as the lead of their film. One of them looked the other dead in the eye and pointed at me and said, "He's good-looking in an ugly kind of way. We will have to surround him with dancers to camouflage him." They then went ahead and did exactly that.

CHAPTER THREE

A TEENAGER LIVING WITH TWO SAINTS

Vir (top row, second from the right) on the Delhi Public School Noida basketball team.

I'm no detective, but I've discovered that the fact that I haven't been settled since I was a child perhaps contributes partly to the fact that I don't currently own a home. As far as the one I rent, I spend about four months of the year in it. I'm used to sleeping in someone else's vibe, accepting their décor, and finding my own little corner inside of *their* world. After boarding school, and when I was a teenager (and at my very worst), I claimed a corner of my grandparents' house and defended it with every single raging hormone I had in my body. Consider this chapter an apology to two dearly departed, generous souls who had no clue what had hit them.

After my appendicitis saga, I got the feeling that everyone was kind of tiptoeing around me. My parents didn't know what to do with a kid who'd voluntarily allowed his perfectly healthy appendix to be removed as an act of rebellion. I think taking me in was my grandfather Baba's way of saying to my dad, "Watch how it's done, son." That's how I went from marching to breakfast like a child soldier to living in a house with two very spiritual, Dalai Lama–esque saints.

In less than two decades, I'd lived in a guarded compound in Africa, a boarding school in the Himalayas, and then finally in Indiana Jones's house in Delhi, if Indiana Jones were an elderly Buddhist leader called Baba. When I was kicked out of boarding school, my grandparents, Baba and Bari Mami, took me in. Which is, by the way, what they did for everyone, throughout their lives. I was accepted at Delhi Public School (DPS) Noida and started attending classes there. My grandfather Baba came from a family of twelve brothers and sisters. My grandmother's family was equally large. There were relatives spread across India, so there was always a niece, a nephew, or a cousin who needed a place to crash, or a room during college, or a place to stay when they were on their way to a smaller city or a bigger country. So, you would think their house was large enough to have rooms for all, right?

Actually, the place I lived in with them was this quaint little home in the trans-Yamuna part of Delhi called Chitra Vihar. Picture a suburb of a suburb of a suburb and then think of the poorer neighborhood right next to that last suburb. That was us. A tiny park that eventually became a parking lot was on one side of the house, and then massive empty lots that were being constructed into something (no one knew what the hell that something was) with a constant layer of rising sand next to them. Desolate, deserted, and hot as hell. Not the best place for a kid to grow up. My closest friend was a thirty-five-minute bike ride away, so my mission became to stay on the school grounds as long as I possibly could to avoid the time suck that was Chitra Vihar.

The house itself was kind of like six different historical eras that went to battle and decided to coexist. There were two rooms on the ground floor—one was mine and one was my grandmother's. Mine was covered in rock posters, hers was adorned with old lady things like an Oil of Olay cream container and two cupboards that smelled like ancient sarees. (There's a particular smell that a cupboard full of sarees, some of them more than sixty years old, emits, like mothballs and generational trauma.) There was a living room on the ground floor that *no one* ever went into because it was like a museum with relics from across the world. Thangka paintings from Bhutan, photographs from Russia, carpets from Lucknow in India, a samurai sword from Japan, two sculptures from London, plus my grandmother's art all over the walls. She was a wonderful artist. She painted mostly Ganeshas and saintly women clad in sarees. I'm sure there's a joke there somewhere, but she's just too talented to parody. Plus, she's my grandmother.

The first floor was my grandfather's domain. He had his own little study with suits and books, and all the artifacts he had collected as ambassador to everywhere. I didn't know it at the time, but those stories and artifacts lit up the part of my brain linked to travel, if there actually is a part of the brain dedicated to wanderlust. I would stare at a Russian painting or a statue from China or cutlery crafted in London and think, "I want to go where these things came from." Each hinted at a new culture or city that I could only imagine, and eventually, imagining wasn't enough. I needed to experience these places.

There was also a TV room. Thank fucking god for the TV room. It's the one place in which we converged. Television time was after 6:00 p.m. Afternoons were just me, a teen boy, alone in this house of relics. My parents were still in Africa (they came back to India when I was fifteen), and my soulmate at the time was our family cook, named Ramesh. I think he was already 132 years old when I got to Delhi. Perhaps I reminded him of his younger self, a teenager who was bored in the afternoons, back when dinosaurs roamed the planet. He taught me how to smoke cigarettes, listened to all my school problems, cooked me lunch, and—most important of all—let me watch MTV when I was supposed to be doing homework. He once told me a particularly graphic story about how his father, also a cook, had poisoned a British army man during the freedom struggle. He said this casually, while preparing my lunch. This moment enlightened me about something very important, which would later come back to me when I was a dishwasher in Chicago: NEVER fuck with the cook.

Here's the thing about Ramesh—he listened (or at least pretended to), and he also never responded. Because of his silence, I had to make a story *extremely* interesting to get a response out of this taciturn man. My stories for Ramesh kind of became afternoon bits. In a way, he was my first audience member, one who paid in food. I have yet to come across a cook as good as he was. One summer holiday I went back to Lagos to see my parents, and when I returned to India, I was informed that Ramesh had retired and gone home to his village. He never said goodbye. No phone call. Nothing. At that time, I was still figuring out how class worked in India, which is to say many people (not just rich people) have "house help," who become like family. They live with us for decades, we educate their children, we enable them to buy land in their hometown, and they stay and tolerate us in the hope that when the time comes, we will do right by them and send them off to relax in retirement. All I knew was that my only real friend was gone, and I would never hear from him again.

Say what you will about boarding school, they kept kids busy in the afternoons with activities or beatings. In Delhi, I was bored out of my fucking skull, and now Ramesh was gone. It was just me and my grandparents.

Before he became a Buddhist, my grandfather worked as a career diplomat. He was a special officer and eventually ambassador to Bhutan. He has the résumé to end all résumés. He started out as a police officer, then became a local diplomat in the Indian Administrative Service, then worked in the Indian embassies in London and Russia, then became the first ever Indian ambassador to Bhutan. He worked with the legendary (and infamous) Prime Minister Indira Gandhi, became the chairman of Air India, and retired as the chairman of the Airports Authority of India. When he retired, the prime minister gave him our highest civilian honor, a Padma Shri, our equivalent of a "Sir" or a medal of freedom, a title of respect that goes before one's name forever. To recap, that's police, politics, foreign service in communist countries and kingdoms, aviation, and airport administration, plus a goddamn knighthood, all in forty years.

Why do I go into such detail about my grandfather's achievements? To give you a sense of how much life he had lived and seen, which, in turn, dictated how empathetic he was with me. I'm a successful/lucky person today, and I try to remember that the more life experiences you gain, the more empathetic you should become. I see too many people hardened by success, chiseled into cynicism. You see it all over Instagram, these "hustlers" preaching hardness. I always think that's a tragedy. When I first arrived at Baba's, I had typhoid and was weak from that and the appendix surgery. Instead of scolding me, Baba showed me sympathy. I arrived feeling judged and ashamed, like a failure. He told me I'd get strong again. He did NOTHING to make sure I would get strong, but he reassured me that it was inevitable. He spent time with me and told me stories from his life. Baba is why I love storytelling. His stories about Russia and Bhutan made me fascinated with the world. The reason I roam so much is because Baba taught me that I didn't have to pick just one country or city to live in. He enriched my young life at the same time that I'm pretty sure I ruined his old age by blaring Nirvana and Guns N' Roses while he and my grandmother were trying to chant.

Oh yeah, the chanting. The rhythmic, relaxing, heavenly, never-ending, infuriating . . . chanting.

At some point in their travels, probably in Bhutan, my grandparents found Buddhism. When I lived with them, they headed up Soka Gakkai, a local society of practicing Buddhists. It's made up of people from different faiths who come together to chant for health, recovery, or community. They chant *Nam-myoho-renge-kyo,* the homage to the Sublime Dharma of the Lotus Sutra, and as they do they create a frequency that is low and raspy and just wonderful. Picture the most relaxing nature sounds, or a white noise machine, or a sleep symphony app that lulls you like a baby. Those do not have shit on six people *Nam-myoho-renge-kyo*ing. The house vibrated, and every piece of cutlery did too. I felt it in every bone of my body, and it put me right to sleep. You know how they say hell is other people? I now believe human beings can also be each other's melatonin.

That low hum of chanting filled the house every day. There were ALWAYS Buddhists there waiting for my grandparents, the way the

British Prime Minister waits for the Queen on a Tuesday. Or is it Thursday? Whichever day, there would be stressed-out people sitting near one of the relics, and I would engage in five minutes of polite conversation with them.

"What grade are you in?"

"What's your favorite area of study?"

"Is that the Salman Khan hairstyle?"

No it's not, lady. I'm not a Bollywood star with a team of hair people. This is a middle part plus a mushroom cut. It was the 1990s! I lived with old people. How was I supposed to know how to style my hair? These neighbors and strangers would come by the house for counsel, and since you usually only seek counsel from wise elders when you're in some sort of crisis, I heard a lot of real-world shit as a young teen. I always wanted to ask the visitors what was wrong with them, but I never did. I (sometimes) knew my limits. But you can feel a crisis in the room. There's an old quote, sometimes attributed to Robin Williams, that says, "Everyone is going through their own battle, so be kind." When you're a kid, life is zero wisdom, ALL energy. I think kids pick up on sadness quicker than most.

It wasn't a huge house, so when there were visitors, there weren't any faraway wings for me to disappear into. Because of that, I listened to everything the visitors said. I heard people telling stories about alcoholism, divorce, death, or money troubles. The house was like a monastery, deep and spiritual, full of people's heartbreak and their desperation to make things right. Maybe it was not the perfect place for a prepubescent misfit who desperately needed to be onstage. Or maybe it was.

Even as an adult who long ago abandoned the mushroom cut, my favorite time of day is 3:30 p.m. I think it started at Chitra Vihar, in this era of my life. My grandparents were usually out doing whatever elders do all day. It was early enough where Ramesh had just given me lunch (before he left), I had a little TV to watch, and all the bullies I hated at school were far away. I knew Baba and Bari Mami would be home soon, and a cup of tea would be made for me and each of the other forty temporary guests in the house. The tragedy-chanting queue had not begun yet. I had a choice of five dusty rooms to eat my lunch in. Afternoon light shone on all the old relics, and I could watch dust particles floating in the sunbeams. At 3:30 p.m. I was still in my school uniform, but my shoes were off and my belt was loose, and I watched MTV in peace. I remember a formative moment, when MTV debuted En Vogue's "Free Your Mind" video, and I decided right then and there that I would have sex with pretty much anyone onscreen. Watching music videos on TV was how I spent that golden time around 3:30 p.m., when the world, or a tiny part of it, belonged to me.

If you had asked my grandmother Bari Mami, she would have told you not *everything* belonged to me. I'm convinced that every successful career diplomat is supported by a spouse who knows how to hold shit down. Diplomats live a luxurious and decorated life, and they retire with almost nothing. That's when the other spouse, the practical one, really takes charge. When Baba retired, Bari Mami counted every single penny that moved through that house. And movement, believe me, was slow. So the bratty grandkid from boarding school moving in was an adjustment for Bari Mami. Boy, oh boy, did we fight, though mainly about one thing . . . air-conditioning.

My grandmother was always doing little things to save money, and the air conditioner was a prime target of her attention. Like every Indian grandparent, she believed that the GDP of our country would quadruple if people just stopped spending all their money on air-conditioning. In her mind, the reason India had not become a global superpower yet was because we had collectively as a nation wasted all our money on air-conditioning. A Delhi summer can get to about 110 degrees Fahrenheit (about 43 Celcius), so cooling off is a luxury and also something that will keep you from dropping dead. But Bari Mami felt that having young blood prevented you from feeling the heat generated by the big ball of fire in the sky. She was wrong.

I had a window AC unit in my room. I am sure every Indian (or New Yorker) can relate when I say that the sound of a window AC is the best sleep device in the world. Second only to fifteen Buddhists chanting away their tragedies. The sound of an AC compressor kicking in while you're already in deep sleep is like the universe, a higher power, reminding you that you're safe and your dream is about to get way cooler. ALL of this went against my grandmother's core ethos, and so, every single morning during the warmer months, she would sneak into my room like a ninja. Soundless and swift, like Bruce Lee in the hall of mirrors, she'd come in at 4:30 a.m. to turn the air conditioner off. So from 4:30 a.m. until 6:00 a.m., when I got up for school, I would wind up lying in a puddle of sweat. It's a weird feeling to wake up in a puddle of liquid that came out of your own body and be instantly mad at someone else for your predicament.

I'd always wake up and turn the AC back on. And when I did, I could hear my grandparents talking in bed. This is the other thing about old people. They wake up early. Baba and Bari Mami would typically wake up at 4:30 a.m., and then they'd stay in bed and chat about the world till 6:00, when one of them organized a cup of tea. You'd hear them discuss their kids, their kids' kids, their finances, their to-do lists, the country, their joints, their pills, the kingdom of Bhutan, geopolitical movements in sub-Saharan Africa, all while staring up at a ceiling in the dark. Maybe that's love. Find yourself someone you can talk to for ninety minutes in the dark with morning breath so that you don't have to say a word to each other for the rest of the day. All after messing with a teenager's body temperature for kicks.

During this time, when I wasn't busy furiously masturbating or blaring "Smells Like Teen Spirit" in my room, I would watch American soap operas with my grandparents at night. Family activities are important bonding rituals, and our ritual was soap operas. Me, two brown grandparents, and some scattered cousins, sitting on a red couch looking at white folks. It felt normal, which was something I had not felt in a very long time. For some reason, we loved *The Bold and the Beautiful* and *Santa Barbara*, the latter of which featured a fictional "supercouple" named Eden Capwell and Cruz Castillo, this gorgeous Latin man who I swear to god looked like he had chest hair on his head. We'd sit and watch these Americans in silence because the novelty of American TV had just entered our lives, and we were basically shell-shocked. Before that, Indian TV would show a Hollywood movie on Thursday nights at 10:40 p.m., or you had to go to the cinema. But here they were, Americans in our living room. We had no frame of reference for how shitty the storylines were, or how bad the acting was, we just knew that Robin Wright, who played Kelly Capwell in *Santa Barbara*, was gorgeous and cut across ALL age-groups. This might be the first time I thought about going to America when I grew up. It was not about academic or career ambitions, it was just: I want to go where Kelly from *Santa Barbara* lives. Thank you, Robin, for the motivation.

Unlike in Africa or at boarding school, I had total freedom at my grandparents' home. There were no gates or guards, no teachers chasing me with hockey sticks. I could wander outside, smoke a cigarette, and wander back inside without anyone beating me. I wasn't great at academics, but I won trophies in debating and basketball, and my grandparents focused on the wins instead of the bad grades. I later realized this was because Baba never did that well in school and he turned out to be a well-adjusted citizen of the world, so he figured I would do okay. At what, none of us knew. Comedy and performing were not part of my plan at that age. Whenever I had to prepare for a debate, I would go to my grandfather, since he was a living, chanting encyclopedia. I would ask him about the ethics of cloning, or the morals of animal testing in labs, and he would light up and say, "Let me tell you a story about Bhutan!" He always came through, and I loved listening to him.

Here's the trick to telling a good story, and I say this as someone who is considered to be good at spinning a tale. You can't tell it—you have to *remember* it. EVEN IF you're telling it, you've got to make it look like you're *remembering* it. That's the Baba magic. When he told you something, you saw him go to a place in his head that you had never been, you saw him see things and people you never knew. You even saw him see things that he didn't tell you about, parts of the story he omitted because you weren't old enough or worldly enough to know. That's why Dave Chappelle is great at telling stories. It's like he's *right there*, wherever the story is. I realize I just compared my grandfather, an old Indian man, to Dave Chappelle. Baba actually seems less cranky than current-day Dave. When I'm onstage, if I'm telling you a story, you don't get eye contact until the punchline. Until then, the story is for me, and then, at the end, the line is for you. Just as it was from Baba, to Vir.

I know I paint Delhi life as if I wasn't really doing anything all day except smoking, talking to elders, and watching soap operas, but this isn't the case. I wasn't doing anything *after* school. At school, I was killing it . . . and dying simultaneously. Debating, dramatics, playing in a band, track, tennis, and basketball were amazing. Every exam I took? Unless it was English, I was failing. The teachers began to recognize that I had talent in certain areas, and they started to forgive the failings because I was bringing the school trophies in debate. Delhi Public School is an insanely competitive academic environment, where teachers are bred to give you a hard time about studying every second of your day, and for some reason with me, they just didn't. As long as I could pass the exam that took me to my next tournament, they were fine. Maybe this wasn't setting me up for success, but it was definitely setting up Delhi Public School Noida for a more competitive reputation. You'd think all of these activities would have brought me some measure of popularity, but I just became the kid who was never there. I cannot tell you how many times a school bus was made to stay back so my debating partner, Ruksh, and I could be sent somewhere across the city to a tournament. Two kids alone in a bus that can hold fifty. If you asked anyone at school, they would say, "Oh, Vir, he's off competing somewhere." It's weird how that line still describes my life.

It took one teacher to set me on that path; her name was Surjeet

Khanna. I've been incredibly blessed to have teachers who fought for me. And I mean REALLY fought for me to get onstage. I'd say she tops them all. No matter how many exams I was failing in, no matter how much I missed my parents, no matter how lonely I was in Chitra Vihar, she would just send me out to debate and compete. She'd say, "You're good at this. Go!" It became my singular focus. My parents didn't come back to India until I was fifteen. During the years with my grandparents, debating is what got me through. By the time my parents got back from Nigeria, Surjeet Khanna had molded me into a performer. In my final year of school, she directed the school play, a production of Shaw's *Arms and the Man*, and cast me in the lead as Captain Bluntschli. I had failed so many exams I was forbidden by my folks from doing any extracurriculars. She fought my own family for me. Ever seen a teacher scream at your mum? The only word that comes out of your mouth is "Bro . . ." We did the production to pretty great reviews that year. This, in an environment where every child was being told to drop everything and focus on their academics in grade twelve. Surjeet Khanna recognized that a child can be dyslexic and unfocused, but talented. May each one of you have a teacher like her.

But back to Chitra Vihar and fourteen-year-old Vir.

Every Sunday, I would talk to my parents on the phone. When they'd ask about my mediocre-to-terrible grades, my grandfather would be like, "But what about the trophies!" I was living in a zone of zero judgment, for the first time in my life. My grandparents didn't mind that my room was plastered with posters of INXS, Nirvana, and the epic Brad Pitt movie *Legends of the Fall*. I also had a random poster of Tom Cruise because . . . why not? And there was music. I loved—I mean fucking loved—music.

If you took a twenty-minute rickshaw ride from the house to Patparganj market, you would find Archies Gallery. It's a shop specifically designed to siphon away pocket money from young kids. They sell plastic roses that play strange songs, greeting cards for every kind of proposal, random teddy bears and cuddly things, and cassettes. Disclaimer: If you do not know what a cassette is, this isn't the place to learn about it, but you should totally google it. Also, I hate you.

Every Friday, Archies would get a new set of English music cassettes. It's where all my money went. From INXS to the Red Hot Chili Peppers, to—yes—even Peter Andre and Mariah Carey. If it was new, I wanted to hear it, and then I'd have Ramesh give it a listen too. I'd spend hours in my room pretending I was a lead singer, holding a hairbrush in my hand like a makeshift mic. By the way, this is still how I rehearse a comedy routine, by walking around the house with a hairbrush, with zero embarrassment. This is because once Bari Mami walked in on me dancing around the room to "Give It Away" with a hairbrush in my hand. I froze in what can best be described as an "ass-out, lips-pouting" pose, and she screamed, "YOU ARE NEVER GOING TO PASS YOUR EXAMS!" Once you've tasted that kind of embarrassment, you're unbreakable.

My love for music as a teenager led to me starting my current five-piece rock band, Alien Chutney. I'm the lead singer and I play the acoustic guitar. We're not playing stadiums, and I'm no Dave Grohl, but we do play college festivals where fifteen thousand kids show up. To this day, playing music is the only time in my life that I feel 100 percent free. When I'm doing stand-up or acting, there's pressure to deliver, to be good. Since I know I'm not great at music, it's purely for the feeling of being onstage, connecting to an audience, and absorbing that energy. It's not like I want to suck onstage playing music, but I can just enjoy it, instead of worrying whether a reporter or a critic is watching. It's a strange energy experience, dancing and playing in front of thousands of people who are also dancing and singing along. It sets you free. Even when you have a deadly, mosquito-borne disease.

Allow me to explain.

In 2013, I tested positive for dengue fever. It's an illness that wrecks your system, so I spent six days in the hospital. Your platelet count drops, which means your body can't fight infections. If your platelet count drops below a certain number, you're supposed to get a blood transfusion, and mine had dropped way below that number. The doctors told my wife, Shivani (spoiler alert: I get married), to start making arrangements for blood donations, and she went out and asked a bunch of comics to donate, which is the absolute worst blood you can give a human being. Luckily, I ended up getting better on my own, so I didn't need any comedian blood in me.

Alien Chutney was supposed to play a big festival called NH7 Weekender ten days after I got out of the hospital. I rested and tried to get my strength up so I could entertain thousands of dancing, screaming people. The day of the show, I dragged myself to the venue and waited backstage as 11,000 people screamed our band's name. It was ten minutes until we were supposed to go on, and the guitarist and drummer went onstage to check their instruments. I stood up to go meet them, and my legs gave out.

For some reason all I could think was "I need to get my shoes off. My shoes are weighing me down. If I get rid of the shoes, I will have legs again!" I was on a LOT of medication. I panicked and asked someone to take my shoes off since I couldn't feel my legs. I drank two Red Bulls and ate four Kit Kat bars to try to wake my body the fuck up. After a few minutes I was able to get my shoes off, drag myself onto the stage, and hold on to the mic stand for support. I ended up singing and dancing on that stage for an hour before our set was over, when I walked backstage and blacked out.

I'm no doctor, but I swear the problem was not the illness ravaging my body but the shoes. I grew up doing my best dancing barefoot, locked in a room. Fuck, if NH7 gave me a hairbrush, I could've done another hour barefoot. Don't believe me? Ask Bari Mami.

Long before Alien Chutney, back in Chitra Vihar, I barely had any friends and no prospect of a girlfriend anywhere in sight. If you saw photos of me as a teenager, you'd realize it was not a good situation. I was awkward and had—no surprise—zero game. I never even attempted to ask a girl out during those mushroom-cut years. It's not as if I was living in a sexy environment. "Come back to my holy home, where my Buddhist grandparents are chanting and neighbors are talking about their gambling addictions!" I think my aura at that time told girls to stay the fuck away.

So because the female population of Delhi didn't know what they were missing, or maybe because they VERY much did, I spent my evenings going to the airport.

While I was living with the saints, my parents were still in Africa, my sister, Trisha, was still in boarding school (she opted to keep her appendix), and we had relatives in Germany and America. People would fly in to visit from all over the world, and they would bring me biscuits or chocolates with labels in different languages. Since my grandparents were getting too old to constantly go to the airport, I happily became the airport greeter in the family. I swear I was there about twice a month. I would go to the visitors' lounge, buy a cup of tea for five rupees, and watch the mass of humanity coming and going. People who looked different, smelled different, dressed different, and carried themselves in ways I'd never seen. I loved it, especially if someone's flight arrived late at night, since that meant I got to sleep in and skip school the next day. I fantasized about being one of the travelers one day. I didn't wander away and hop on a plane by myself, since I still had basketball and debate trophies to win. But I started to sense, during those airport visits in the years I lived with my grandparents, that there were bigger things out there waiting for me. One of those things would be standing completely naked on a stage in Galesburg, Illinois (stay tuned for more on that).

Those teenage years living with my grandparents were the only time in my life that I had a stable, long-term sense of home. They didn't move houses; they didn't even rearrange the furniture. We watched soaps and talked about Bhutan. As an adult, I look back at those years with my grandparents as a magical time. In my career, I'm never really in a place for long at all. Being at Baba and Bari Mama's might have been the only time (since I don't remember much before boarding school) where I knew I wasn't going anywhere, except maybe to the Delhi airport to dream about one day seeing the world. I liken that experience to living in Forrest Gump's mother's house. There were always interesting people passing through, heading to faraway places that inspired Forrest (and Vir) to fantasize about exploring the world and having wild adventures.

It's weird to talk about your formative years in retrospect. It feels like those years are just waiting to be judged, to see if they qualify as a decent childhood or not. My childhood was certainly not normal, but does that mean it was bad? I had Ramesh's food, Bari Mami's AC (sometimes), Baba's stories, American music mixed with Buddhist chanting, and a tiny corner of an overpopulated house. Would it have been any better with just me and two parents? I don't know. Perhaps I don't know any better. Perhaps that's exactly the lesson it taught me.

You're not normal, this is not normal—now deal with it. And head to the airport.

A SHORT DOSE OF GROUNDING

I was a national gymnast when I was in Sanawar in grade six. We went to Cuttack in Odisha from Himachal Pradesh, which was a forty-eight-hour train ride, to compete in the All India Nationals. We came in second to last.

CHAPTER FOUR

FOOL FOR LOVE

Vir and Shivani at their wedding in Sri Lanka.

Close your eyes, take a deep breath. Now, when I give you your mantra, I want you to repeat it to yourself and let it sync with your breath . . . Eventually you will find that you are thinking rhythmically and the mantra will move to the back of your mind.

A fun fact that is not on my résumé, since I'm a comedian and my résumé is basically one promoter telling another promoter that I'm funny, is that I can teach Transcendental Meditation (TM). Well . . . I tried to teach it. Instead of making me relaxed or wise, though, it just made me sleepy. Honestly, I didn't learn it for a noble reason. I only learned TM for the money and the girl. That's something not too many men get to say: I meditated for a girl.

Pretty much anything good or bad in my life, I have done for a girl. I'm an idiot when it comes to love. A pushover, a carpet, a doormat, a hopeless romantic, an impractical fool, and, yes, a Transcendental Meditator. So I can teach you to do TM not because I love a silent repetition of sound. It's because of Aarti, and my undying (at the time) love for her. See, I went from being that kid with the mushroom cut to a guy who convinced girls not only to date him but to enter into actual, committed, long-term relationships with him. And when I'm in love, I'm all in. It's my nature to be 900 percent committed. After spending many years in which my relationship was with a stolen issue of *Penthouse* magazine, I grew up to be a total romantic. I turned into the guy who orchestrated a complex, multipronged marriage proposal that involved four thousand roses, a treasure hunt, and not just a single soufflé but handpicked desserts from ten different restaurants (more on this insanity later).

I love women, and I love being in love. The problem is that I have no idea when I am being hit on, how to hit on someone, how to take charge of a date, how to show women the strong man figure that 99 percent of Instagram videos preach you should show them. I have none of it. I kind of stumbled into sex like you would into a nice restaurant in the West Village in New York. We don't know how we got here, but let's try it. Every single woman I have ever been with has had to make the first move, without exception. Getting up in front of nine thousand people and doing that first joke? Not a problem. But saying one sentence to one person about my romantic intentions is pretty much impossible for me.

I guess this chapter is the tea when it comes to my love life. Let's spill some.

The first girl I ever dated was named Sara. We met when I was in grade twelve and she was in grade eleven. It took me seven months to ask her out. When I eventually did, it was because we were on a school trip and she had fallen sick. I sat down next to her on the bus when she wasn't feeling well and let her put her head on my shoulder, and it eventually landed on my chest when she fell asleep. Guys, do not underestimate the "shoulder to cry on and occasionally vomit on" move. It's very powerful. If your woman has a male friend who shows up a lot when she is sick, get that man the fuck out of your life.

When Sara's clammy, contagious head fell on my lap, I remember every molecule in my body going stiff because I had never had a girl lean on me before. Everything about this bus ride felt magical—the smell of her hair, how she kind of adjusted herself and held tighter when the bus took a turn (thank god for hilly roads). But more than anything, I loved the feeling of being someone else's safety zone. The fact that holding on to me made her feel like she was going to be okay? That felt like the most massive privilege in the world. All I wanted to do was protect her, while secretly wishing she never got better so this moment could continue.

After she recovered, we became boyfriend and girlfriend. When the final bell would ring in school, we would meet outside and hold hands for twelve minutes while we walked to our school buses. This was all the physical contact we ever had, and it was all I could manage. I believe the word "coward" applies here, although in the 1990s we called it "being respectful." Sara was from an orthodox Muslim family. I knew her mother had passed when she was only five and she lived with a very strict father and brother. They didn't know about me, and I was assured that if they found out it would be a massive problem. It's weird how these little realities of the world don't hit you when you're seventeen and in love. Or maybe they don't hit the person they're not a reality for. Sara would have this little sadness in her eyes when she told me about them, as if she knew this relationship was doomed. So for twelve minutes a day I would hold her hand, and our religions and our very different realities wouldn't matter.

Despite the fact that our love was doomed, one day Sara said, "Why don't you ever kiss me?"

We were about thirty feet away from my bus, which was getting ready to leave. I was going to graduate soon. I had my final exams in one week. Both of us were secretly worried about how we were going to continue with me leaving for college and her still being in school here. I fumbled and said something like "I didn't know you wanted me to." She smiled gently and said, "I REALLY want you to."

I said, "Fine, next week I am going to come over to you and kiss you." Sara was leaving to go to her family's house for the summer, which was far from school. I didn't know where they lived, since we never hung out outside of school, and then of course there was the issue of the dad and the brother. But what's reality to a young guy who is about to have his first kiss? I don't know why I needed to wait a week to make this kiss happen. Maybe I needed seven days of prep time, since I'd been fantasizing about kissing her for weeks.

The next week couldn't come soon enough. I lied to my parents and told them I was going to a group study session. I took three buses for over two hours to the Badarpur border to a colony called Charmwood Village, which was sort of a perfect suburbia. It was summer and about 102 degrees Fahrenheit (38.8 degrees Celsius). I carried flowers and a card from Archies Gallery. When we met, we walked around in the heat for a bit until she said, "We have to find a place to hide. Everyone here knows my father."

Charmwood had these apartment buildings with shaded staircases, and we found a staircase in a building far away from hers. We sat down and talked for five hours. Finally, she put her hand on my knee, and then her head on my shoulder. She looked at me like she expected something, and that something was a kiss. Time stopped, as did my lungs, my brain, and my extremely frozen arms. She started to laugh and then pulled me in and kissed me. Then she said, "You look terrified." The kiss must have lasted all of eight seconds, and then I had to go. I spent two hours on a bus home with a giant, stupid smile on my face. I couldn't wait to kiss her again. I planned to go back the next week. At that point I would have climbed Kilimanjaro if it meant I got to kiss her again.

The next day I got a phone call from Sara. She was crying.

"Someone saw us and told my dad. I can't see you again. I can't be with a Hindu boy. He's really upset. He's threatening to pull me out of school."

Fuck.

I don't remember what I said, but there wasn't much of an argument to be had. She had told me this day would come, and her dad did exactly what she had said he would do. I had just graduated, and she had another year left in school. We cried, and she told me to work hard in college.

That night I went out and got drunk with friends. I felt sorry for myself for a long time. My heart was broken. Sara had one of the gentlest smiles I'd ever seen. It was the first time the adult world had slapped me around a little bit, besides those lashes in boarding school, I guess. Now when I think about it, I can't imagine what she went through at home. Maybe today we'd have had a chance at convincing her dad I was an okay guy. Maybe I should've been a man and kissed her sooner. Maybe the Hindu-Muslim divide is too wide for two teenagers to fix.

About fourteen years after I last saw Sara, I was promoting my first Bollywood movie, *Delhi Belly*. It was my first big release as a movie actor, and it kind of made me who I am today. Aamir Khan (an iconic Hindi movie star), Imran Khan (another gigantic Hindi movie star), Kunaal Roy Kapur (a new guy in films then), and I (also a new guy) were sitting on a news set doing a live interview. By this time Kunaal and I had gotten used to not being asked a single question in the one hundred interviews we'd done so far. Then suddenly, one of the two female anchors looked at me live on the news and said, "Vir, when did you come out of your shell? You were so shy in school." My coactors looked at me in shock, since this was the first question I'd gotten during our press tour. I certainly hadn't expected to be asked about my past when in the previous hundred interviews no one seemed to know who the fuck I was. And then the anchor smiled. One of the gentlest smiles I've ever seen. Live, on the evening news, I realized I was sitting in front of my first girlfriend, Sara. Her face had changed, her smile hadn't. I managed some sort of a generic answer: "When I started performing stand-up . . . blah . . . blah . . . blah." When we finished the interview, we immediately hugged each other—to the surprise of my crew and hers. She told me she put herself through journalism school, stood up to her father, and married a Hindu boy who was a journalist. I held her hand and told her how happy I was for her, how I was with someone wonderful too. I didn't see a grown woman in a power suit in an expensive news studio; I just saw a girl in her school uniform. Yup. Should've kissed her sooner.

Despite being a coward in my younger years, I'm with a wonderful person today. Shivani, my wife and copilot on this crazy ride, is this perfect mix of running hot and keeping me cool. It's like god took all the passion he could from seven thousand human beings and put it in her without compromising on any practicality. Her passion is contagious, magnetic. She owns every single room she is in. It's really a marvelous thing to watch. Which I do a lot. Sometimes I will just sit back and watch a room gravitate toward her. We're this huge contradiction, where I'm an awkward introvert who is a magnetic force at work, and she's an amazing extrovert who works with animal welfare organizations and stray dogs, where she could not be more gentle. We're complete opposites, and it has taken me a while to understand that that's what is required for someone like me. I sometimes say that I made a calculated decision when I chose her. But the truth is, I lucked out and stumbled upon her like I always do. This only happened after many years of dating . . . and dating badly.

For a guy who loves to travel and roam, to remain untethered to a single location, and who feels most alive when he's boarding a plane, it's almost miraculous that I love LOVE as much as I do. I'm not just talking about fleeting love, but long-term, committed-relationship love. I love to pack a suitcase and grab my passport, but I also love to go home to Shivani. It's a cliché to say that when you find your person, it feels like finding your true home, but in my case, the cliché is true. My relationship keeps me grounded; it gives me that sense of stability that my grandparents' house in Delhi once gave me. Before I got lucky enough to find someone who would become, in a sense, my home, I had to get smashed on Long Island iced teas, throw up, and make it through what I believe is the worst first date in human history.

This is where Aarti comes in.

It started at a nightclub in Delhi. Picture this: There are flashing blue lights, young people dancing, girls in tight clothes that they're a little uncomfortable in because it's a little too hot and crowded in there, and guys in the one set of "going-out clothes" they have who are also uncomfortable, because drinks are really fucking expensive. I was in my first year of college in India, trying to figure out what to do with my life, and looked like a Backstreet Boy fucked a runaway child. I had a middle parting (still) and a baggy-jeans situation going on. The 1996 song "Return of the Mack" was playing. I'd known Aarti for a while because we played basketball together, and I'd had a crush on her through many dunks and three-pointers. She told every single one of our friends that she wanted me to ask her out, so it became a running joke in our college that I did not have the guts to ask this girl out, even though she made it crystal clear that I would get a YES if I did. That night at the club, I finally gathered the courage to walk up and flirt with her for the first time. When I asked for her number, I didn't pull out a phone or a pen. I was way too cool to *record* her number. My powers of memorization would surely make me seem like a Marvel hero to this girl. Like an Indian Doctor Strange, an all-powerful dude in a Delhi club with a photographic memory. I asked her for her number and just stood there with my arms by my sides.

"Don't you want to write it down?" Aarti wisely asked.

"Nah, just tell it to me."

"Okay. 2752812."

"Cool. I'll call you."

And then I walked off, looking totally smooth and supremely confident in what I'd just done. Secretly my hands were shaking, my legs were shaking, and my memory was . . . blanking? I completely forgot her number three seconds after walking away. I'm dyslexic, so I'm not sure why I thought I could pull off this trick. Instead of heading out of the club and swallowing my pride, I turned around and approached Aarti. Again.

"Hey. Um. I forgot your number. Can you say it one more time?"

This was not a good look, obviously, but she agreed.

"Do you want to write it down this time?"

"No, I got it."

I still refused to write anything down, so I guess my pride was still largely intact. She said the numbers again, and this time when I turned and walked away, I repeated *2752812 . . . 2752812 . . . 2752812* until I could exit the club and lunge for the nearest pen. Think about it from her perspective: A dude asks for your number twice in thirty seconds and then walks away reciting it like it's the answer to a fucking exam question.

It only got worse from there.

I called Aarti and arranged a date. I would take her to—wait for it—TGI Friday's. What can I say? I was a broke college kid, so it's not like I could escort her to a Michelin-star spot with white linen tablecloths and a paupiette of Chilean sea bass. TGI Friday's was as good as it got for me at that time. I put on my best shirt, which was actually a sweater. This might not seem like a strange choice, but it was summertime in Delhi, which means it was eight thousand degrees outside, even at night. I figured Aarti wouldn't even notice. Fifteen minutes before I was set to pick her up, as I was driving to her house, I decided to call her.

"Hello?"

"Hey, it's Vir . . . Remember me?"

"Yes, Vir. We have a date in fifteen minutes."

"Cool. Cool. Just making sure. See you in . . . fifteen minutes."

Now, I had a damn good reason to make that call. A few weeks before, I'd asked another girl out, and when I showed up at her door all dressed up for the date (not in a sweater, mind you), she was wearing denim shorts and a ratty T-shirt, and her hair was in a bun. This wasn't because that was her style, it was because she'd forgotten all about our date.

"I'm sorry, Vir," she had said. "I totally forgot. Can we do it another time?"

"Sure, sure. Cool." I played it off like this happened all the time. I kind of looked away and pointed down her street like I had some business there anyway. *This isn't about you, lady. I was just in the neighborhood running errands and I decided to knock on your door and see if there was any soul-crushing rejection available.*

See. Doormat!

That girl was high all the time, so I just assumed that's why she had completely blanked out on what would have been an epic night with one of the most eligible/eager bachelors in a city of millions. I never went out with the stoner girl, but maybe now you can understand why I felt the need to call Aarti minutes before our date to see if she remembered that I existed? No? Okay, we'll move on.

When I picked Aarti up, she was in a short dress and heels. Thankfully, she was dressed for a date.

"You look lovely," I said.

"Nice sweater," she replied as sweat dripped down my back, neck, and face. I liked this girl.

We walked to my car, and as she started to get in, I realized I should probably be a gentleman and open the door for her. I unfortunately realized this only after I had begun walking to my side of the car. So, to play it cool, I proceeded to walk to my side of the car, and instead of getting inside, I continued walking around the car to her side. Halfway through this I realized I looked fucking idiotic and so I panicked and did ANOTHER circle around the car. It must have looked like I was doing some sort of good-luck ritual stroll before I got in. Again, imagine it from her perspective: This dude who recites her number walks around his car two times before opening her door. Luckily, my circumlocution didn't seem to bother her, so off to the restaurant for giant onion rings and crispy potato wedges we went.

Like a pro, I decided to have two Long Island iced teas with my meal. If you've never had one, just know that there is zero iced tea in it, but to make up for that lack there is plenty of vodka, rum, tequila, gin, triple sec, and a splash of cola and sour mix. I got up to go to the bathroom so many times, I'm sure she thought I had a severe bladder issue. On not one but two of those bathroom stops, I threw up. No big deal though. I ate two mints and returned to the table a new, refreshed, less drunk, and only slightly smelly man.

I don't mean to boast, but this is my book, so why not? I'm charming. Charming enough to overcome numeric recitations, car rituals, and a hint of vomit mixed with spearmint. I just asked her about herself, and really listened despite my two-drink haze. I was funny, and I could tell it was going well because she was laughing. I was also laughing, having a great time, and then . . .

Aarti suggested that we go back to her place after dinner.

Fuck. This was going so well.

"Or we could go to a club, or go see a movie," I said. Remember, I was new(ish) to dating, so the idea of going back to a girl's place seemed scarier than walking into a Turkish prison cell.

"We could," Aarti said. "OR we could go back to my place . . ."

Again, when I am faced with clear interest from a girl, I will absolutely do my best to find a way to sabotage it.

When we got to Aarti's house, she leaned in for a kiss. You know how a girl will let you know when she wants to be kissed? She will look at your lips, and kind of sigh deeply and do a head tilt while every bit of subtext in the universe is screaming MAN UP, MOTHERFUCKER! And what did I do? I bolted into her bedroom. I didn't flee so I could lounge on her bed naked like an Indian Burt Reynolds posing on a bearskin rug (google it if you have no idea what I'm talking about, and thank me or curse me later). I fled because I was freaked out. Undeterred, she followed me into the bedroom, sat on the bed, and gave me a look that very clearly said, "YOU MAY KISS ME NOW." So of course, I leaned away and leapt up again, this time to peer at the wall.

"Look at these photographs you have!" My self-sabotage was on point.

She looked frustrated with me and said: "Vir, is there a problem?"

"What do you mean? I'm just looking at this picture of your great-grandparents here. What could possibly be wrong?"

"Well . . ."

"Okay, look. I've been trying to find a way to kiss you, but I can't find a good segue into the kiss."

Yes, I actually used the word "segue." You didn't think that word could be romantic, did you? Yeah. It isn't.

After that, she kissed me, and clothes started flying off. This was all great, it was amazing, until her mother walked in just as my pants were unzipped. Even though I knew she lived with her parents, I panicked, but Aarti looked totally relaxed. Her mom was squinting in the darkness, trying to see what was happening.

"Mom, I'm fine."

"Okay. Good night."

It was at that moment that I realized she wasn't worried because her mom was half-blind and couldn't see anything without her glasses. Which is why this probably ranks up (or down?) there as one of the worst first dates ever.

We dated for two years. And we fought ALL THE TIME. We were The Couple That Fought. I don't think "toxic" was a word back then for anything other than chemicals and paint, but that was us. Constant cat and mouse, anger and apology, with me being . . . the apologizer. I have apologizing down to a science and an art. I have to; I like fierce women. It's my thing, unfortunately. It ain't easy, it's hugely inconvenient, but my life transacts in passion. Aarti was the beginning of this, and when I finally met Shivani, my wife, I realized that passion could be paired with compassion. Who knew?

Back when I was dating Aarti, she got into Pace University in New York. I was so romantic that I raised my fist to the sky like the hero of a rom-com and declared, "I will follow you to America!" And I did. Put that in your fucking movie. A young man with no money made a promise to a young girl who had money. He moved the earth to move continents, and he showed up in America with zero concept of how large the fucking country was. That she was in New York and he wound up in Illinois was a minor inconvenience.

This is how I ended up in Galesburg, Illinois, which was an epic adventure that you will hear all about in the later pages of this book. Remember when I said I could teach you Transcendental Meditation? Well, it's because my parents had lost everything, and I was broke. In order to get enough money to go to college in America, I needed a job. The Maharishi Institute of Management in Safdarjung, New Delhi, offered up to five thousand dollars a year in scholarship funds for students to complete their meditation course. I went through the training, sacrificed my sanity for love, faked my way through the entire course, got the money, meditated a lot, and FOLLOWED HER TO AMERICA!

What have you done for a girl, huh? Emptied your bank account? Changed cities or jobs? Have you ever recited a mantra for ten hours a day and stared into the void of your soul when you're twenty years old and should be out smoking weed, which you're going to do later anyway?

One thing I didn't think about when it came to this plan was that there were other boys in America. New boys.

I applied to NYU, to Brown, to all the big-name colleges. I actually got into a few, and they wrote back and said, "We would love to have you—we just need money." I applied to Knox College in Illinois because a friend told me they were legendary for giving a lot of aid to students who could not afford school. In June, I got an email from Knox saying that if I could muster up five thousand dollars a year, I could go to America. I sat in front of my computer and cried, for two reasons. First, I had made myself and someone I loved a promise, and I had to come through on going to college, to America.

Second, because five weeks before I got this email, Aarti had cheated on me and told me she was leaving me for another man.

It's not insignificant that every single one of my relationships, including my marriage, has been long-distance at some point. Offstage, I don't have a large personality, but I have a large dream, and if someone is not secure with that, then it's a problem. It's not an easy gig, and I get that. You need someone secure in their own dream. You need a Shivani.

Aarti and I went back and forth like this for a while: her cheating on me, us taking a break, me rebelling.

Part of that rebellion included me dating a stripper in Peoria for a few weeks. I mention this not as a cool story but because of what it taught me. I was taken to a strip club in Peoria for my birthday, and my friends bought me a private lap dance. As you might imagine, I was terrified. I just kind of sat there frozen until the stripper started to laugh and said, "You can put your hands on me, you know?" I did, reluctantly. And for some reason, because I thought it would make it easier, I said, "What's your name?"

"Mercedes."

The dance continued. I said, "No, I mean your real name." We made eye contact and had a real moment because I guess I had just broken protocol. But it seemed to be the only option for me: If I'm going to touch your breasts, I'm sorry but I need something real, like a name. She looked—and I say this with a lot of respect—better than the place she was in. She said, "I don't tell people my real name on the first date, sweets." She actually called me sweets. I liked that. So the next day, I went back. I bought myself a private dance on a Sunday, when the club was a lot slower, and as she sat down, I said, "It's our second date. What's your real name?" She told me, and I'm not telling you. Sorry. That's our secret.

We went out for Cinnabon when she finished her shift, and I woke up the next morning in her house to the sounds of a small child. Mercedes—which was her stripper name because she loved Janis Joplin (*Oh lord, won't you buy me a Mercedes Benz . . .*)—was the mother of a four-year-old. She was putting herself through community college, earning more than a hundred thousand dollars a year in cash, and she was twenty-one, one year younger than I was. I never took my freedom, my youth, my college, or my circumstances for granted ever again. I saw this wonderful, beautiful, intelligent girl doing her best to pull herself out of an immeasurably tough life, which I like to think she did eventually. We dated for about a month, but I just didn't have the money to keep commuting to Peoria at 2:00 a.m., and I knew nothing about real life and kids at the time. She wished me well, and there were no hard feelings. If she's reading this, her kid is probably in college by now. So, Mercedes, you did good!

My next significant relationship was with Swara, whom I'd met long after Aarti and I broke up for the fifteenth time, and after I'd finished college in America. We met while on vacation in Delhi. She had heard I was in a couple that fights a lot, and she had been in one of those too. We clicked.

She was a wonderful, gentle girl who came from a background significantly more privileged than mine. Her father was an Air India pilot, and her family was into aviation. They were serious people who looked a little more serious when their daughter's boyfriend said he was moving to Mumbai to become a VJ and a comedian. More on that soon. To their surprise, this privileged, kind girl said she was moving *with* him. They of course said, "Absolutely not. You can stay with Vir a few nights a week, but you will officially live with your father in Mumbai." So Swara shuttled between Pali Hill, probably the third most expensive area in Mumbai, and my studio, between privilege and struggle, from father to lover, three days a week.

When I say my apartment was small, I mean that if I was lying on the bed, I could touch the TV, the gas stove, the air conditioner, and the bathroom door with my foot. It was one room on the ground floor of Dr. Russell Pinto's house. If I had a fight with my girl, Pinto heard enough to give me advice the next day. The place was a dump, but Swara and I were two twenty-somethings in Mumbai and we just didn't care. Life was good. There was no conflict, no constant fighting, no tumultuous relationship status, just caring and comfort. I think people who come from generational wealth tend to go one of two ways. Either they become callous, or they soften and become kinder for it. Swara never wore it on her sleeve, but you could tell that she didn't sweat life too much, and that allowed her to be empathetic to people who didn't have her background, myself included.

We built this little world for ourselves in a four-kilometer radius in the by-lanes of Bandra. Truly just filled with a lot of love and a lot of kindness. Swara was—and I don't mean this as a knock—a homebody.

Extremely house-proud, extremely nurturing, obsessed with cleanliness, and kind of always making sure people were well fed and taken care of. Our tiny flat became the place people congregated in because she was there, and that meant they would be cared for.

It all made sense. It all fit. And so I decided to propose. It took me a long time to realize you don't propose because it makes sense with someone—you propose because none of it makes sense without them. But the former was my mindset when I started looking for a ring.

Swara had to leave for Rotterdam to get her MBA. It was a two-year program, and I figured we could handle a temporary long-distance engagement. I was starting a regular gig at CNBC in Mumbai as a TV comedian. Money was coming in, I had moved us into a better place, and it was time. *It all made sense.* Propose now, get married when she comes back in twenty-four months.

The thing with some proposals is they can feel performative. I know that sounds ridiculous coming from someone who performs for a living, but there's just something about making a spectacle of love that feels a little inauthentic. At the time, though, I thought I was taking my Archies Gallery game to the next level. I booked the Presidential Suite at the Grand Hyatt hotel. I set up a series of questions and clues that led Swara from a clothing shop, where she was to pick up a dress with her friends, to a salon, where she could get her hair done, to the lobby of the hotel, where she was to take a math quiz consisting of cute questions like:

Multiply the day we met by our age and that's the room number you should come to . . .

Too much? Oh, there's more.

In the suite, I had four thousand roses set up, and not plastic roses that played "Fleur de Lis." And, yes, the roses were insanely expensive. I ordered a dessert from each of her favorite restaurants and had them all set out for her. She took a really long time with the romantic math exam, though, because I remember watching the ice cream melt and thinking, "Fuck!" Anyway, I was twenty-six years old, and I thought this was how you were supposed to pledge your love. When she arrived, I got down on one knee and proposed, and she said yes. We cried, we kissed, we slow-danced to "Saiyyan" sung by Kailash Kher (look it up, great goddamn song). We planned an entire wedding. If you're not familiar with traditional Indian weddings, let me tell you that means we sent invitations to thirteen hundred people. This was not a mellow trip to the justice of the peace with our dog as our only witness. When we met, we were kids. Now, though, we were each pursuing a career, growing into adults, and she was off to Rotterdam to get her MBA. In the end, all the musical greeting cards in India could not have saved us, since she broke up with me from Rotterdam . . . via Skype.

We had outgrown each other. But still . . . fucking Skype?

Have you ever been broken up with via technology? I don't mean by someone you went on a few dates with and didn't even know enough about them to remember what city they were from. I mean have you ever been broken up with via technology by someone you'd given four thousand roses to, and *also* pledged your undying love to? If that's not humiliating enough . . . she *typed* her breakup. We had even booked the venue and the pandit who would officiate the wedding ceremony. We were staring at each other on our laptop screens, the volume was working, and instead of saying the words, she chose to type it.

S: I'm breaking up with you. I cheated.
V: Oh?
S:
V: Well, have a nice life, then.

Once we ended our silent call, I proceeded to get drunk and smash up my apartment. Then I did what any self-respecting person with a bruised, battered, broken heart must do—I rebounded like a madman, dating and going out, all while starting my first movie. It was this weird moment where, a decade later, the universe had set me free. I was free to be ambitious, to be exposed to show business and have the bandwidth to really understand what it meant. So, I threw everything I had into working.

Almost resentful, if I'm being honest. It's like the universe had given me a chance at domesticity and I had fucked it up, so I had this sense that maybe I didn't deserve it anymore. I'd forgotten that I wasn't "normal" and wasn't entitled to normal joys and comforts. I'd lost the girl because I wasn't good enough at normal. The guy she was with probably was. Took me a while to realize it wasn't anyone's fault. She just grew up. We were in a relationship where I was the only one taking chances. Those chances kind of eclipsed her; she'd been protected her whole life and needed to take a few of her own.

Relationship-wise, I was a broken man. A shell. A drunken shadow boxer alone in his apartment. Career-wise, I was the opposite. I had been gaining a following as a comedian and had just been cast in *Delhi Belly*, my first movie role. The movie went on to become a huge international hit, but I spent that entire shoot heartbroken. I still learned my lines, showed up on set, and did the work, but it was rough.

I saw how hard these people worked, how this industry was full of people from small towns who showed up to believe in some sort of magic bigger than themselves. We did eighteen-hour shoots, we busted our asses without knowing if any of this would work out. Making movies is literally making magic out of thin air, running on fumes and pure conviction. I fell in love with the business.

I was a comedian gaining steam who had just been cast in a hot movie. So, I had a little fun. I dated, casually hooked up, found that I liked it, and told myself I would continue having fun. I felt confident as a man for the first time. I also felt wanted for the first time. This was to be extended and enjoyed. This was not to be rushed. I pledged that I WOULD NOT UNDER ANY CIRCUMSTANCES fall for anyone. I would be a dating machine, a lone wolf, a romantic bandit.

A week later, I met Shivani.

I had spent the entire time with Swara saving money for the life we would have when she got back from Rotterdam. For a year while she was away and for two years before in prep, I had spent NOTHING on myself. So, freshly dumped, I got my first-ever nice apartment and went to fucking town. My best friend Sahil showed up and helped me set up the bachelor pad of all bachelor pads: big TV, surround sound, nice rugs, cool art, massive kitchen, stocked bar. This is where the ladies would find out I was a man of substance. This would be a high-traffic area. God only knows the number of women that would come through here! Should I put a "Heathrow" sign on the door?

Then I went and fell in love at my own housewarming party.

Shivani gate-crashed the party. Our friend Kabir brought her over just so we could meet each other. I walked into my kitchen and saw this beautiful, feisty, magnetic, five-foot-two Delhi girl who was owning a conversation and smoking a cigarette. It was game over.

She was an event manager who used to run *Rock Street Journal*, India's equivalent of *Rolling Stone* magazine. She had single-handedly organized concerts for everyone from Megadeth to Herbie Hancock. She had spent a lifetime around rockers and artists and wasn't fazed by any of them. She knew what it took to be an artist, and the kind of work it took to make them shine. Like I said, game over.

She was from Delhi like me, didn't fully lose herself to Mumbai like me, valued family but didn't always see eye to eye with them, a lot like me. She had escaped the house and fled to London for a boy who broke her heart, her family did not understand her choices, and her career was entirely self-made. Game over.

She listened to hard rock music, smoked Classic Ultra Milds, and loved to dance. Game fucking over.

I went to Kabir's house the next day and took her out. After a night spent talking and beating around the bush, I looked at her and said, "I wanna kiss you . . ." So *she* leaned in and kissed *me*.

She had just had her heart ripped open by the boy in London, and our friends were like, "Please do not fall in love with each other. Just bang and move on." I think they figured we were both so messed up from our breakups that it would be a disaster if one of us fell for the other. We took their advice to heart and just casually hooked up for two months, both of us stating that we did not have an emotional connection, it was only surface, we felt nothing—all the bullshit you tell yourself when you actually are falling in love and terrified about what that means. Still, neither of us put pressure on the other, so we were able to just get to know each other and have a good time. She'd come over after work and roll me a joint, and then we'd go up to the terrace of the building and get high and look at the stars and talk for hours. I'd show her my writing, she'd show me hers. We'd get high and order Baskin-Robbins Bavarian Chocolate ice cream. And she'd stay the night.

I'd go off and shoot the movie. Also, because of the movie, I had to completely shave my head. Gotta hand it to her. She slept with a cute boy with nice hair, and the next day he showed up bald and stayed that way for five months.

We never really had the "are we exclusive?" conversation. We would go on dates with other people, which was totally cool with both of us ... until it wasn't.

While hooking up with Shivani, I had gone on a few dates with an Iranian lingerie model. No, that's not a typo. Me, Vir Das, the sweater-clad kid who puked at TGI Friday's, was going on a third date with a model. Not a hand or foot model, but an ex–lingerie model, who was going to be launched in Bollywood soon. We met at a film slate announcement. Now keep in mind this was someone whose whole body (not just an appendage) was seen as some sort of otherworldly gift to mankind. Now, there is a certain type of self-assured, confident man who is able to date people in this upper echelon of biology. I've looked in the mirror and at my bank account. I am not that man. You can't have impostor syndrome on a date. I had it written all over my face. One night I took this model to Club Zenzi, located in Bandra, Mumbai, and after we'd gotten our drinks and sat down, I spotted Shivani there with another guy. I saw him put his hand on her shoulder. Maybe he was just asking her what she wanted to drink. He was a nice guy who I actually knew, and now wanted to brutally murder. I went from being oblivious to my feelings for Shivani to feeling a fuck of a lot of things. When the model and I finished our drinks, I left the club, dropped the model at her house, and immediately texted Shivani:

I will be at your door in twenty minutes . . .

If you think this is the Hallmark movie ending right here, the one where I show up at her door and we fall into each other's arms and declare our love . . . think again. Yes, we hooked up that night. Yes, we continued to have fun and hang out, but it was becoming harder to pretend we didn't have feelings. Being two strong-willed people, we still tried every form of denial that two humans could conceive of. While this dance of denial was happening, Swara reached out to me from Rotterdam saying she was sorry, and that she wanted to work things out. We'd canceled a wedding, she'd cheated on me and torn my heart apart via Skype, but sure! Why not work it out? That seemed like a good choice.

So, like an idiot, I bought a ticket to Delhi, where Swara was now living, and told Shivani about it. Instead of freaking out, Shivani responded, "Cool. Good luck with it."

I told you, we were committed to our vows of pretending not to have deep feelings for each other.

"Good luck with it. I just want you to be happy." I had never had someone care for me enough to let me go in order to put my happiness above their own. You could tell she was heartbroken, but she's the strongest person I've ever met, so she didn't show it. This is a person who, like me, has been fighting against everything from family expectations to schools to society since she was seven years old. We won't give you the satisfaction of seeing us crumble.

When we said goodbye, Shivani just kissed me, hugged me, and told me I deserved the world. And then she handed me a book that she'd contributed a chapter to, and that chapter was all about what she perceived love to be, how it felt to her, what it meant. She said it was a parting gift, and that I should wait until I was on the plane to read it. It was a book about the idea of love, with seven female authors talking about their damage, their trauma, their desires, and the kind of love they wished for. She said, "If you're going to get back with her, I think these stories are the kind of love you deserve. Make sure she gives it to you."

I boarded the airplane with her book tucked under my arm.

The flight took off into the sky, heading toward Delhi. I started to read how this woman described love. This woman whom I had spent four months dancing, laughing, talking, smoking, and growing with. This woman who wasn't perfect, but who wasn't hiding her scars. This woman who knew what it was to be passionate about art. This woman who does it all by herself and tells herself she needs no one, needs . . . me? This woman who owns the room.

She described love and hurt better than I have ever seen it described. I sat there on this plane headed to Swara, and it was like I understood what love was supposed to be for the first time.

I was in love with this woman. The one I'd sworn I had no real feelings for. The casual hookup. The woman who'd said, "Good luck with it," when I told her I was leaving to get back together with my ex-fiancée.

Fuck.

The plane landed in Delhi. Keep in mind this was not a quick forty-five-minute flight. This was two and a half hours on an airplane. Two hours to drive to her house. Enough hours for me to agonize over what I was doing, and feel terrified about where I was headed, knowing that my home wasn't settling with Swara. It was a crazy adventure, with Shivani. I told Swara what had happened. I told her I was in love with someone else.

I got on the first flight back to Mumbai. When I saw Shivani, all those attempts to tamp down my emotions were obliterated. It was intense. It was terrifying. It felt like home.

I told her I'd read what she'd written in the book. I told her I loved her. I told her, "It's you and me." She burst out crying. She'd said goodbye to me ten hours ago. It was 3:00 a.m., I was on her balcony, and I wasn't going anywhere. There were purple fairy lights that she'd put up twinkling, and we lay down on cushions on the balcony and held each other. Some music trickled in from the bedroom. Mumbai was silent, and so were we.

I know it sounds like a movie. But it isn't. It wasn't. It didn't feel dramatic or performative. It just felt right.

She gives kindness without indulgence. She gives sympathy without weakness. She tells me I'm meant for greatness and then tells me to walk the dog. I make her believe that anything is possible. I show her that a hard life can make a soft existence. We love, work, fight, and live passionately.

Neither one of us has a domestic bone in our body. We would fuck up toast if you let us. Our house is a collection of many items from lives well lived, in a disorganized mess. We're a mess. But we've seen the world more than most and lived more stories than ten books can fit. We're all in, all the time.

I have a tremendous amount of respect for the women I have loved, but I am in awe of Shivani. She's the first one I really admired. I look at her sometimes and just think, "Fuck. Look at what she's been through. Look at what she became. What a force."

Shivani lost her mother when she was eight, grew up in a house with a very complicated dynamic and a father working his butt off to raise two girls. I left home when I was nine. Neither one of us has known normalcy in family, and the little we have, we have found in each other. I am proud to say, whatever we are, we are self-made, together.

I didn't get her four thousand roses and multiple desserts when I proposed. I actually proposed to the love of my life on the way to our wedding. Meaning, we just decided to get married one day, she picked a ring, and that was it. In the car on the way to the airport, as we were about to fly to Sri Lanka to get married on a beach in front of eighty of our closest friends and family, I said, "Wait? Should I formally propose? Will you marry me?"

"I think I kind of have to at this point," she said. And it was more romantic than any grand gesture could ever be.

Our wedding was a gathering of artists, deviants, rockers, and parents who were told to put their phones away for seventy-two hours on a tiny beach in Sri Lanka. At some point we kicked the local wedding band offstage and the rockers took over. I gotta say, it was the most professionally managed event I had ever been to. Shivani handled it all. Treated it like a Megadeth concert. It ran like clockwork. We agreed on no gifts and tried to pay for most of the wedding ourselves.

I wrote her a song. I sang it barefoot, because we were on a beach.

Ten years later, I'm still uncomfortable writing about it and her. None of it is normal, but she's my normal. I feel protective of that story.

My work life is so much about being loud and audacious and not chill, and I've learned that my personal life is much better without all that noise. We're together, but we're also each on our own journey, and it works for us. Not everyone could stay with a guy who is flying from India to America, Australia, and Europe, sometimes within the span of a week. I do know that on my deathbed, I probably won't be saying, "Oh man, that gig at the Sydney Opera House was amazing!" I'm pretty sure what I'll be thinking about are all the trips I made home, and the person who was there waiting for me.

A SHORT DOSE OF GROUNDING

Mr. Amitabh Bachchan is one of the biggest Indian superstars to ever walk the planet. He's kind of like our Pacino, De Niro, Streep, Olivier, and Denzel all in one. He once saw me perform at an awards ceremony and came up to me and said, "You were funny on that stage." I was so nervous to be in front of Amitabh Bachchan, who, by the way, is six foot two but feels like he's eleven foot nine. I looked him dead in the eye and blurted out, "I agree!" I agree? I *agree*? Then he walked away before I could say anything else, and I didn't sleep for five days.

He hosts a show called *Kaun Banega Crorepati*, which is our version of *Who Wants to Be a Millionaire*. In one episode, there was a question about comedians winning Emmy awards, and my name was the right answer. *He said my name.* I teared up. Mr. Bachchan said my name on *KBC*. By the way, he says five thousand names a week on the show. But if you're Indian, you know what that means to you. If you're not, it feels like Dylan wrote a song about you. I replayed it on my TV and recorded it with my phone.

CHAPTER FIVE

GO WEST

Vir on stage at Carnegie Hall.

All I really knew about America was what I learned from U.S. soap operas and other shows, and from that, I knew I'd like to go there one day. I didn't know *why* I would like to go. I didn't know *where* I would like to go. What I also did not know was that America is *a lot*. A lot of *Real Housewives*, blond comb-overs, rap beefs, extra-large, more sugar, 60 percent off, 789 easy payments, grade A, rotten tomatoes, grass-fed, farm-to-table, two party, 5G, aerial drone, Cybertruck, Russian bots on dating apps . . . It's madness.

But when I first went to America, it represented one thing and one thing alone: a promise.

The promise of America. In most countries outside of the U.S., you are conditioned through years of family stories and pop culture to believe that when you show up and do the work, you'll be able to make a choice about who you are going to be. It's just assumed that anyone not in America wants to go to America. You may not become a huge success there, but you can go to sleep knowing that on some level, it's going to be all right. The lights will stay on, the ambulance will come, the bridges will work, the vending machine will spit out the chocolate bar.

I came to America because of a promise. Not a promise of big dreams and stocked vending machines though. It was because of that promise I had made to Aarti. I pledged I would come to America for her, and I delivered.

Every molecule in my body was happy for her that she was going to Pace University, and also heartbroken. So one day, while we smoked in a small café outside Sri Venkateswara College in Delhi University's South Campus (when we should have been in class), I said, "I'll follow you. Wait for me." She kissed me, even though I'm sure she knew my plan was unrealistic.

I'd already been disappointed about America before, when I'd learned I couldn't afford college there. I had gotten through Delhi Public School Noida telling myself I was on my way to Brown or NYU or some cool place that I had seen in a movie. This was my personal "Tim Robbins from *The Shawshank Redemption*" promise to myself: Focus on the escape.

When I was seventeen, my father sat me down and told me we didn't have the money for college. In his defense, I should've guessed. We were living in a massive house, which we'd built when they were rich, with only enough furniture for two of the five rooms. My father packed it all up and came back to India to work. He'd gone from driving a Mercedes to a Maruti 800, which is basically a roller skate with an engine, and then slowly, gracefully, silently, he built himself back up to a fancy car. We hadn't taken a summer holiday in forever, not even to a neighboring town. We were slowly selling some of the items we had brought back from Africa for money. My mother, whom I had never seen set foot in a kitchen during the first fifteen years of my life, was cooking for us.

I didn't notice we were struggling for two reasons. First, I was completely lost in the women in my life. I was producing enough testosterone to kill a forty-year-old man. I was deeply and blindly in love. My days revolved around getting to college, spending the afternoons with Aarti, playing basketball in the evenings, and saying a quick hello to my parents before either passing out or heading out.

My sister, Trisha, who has always been my reality check, was making documentaries with my mother. And if I'm being honest, we weren't getting along as a family. My parents had shown up in my life again when I was fifteen, and by this time I kind of was who I was going to be for the next ten years. They got to show up and say, "You kind of turned into an asshole." And I got to say, "Well, you just turned up. I've been building myself *by* myself since I was nine years old. So maybe let's all get along until I go to NYU, and I'll be out of your hair."

They were right. I was a right asshole. In my defense, name a hormonal seventeen-year-old that isn't.

Starting at the age of thirteen, I'd been told I would get to go to college. And it was the one thing that had gotten me through the muck and given me hope. I came to feel like I was *owed* college because of what I had been through, and to me, college meant going to the U.S.

So on the day my father looked at me kindly and said, "We don't have the money. You're going to college in Delhi," something in me just caved. It was like there was no justice in the world. From that moment, any interaction I had with my parents was at arm's length and with distrust. Me, the hormonal victim. I was fed a dream, and then, like the world's most depressing magic trick, it disappeared.

Believe me, I am fully conscious of how spoiled I sound.

It took me more than a decade from that day to really see my parents and appreciate what they went through and how unfair my reactions and hostility must have seemed. How judged they must have felt for having a tough go of it. The main reason I just assumed this dream of America would happen was because my father hid any suffering or struggle. It's the thing I envy and admire most about that man. He has the ability to be good-natured and warm in the face of any kind of adversity. He never shows how hard his life is. He is not, as I was, spoiled. Some people might say that being stoic is unhealthy, but it's not that my father is cold or in some kind of denial. In my eyes, he's strong. He's taken hits, and he understands that the world doesn't always want or need to hear about your problems.

So given that I wasn't going to America, I shifted my entire focus to the woman I loved. To Aarti. And on the day she told me she was leaving, something in me woke up after two years of sleep, and I just decided I was going to follow her, despite my dad, despite the money, despite Delhi University. I was going to America, and the universe would have to deal with it. Fuck ambition. Hormones and the threat of heartbreak are the most powerful forces in the world.

When I raised my fist and proclaimed to Aarti, "*I will follow you to America!*" I did not mean I would follow her to a small Midwestern town on the edge of the Rust Belt whose main industries were a tiny college and a Maytag factory. I watched movies like *With Honors*, where Brendan Fraser is a Harvard student whose thesis paper is held hostage by a homeless man played by Joe Pesci (this plot did not age well). I also saw *National Lampoon's Van Wilder*, where a perpetual college student played by Ryan Reynolds has to figure out how to pay tuition when his dad cuts him off. He wants to stay in school so he can keep partying. These movies showed terribly romantic images of American college life—pristine snow, historic buildings, a 2002-era Tara Reid in knee socks and a miniskirt. No movie ever says these people don't exist and this shit is severely overpriced. By the way, 98 percent of American colleges do not offer this experience, and they don't tell you that Tara Reid would probably think your accent is creepy.

When I dropped Aarti off at the airport, we both sobbed. I told her to wait for me. She promised she would (we all know how that turned out). I sobbed at home for another seventy-two hours and then . . . I packed a backpack and headed not to the U.S., but to the USIS.

I took two buses from Noida, on the outskirts of Delhi where we lived, into the heart of the city. We called it Lutyens' Delhi, after the British architect Sir Edwin Lutyens, who created the buildings, monuments, and arches that have defined the area for a century. I went to the United States Information Service, which is the place that kids go to talk about their SATs and TOEFL exams and learn about colleges. If you want to weigh yourself down with five hundred brochures, USIS is your spot. I remember going into the building alone, looking at the kids who were there with their parents, kids who had money and who were on a totally different journey than I was. I didn't come from that level of privilege anymore. It's one thing for privilege to seem alien because you don't recognize it, and another for it to seem alien because you *do* recognize it, and you used to be part of it.

These excited kids were there with their excited parents, going through university brochures like they were picking flavors at Baskin-Robbins. I hated them. I don't know how else to describe it—they just looked *shinier* than me. Which is ironic because after taking two unair-conditioned buses from Noida to Connaught Place, I was the one shining . . . with sweat.

I paid the SAT fee myself and took the TOEFL (Test of English as a Foreign Language). The TOEFL had reading and writing exercises like "John and Mary went to the market . . . they bought custard apples. The apples were tasty. What is the adjective that describes the apples?" So I aced that one. We all know it's "custard," right?

It really is an insulting exam. I'm not sure if it's required to go to an American university anymore, but just so any Americans reading this know, a lot of people taking this exam laugh out loud because it's supposed to represent your idea of good English. We think you're hilarious.

In India you take board exams during your last year of high school, and your scores dictate what you get to study. You have to get above 90 percent to study science or engineering or English. I got 53 percent, so once again, everybody was like—*this kid is fucked.* My extracurricular scores saved me: 10 percent for dramatics, 10 percent for debating, and 10 percent for basketball. I got up to 83 percent and was able to enroll and study political science starting as a freshman. So the three things my parents had told me not to focus on since I was a kid in Lagos kind of saved my ass. But they also kept me busy as hell. I want to say that in the two years I was at Venky (that's right, that's what Sri Venkateswara College was nicknamed), I might have had 20 percent attendance and scored like 43 percent on my exams to barely pass, since 38 percent was the passing grade. But again . . . I had trophies. My high school debating partner, Ruksh, was also in Venky, so Ruksh and I were a force to be reckoned with.

I spent a lot of time at the USIS. It's free and open to the public. They've got massive catalogs and brochures for every university, computers you can use for research, counselors you can talk to. My grades and my dad's admission that we had no money for an American school did not stop me. Go big or go home, right? Actually, "stay home" is what they told me to do. My acceptance required me to pledge that I could pay a certain amount of money toward my tuition. It's a pretty brutal question to ask an eighteen-year-old. "Hey, how much money do you guys have?" I don't fucking know. How much money do YOU guys have? That's the real question. So my father agreed to spend between three and four thousand dollars a year—an amount I now know he didn't have. We just needed to put something on the form, to show them we could pay *something*.

I kind of became this running joke at the USIS. I was the Kid Who Had No Chance. I remember this American lady who ran the place took me aside one day and said, "You know, it's just not meant to be for some folks." Two things stand out here: She said, "some folks," which she tried to say with kindness. That's something I appreciate today and didn't quite notice then. The other thing is that she smelled like bubble gum. It was 3:30 p.m. It was hot outside. The USIS had near-perfect air-conditioning and wooden shelves full of pamphlets. Light peeked in from beyond a well-manicured garden. It was beautiful. If I was putting this scene in a movie, someone would get wonderful news; they would hear the words "Yes, you're going to college in America!" The light would dance across the shelves of pamphlets! But all I got was "You know, it's just not meant to be for some folks," from a lady who smelled like bubblegum.

A year passed this way. Aarti and I grew more and more distant. We'd talk once every two days, but this was in the era of no cellphones, so it cost a bomb. Plus, she was off finding herself, doing what college kids do in America. It was terrifying to feel her slip away with every passing phone call. Because she sounded more distant, I knew something was up. I needed a miracle.

Instead, I got two.

A friend I played basketball with named Abhik told me he was applying to this place in the Midwest called Knox College. I didn't know where the mid or the west of America was, much less some region that combined the two, but he told me they gave a ton of financial aid. As soon as I went home that night, I wrote a college essay that I am still proud of. For some reason, I included a paragraph about the fact that they were going to reject me because I didn't have enough money. You may call this self-deprecating humor, but comedians call it a self-aware callout. It's what you do when the gig is going very, very badly. You turn the mic on yourself so that you and the audience are thinking the same thing. It's a desperate move, but the gig was going very, very badly.

In the quest to attain my second miracle, I went to Vaishno Devi. For those of you who do not know, Vaishno Devi is a holy shrine up in the mountains of Jammu and Kashmir, dedicated to the Mother Goddess, whom devotees call Mata. Reaching there entails a thirteen-hour train from Delhi to Jammu, a three-hour bus ride from Jammu to Katra, and then a six-hour trek *on foot* up the side of a mountain. They say that if you make it to the shrine, whatever you ask for will be granted by the gods. But if it is not meant to happen, you will not make it to the shrine. The entire trek up is filled with beautiful people, in every devotional color, singing, laughing, helping each other, and chanting "Jai Mata Di." Each one of them feels like they are answering a heavenly calling. I wish everyone could experience the journey up to the shrine at least once. Like most things in life, the journey is far more beautiful than the destination.

I knew in my gut that Aarti was cheating. I was desperate (remember, I'm a hopeless romantic), and so the shrine was my only hope. I used some of my pocket money savings to buy a train ticket, and told my parents I was spending a few nights with my friend Sahil.

Let me tell you about my other best friend, Sahil. To this day, I believe that he's the one who should have become the comedian. When it comes to the three of us (Sahil, Nikhil, and me), I'm the immature, suffering artist, Nikhil is the grounded parent, Sahil is the funny, charismatic one. Sahil and I met on the day his father died. I drove his then girlfriend, who I knew in college, to his house in an area called Gurgaon. It was a serious trek from Delhi, but I had a crying girl in my car, and someone I didn't know had just lost his dad, so I drove. Was I going to gate-crash a funeral? I had no clue. We arrived, and it was silent and sullen in the house, and here was this kid, smiling, making sure everyone felt at home. Sahil was cracking jokes. I cracked jokes back and tried to make him laugh. It was like a comedy duel, and the dude whose dad had died was winning. I stayed the rest of the day, and we've been best friends since. He's always the reality check when I need it. He's told me every shit movie I've been in was shit, he understands comedy as well as I do, and we have an emotional openness that men don't typically have in their friendships. It isn't the "let me call you a pussy, or get you smashed, so we don't have to talk about our feelings" vibe. It's "Let me call you a pussy, and let's drink, and then let's talk about all our feelings." We are each other's first phone call.

So in 1999, me going to Sahil's house for a few days wouldn't seem unusual at all. I told him to lie for me in case my parents called. It was time for the gods to fix my relationship and help me reach my goals.

I rode the train for several hours. At two in the morning, I got off at the first station to wait for the next leg of the journey. Did you know that if you get off at a platform to stretch your legs and don't pay attention when the train starts moving again, the train will just fucking leave? Not one sign says that shit. So as I stretched, I started chatting with people—and missed my train. The station agent in charge of the first stop told me to follow a bunch of farmers along the tracks, because the next district had another train I could catch. We walked by moonlight for two hours. The farmers taught me how to carry my rucksack on my head because my back was tired. I told them I was going to America, and they believed me.

I caught the new train and headed up to Jammu. As you well know by now, I was at this point a city child who had neither the body, nor the stamina, nor the mental fortitude of an Indian farmer. I was dehydrated, sleep-deprived, and unprepared. When we got to the Jammu platform, I blacked out.

I woke up in an army truck, still dehydrated and tired, surrounded by five soldiers who took pity on a lovestruck Indian kid who'd been lying unconscious on the platform. They took me to Nagrota military hospital, where I got an IV and fluids. I told them all about Aarti and America. They seemed more invested in our national security at the border, which is fair enough. We all have our duties. My only crystal clear memory of those soldiers is that they looked like I thought men were supposed to look like. It's weird how you can see honor in a human being's face. I wonder what they saw in mine. Desperation? Blind hope? The look of a dude who was being cheated on?

The soldiers told me that Nagrota had an STD booth. Now, kids, this is not a booth where you get chlamydia (terrible business idea)—it's a phone booth where you can spend money and make international calls. I had 2,000 rupees, which would cover a 500-rupee phone call to Aarti, plus the cost of the pilgrimage, my food on the uphill and downhill treks, and my return on the train the next morning. I called Pace University in upstate New York, from somewhere in the mountains in northern India. I didn't know it would cost triple to call from the mountains.

Thankfully, Aarti answered. After three weeks where she was never in her room at night, she answered. My luck was starting to change.

But wait a minute. I looked up at the STD payment counter. Did it say 500 rupees already?

"Hello?"

"Aarti! I finally caught you!"

"Oh. Hi, Vir."

600 rupees.

"I love you! I'm on my knees, in the middle of the mountains, I cannot begin to explain . . ."

900 rupees.

"Look, I don't know what the hell is going on with you and me . . ."

1,100 rupees.

"Just know that I love you and I believe we can work . . ."

1,300 rupees.

Instead of hearing Aarti declare her love and reassure me that everything would be fine, I heard a guy's voice saying, "Aarti, just tell him."

1,500 rupees.

Fuck.

1,700 rupees.

"Vir, I met a guy. His name is Azar and we've been seeing each other for a month and a half. I can't do this anymore."

1,900 rupees.

Click!

Here's the thing about screaming into the mountains. No one can hear you, except for you when your desperation bounces off another fucking mountain. Nagrota is three thousand feet above sea level. I sobbed into a thousand-foot hillside. My heart was broken. It was over. The gods and the shrine would have to wait. Right now, I just wanted my mom. I wanted to go home.

I believe in a higher power, and after that phone call I didn't think it was on my side that day.

But I was wrong.

I caught a lift in an army truck back to the Jammu platform. There was no more money for a pilgrimage. I needed the one hundred rupees I had left to take an auto-rickshaw home from the train station in Delhi, *if* I ever made it back to Delhi. I had to wait all night for my train, which would leave at 6:00 a.m. Mythological music remixed with Bollywood music played on a speaker from a shop nearby. It was cold, and I was thankful for the number of pilgrims at the platform, since they brought some semblance of warmth, some company. I wondered how many of them had actually made it to the shrine. I found a quiet bench, where I curled up and cried.

About an hour later, I felt a hand on my forehead. I opened my eyes and saw an older Indian man, an "uncle," sitting next to me on the bench. I sat up, panicked. He looked at me and smiled, and his gentle tone put me at ease.

"Tu theek hai?" (Are you okay?)

I nodded yes.

"Pepsi peeyega?" (You want a Pepsi?)

I shook my head no, even though I really wanted a fucking Pepsi.

"Jo bhee ho, usse jaane do. Saans lo. Rona bandh karo." (Whatever it is, let it go. Breathe. Stop crying.)

He put his hand on the top of my head. What a counterproductive move. It only made me cry more. He lowered my head onto his knee.

"Chal. So ja." (Come on. Go to sleep.)

I know how creepy this sounds. An old man offered a teenager a fizzy drink at a train station and held him as he wept. It wasn't creepy though; it was just warm and safe. He was so old, and something about his face was so incredibly kind, I shut my eyes.

I do not know how long I slept, or if I slept at all. From my perspective I closed my eyes for exactly one millisecond, and when I opened them again, he was gone. He had vanished into thin air. I looked around the platform for him, but he wasn't there. I don't know if he ever *was* there. I don't know if he was a spirit, or a mystic, or a ghost, or just an uncle who liked Pepsi more than Coke. All I know is he was a godsend. I don't mean that as a figure of speech. I mean a higher power knew I was alone, and knew I needed something, and that higher power sent an uncle.

Thanks, Mata. Even if you're outsourcing your work, I appreciate it.

The train left Jammu for Delhi at 6:00 a.m., which meant it would arrive at the station at 4:00 a.m. the next morning so they could clean it for two hours. I took my seat at 4:30 a.m., even though I knew I'd be sitting there for ninety minutes. I didn't care. The lights in the train weren't on, so I sat there in the dark, watching them clean until the sun started to rise. You know how a train rolls backward a wee bit before it jerks forward? There's that gentle push off where your body slumps forward and back. I felt months and months of worrying and wondering leave my body as the train lurched forward. Years later, when I saw Aarti again, I told her that when that train pushed off, I left her behind, at that station.

That wasn't the last time in my life I had to deal with someone betraying me and cheating on me. Every time it happened after that, I wished for a moment like I had on that train. It never came. Maybe you've got to go up to the mountains. Maybe Mata just allows you the one time to experience it and then you need to find a way to hold on to it for yourself.

The train arrived at Nizamuddin station in Delhi in the middle of the day. I took an auto-rickshaw from there to my home in Noida, spending the hundred rupees I had left. I was starving, hoping for food when I got home. I was also thinking of the lies I would tell my parents about my "weekend at Sahil's house." I wasn't sure which lie would work best, but I was certain of one thing: Despite what happened with Aarti, I was still going to America, not for her but for me. For the first time, I truly believed it was going to work out.

I spent the next two months smoking, sobbing, and going crazy. What do young romantic college kids do when they've had their hearts pulverized by a girl? We go to house parties, get blind drunk, make out with strangers, and then go home and cry ourselves to sleep.

The other thing that kept me busy was a rock band. I was the vocalist and front man of a band called—wait for it—Bad Attitude.

Don't judge me. Or do. It's fine.

We did covers at rock festivals. I can kinda sorta maybe sing, but I need to be camouflaged by very good musicians. Because of this, you'd think our set list would have consisted of songs for people with a limited vocal range. And yet, this was our setlist:

"Don't Cry"—Guns N' Roses

"Suck My Kiss"—Red Hot Chili Peppers

"Jump"—Van Halen

"Whiplash"—Metallica

"Love Is on the Way"—Saigon Kick

"Give It Away"—Red Hot Chili Peppers

"Sweet Child O' Mine"—Guns N' Roses

"Killing in the Name"—Rage Against the Machine

Bad Attitude played at any college festival that would have us, and if there were girls there, even better. We were high, a *lot*, and we had fun. I love being a front man. It's the thing I'm worst at onstage, so there's no place to go but up. Watching live music is the only environment where I cry.

When I was in Bad Attitude, I was twenty years old. If I'd stayed in college at Delhi University, I would've met someone else. I imagine we would've been happy. Delhi University lasted three years, and I only had one year left at this point. I was a political science major who possessed charm and eloquence. I had a great story about farmers and the border that I could use in job interviews. Eventually I would have stopped doing the theater and the debating and maybe started thinking more seriously about a marketing job or an MBA after college. Maybe an ad agency would have scooped me up. Me and the girl—whoever she might have been—would have eventually started thinking more seriously about each other. Married by twenty-six or twenty-seven, kids by thirty, and then maybe I'd take the kids to movies and debates and tell them how their dad was really into both, and how he and Uncle Ruksh really were a force to be reckoned with on their empty school bus. I would get home after work and take the kids to see Baba. I'd put on the dad bod and start wearing three-quarter cargo pants. I would get promoted to head of the agency where I worked by forty-five years old. One day, a young kid would come in, heartbroken and distracted, and I'd call him into my office during lunch and tell him the Vaishno Devi story. He'd hate it and think it's lame, but I'd be the boss, so he'd listen.

That all sounds pretty good, actually. As I write this, I'm in a hotel in Kuala Lumpur by myself. I've just been to Sydney, Perth, Melbourne, Tokyo, and Hong Kong . . . in eight days. I'm exhausted, jet-lagged, my voice is hoarse, my wife misses me and I miss her. Tomorrow, I have to make four thousand people laugh, after which I will eat a chicken breast in silence, alone in a hotel room. The room has fancy wooden blinds, which match the floors and the wood on an antique ceiling fan that give it a colonial touch. I never thought I'd be in a nice room like this. I've seen the world three times. How many people get to say that? I've seen more joy on more faces than any human being deserves to see. It's truly a blessing, a gift, a godsend . . . and all because after my attempt to reach Vaishno Devi, a miracle occurred.

I got an email from America.

A SHORT DOSE OF GROUNDING

Weed just makes me horny. I'm not high, just hard. Once upon a time, I did not know the difference between a THC gummy and a CBD gummy. On one of my tours, I took a bunch of gummies for jet lag that I thought were CBD but ended up being a total of thirty grams of THC. I paced up and down naked with a boner in my hotel room for six hours. I did push-ups to try to "sweat the weed out," not knowing my dick was clamming into the floor repeatedly. The next day I went on Conan O'Brien and acted casual, even though my dick hurt the entire time.

CHAPTER SIX
THE MECCA OF THE MIDWEST

Vir at Knox College.

It was 2:00 a.m. in India. I turned on my computer and waited for the dial-up connection to work. I wasn't sure if I was feeling depressed because my girlfriend had cheated on me or because I wasn't going to college in America, or both.

But then everything changed with one email.

The message was from Dean Tony Franklin, and it said that Knox College in Illinois would be happy to offer me admission, plus a 90 percent aid package. They knew I only had three thousand dollars, but if I could come up with five thousand, I was in. I had no idea where Illinois was or what it was like. The dean's email included a personal note from him about how he thought my essay was hilarious and how my signature was very cool. They look at signatures? Now THAT'S fucking cool.

I sat there, frozen at my desk. I was afraid my dial-up connection was going to get cut off, or electricity would go out in Noida and the inverter would kick in and the email from America would disappear without a trace. I had a choice: I could spend one more year in college in Delhi or I could start a new life in America. I'd been dreaming about this for so long, but when it was right in front of me, I had no clue how to handle it. So I woke my parents up.

I remember how nervous I was as I knocked on their door at 2:30 in the morning. That walk down the hall to their room was the first time I fully realized how much they had been struggling financially. I knocked.

"Vir, are you okay?"

They thought I had fallen sick.

"I got into college at Knox. The one I'd told you about. They're giving me twenty-nine thousand dollars in aid. We need to give them five thousand. I know we said we only had three, but they really want me!"

My dad, in his pajama-kurta, groggy as hell, told me he would figure it out. He would find two thousand extra dollars. We hugged for the first time in a very long time. I think they were just relieved at the thought of not having a weepy, club-hopping son moping around the house all day. They went back to bed. I headed back to my room. I was so revved up I thought I would never sleep again.

I sat down in front of the computer. Without knowing where the other two thousand dollars would come from, I immediately replied, saying I would accept admission, and the five thousand dollars was going to be fine. And then I sobbed. I had seen movies where people cried just because they were *so happy*, and I always thought that was utter bullshit. All my crying so far had been strictly related to sadness and pain. Yet there I was, blubbering in front of an ancient dial-up modem. These sobs were not from heartbreak; they were from relief. I had wanted this for so long. Just when I'd convinced myself that I didn't want it, there it was: America. For five thousand bucks.

There was no girl, there was no plan, but I was getting out. For me.

It's weird to attach childhood beatings, and family rebellion, and long-distance parenting, and all these other things to a single nation and just assume that if you show up in a new nation, those things from the past are just going to go away. But when you're a kid and you're scared, you cling to things. I clung to this American dream. For some reason that was the haven my mind had conjured up. Even when it seemed entirely out of reach, it stayed there in the dark recesses and refused to leave. Perhaps this is what Gen-Z and the 6 million wellness/motivation grifters on Instagram call "manifesting." I'm on the side of Andy Dufresne from *The Shawshank Redemption*: "Hope is a good thing, maybe the best of things, and no good thing ever dies."

So it was decided. I had a few months to make enough money to make this dream actually happen. My desperation, my desire to impress my ex-girlfriend who was already in America, and my lack of funds led me to a Maharishi Institute Affiliate in Safdarjung, New Delhi. My acceptance email came in late spring, and I had to be on campus in Illinois in August. Like I said before, I completed the course to become a Transcendental Meditation instructor and worked all summer to make money for college. My sister, Trisha, was working as a documentary filmmaker with my mother, so they put in a few thousand as well. In the end, I had seven thousand dollars. It was a huge sum of money for us. I have never forgotten what it meant for Trisha, at age twenty-five, to pay two thousand dollars a year for her brother to go to America. Maybe seven grand doesn't feel like a lot to you, but to us it was a massive sum.

Once I had the funds, in a gesture that I will remember forever, my dad came with me to America, to see me off. It wasn't the first time he'd traveled with me to go to a college. Before I got into Delhi University for political science, I thought I might try being an engineer. I had taken science courses in school, and fucked up my board exams, but someone convinced a tiny engineering college called Bharati Vidyapeeth in the city of Pune to give me admission. My dad came along to drop me off. From what I remember, the college was a single building with a disheveled basketball court and some very unhappy-looking kids. I have no clue what it's like now. As we walked around the campus, my dad looked at me and told me that I was not meant to be an engineer, that I would never be happy there, and that none of my talents would come to use in that place. I looked at him, shocked. I had no idea he knew who I really was, or that he thought I had talent. He saved me that day.

I think that's why he wanted to come to America. "Hey, I saved my son from a place he didn't want to be in, so I want to be part of the good stuff too."

And so, one fateful day in 1999, we flew to Chicago. Then we waited in the afternoon sun for a bus from O'Hare Airport to Peoria, Illinois. We boarded the bus and watched the impressive buildings of Chicago give way to corn, and more corn, and more corn, and ads for strip clubs, and various McDonald's arches, followed by more motherfucking corn. We then took another bus to Galesburg, Illinois. Three hours of flat cornfields did not match the view of America that Hollywood had fed me, but I was *so* in at this point, we could have been driving across a barren desert littered with vultures and I would still have been thrilled. As we drove past the never-ending ears of corn, my dad tried to keep a straight face. I think *he* knew where we were going, and he knew that *I* had no clue. I also had no clue that my new college was about 950 miles from Pace University, where Aarti was. We had broken up, but I was still determined to find her and win her back.

Knox College has about 1,100 undergraduates, and Galesburg has a population of about 29,700. That may sound large if you're from Hooppole, Illinois (pop. 180), but I was coming from Delhi (pop. approx. 15 million). So, we got to campus, and there were a bunch of other international kids who looked as shell-shocked as I did. Knox has a reputation for being this little liberal arts oasis of diversity in the Rust Belt, a place where kids from India, Africa, China, Chile, and Vietnam all come to study (and party). The school prided itself on the fact that Harvard students read 480 pages a week, but Knox students read 520 pages a week. That is their bragging point. When we arrived, no other students were on campus yet, since this was our orientation time to learn about America and find out what to expect. I made friends in an instant.

We were all scared and disappointed that this wasn't like the movies we had seen, so that was all we wanted to talk about. I met three girls, Nalini, Riddhi, and Schonali, who are amongst my best friends even today. I was so excited, I forgot my dad was even there.

Let me tell you about my three female best friends, Nalini, Riddhi, and Schonali. Through my college years and beyond, I have been counseled, fed, and cared for by these three wonderful women. Nalini is a child of diplomats who grew up all over the place. She's a legit genius who's aced every test she has ever taken, and she's probably one of the most principled people I've ever met. She's five foot eleven, and the entire college thought we were dating and wondered how that was geometrically even possible. She eventually met a gorgeous, tall white guy named Josh Hart, a football player from Wisconsin, whom we judged at first and then basically made an honorary Indian. Josh became my roommate after graduation, when I lived in Chicago. They're now married with two kids, and we have an annual reunion. Once during a film awards ceremony I was hosting in Tampa, I put Nalini and Josh in makeup and made them walk the red carpet. The paparazzi saw a six-foot Indian girl with a blond-haired, blue-eyed white guy and thought they were movie stars and took their pictures.

Riddhi is one of the heads of the psychology department at Columbia University. A legit doctor, not an honorary PhD like me. Did I mention I'm Dr. Das? Although I often remind her that I'm the one saving lives, just to annoy her. She was simply the most popular kid in the history of Knox College. She knew everyone's name, was loved by everyone, and got invited to every single party. She exudes this crazy life force, and she now teaches, something I look upon with admiration and envy. She's also a shrink, so she will tell me the things *my* shrink doesn't tell me. One day we were grabbing coffee in the Village and she looked me dead in the eye and said, "Your definition of love is withholding. That's why you gravitate toward women who mistreat you and you try to get love from strangers. Easily available love, you don't notice or accept. You need it to be hard." Talk about a punch in the gut. But spot-on. That's about nine sessions of work, for free.

Schonali is from Bengaluru, and the party person in our group.

> I'd say she's the only one among us who has a hustle like myself. She is 900 percent all in for a good time, at all times. She can show up in a city and just make things happen because of sheer positivity and life force. She's been a waitress in Canada, a club owner in India, a writer for a women's magazine, worked in the pharma industry, and now works in the automotive field. I stopped asking her what she was doing a long time ago, since her increasingly impressive answers give me whiplash. Schonali is the one friend who knew I basically had no money throughout college, so she was generous with food. I could not afford the meal plan, so I fended for myself. Once every ten days, she'd take me out to the Ramada's all-night breakfast in the center of town because she knew I was down to one meal a day. She always paid, and never made a thing of it.
>
> These three women got me through college and more.

But I digress. I arrived at college, fresh off a plane ride and a road trip through the Illinois cornfields.

The campus had quads, and clean water fountains you could drink from, and everyone wore sweatshirts with KNOX written in gold. And the girls were pretty. There was actually another guy from Noida there, named Abhik, and we shared a jail-like concrete block of a dorm room with plastic mattresses. As I've said before, he was my basketball buddy from back home who told me about Knox in the first place. To be this excited, to feel optimism, to feel fresh, to feel free. College felt totally alien to anything I had ever experienced in a school.

It felt like justice.

At the end of the first day of orientation, when my dad saw the burning elation in my eyes, he said, "Vir, I think I'll leave a day early. I think you've got this."

I walked him to the bus station the next day. Before he went back home, my dad left me with a parting note:

Vir, I love you from the bottom of my heart.

Don't mess this up,

Dad

He's never said words of love like that openly to my face. He couldn't manage it, plus he knows I wouldn't be able to handle it. He had to write a note and fly seven thousand miles away to be able to say it. I sometimes think about what he felt on that long journey back home. I hope he felt like he did good, like he came through for me. I hope he felt proud of himself. I was proud of him. Proud to be his son. Never mind the boarding school, never mind the appendix, never mind all the fights, never mind the lack of finances—he got his son to the place he'd always dreamed about.

Knox changed everything. I found the arts, theater, and stand-up. I found a voice. It changed the course of my life, and I have my dad to thank for leaving me that note and giving me the confidence that I was doing the right thing.

I'm a stubborn son of a bitch. Some would say I've had this quality for a long time, and it's because I was shown very early that if you refuse to take no for an answer, things will eventually align. There is no way in hell a person from my background, with our situation, should've wound up in America in 1999 with the dollar and the world being what they were. But by the time I was twenty-one and having a drink at Cherry Street in Galesburg, Illinois, the universe, the Vaishno Devi shrine, and my family had shown me that ANYTHING was possible. I believed it then as I do now. I was FINALLY in America.

To that, let's raise a Miller High Life and say, "Cheers!"

So there I was, in the Mecca of the Midwest, with a scholarship to study . . . economics. It wasn't my choice, but I promised my parents I would study something practical. Instead of focusing on econ, though, I played into every American college kid trope you can imagine. On the very first day of class, I got high as balls with a bunch of Americans who had an apple bong. Later I joined a frat called Sigma Nu, which was full of dweebs who liked to party. I became the rush chair. I had never hooked up with an American girl, so I accomplished that goal on day two of college. As soon as that happened, all of the Indian and international girls were like, "This kid is a problem." Her nickname was Tiger, because she had a tiger butterfly tattoo downstairs, which I got to see forty-eight hours into my college experience. It ruined my reputation with the Indian kids, since I was the brown kid who lost himself in forty-eight hours. What they didn't know was that a few weeks in, they'd all lose themselves too!

After that whirlwind hookup ended, I met my first college girlfriend, Teresa, an evangelical Christian from Malawi, Africa. She came from a family of ultraconservative white missionaries, and if you're wondering what we had in common, we both liked dancing and making out. She was a brilliant biochem major, so I was also fascinated with her brain (I swear). She had about ten churches to choose from in Knox, and she would pray for my soul every week. I had to leave her every Sunday morning so she and God could have alone time. I was going to hell if I didn't accept Jesus as the son of the lord because all other religions were subtle manifestations of the devil's deviousness. Fair point, but man she was so beautiful and sexual. She wasn't allowed to follow through with those impulses, so our make outs were limited. In the end, I was competing with Jesus. I didn't stand a chance. So we'd make out for like four hours, and I would just be hoping, praying, that she would give up on her religion. Which, in retrospect, is kind of messed up. She never did. It was the first time since Sara in India that religion really came into my relationship as a roadblock. We have this stereotypical pop culture version of a blond-haired white woman as someone liberal, bohemian, and sexually liberated, who is casual and noncommittal about it all.

That has not been my experience. With most of the white girls I have dated, I was the one flitting about while they looked for something real and committed. I try to keep that in mind every time I write a white character in a script.

There was so much diversity at Knox. It was this safe little bubble of ultra-intelligent people, which leaves you entirely unprepared for the real world. It's a tiny campus, but it's full of very big opinions and loud conversations. It is freezing and covered in snow for half the year, and then hot as fuck the other half. There's little or no contact with the "townies," or more politely, the locals. But it was this amazing escape where I truly lost myself, in a good way. I just wasn't used to talking about ideas with that kind of openness and conviction. Certainly not with other kids my age. I'd only had that with my grandfather Baba before. This felt like one constant, all-day debate club where we all hooked up after the debate because our brains hurt.

I remember one day writing a philosophy paper linking Plato's *Republic* to *The Matrix* and the caste system in India, and arguing how they were all structurally basically the same. I stopped myself in the middle and just thought about how utterly insane it was that I was able to do this at all. In Indian academics there is no room for opinion. There is a right answer and a wrong answer, and a smart student is able to fully memorize the right answer.

I got to study philosophy, psychology, science fiction, jazz history, literature, creative writing. All of this along with the economics and calculus I needed for my degree. Indian kids came in better prepared for undergrad. We had been trained to memorize for twelve years.

We could also take an exam anywhere on campus. Like, walk out with the paper in hand and sit in the sun on the lawn and take a final exam. Not cheating was basically an honor system. Are you fucking kidding me? For my final economics paper I remember that the professor, Roy Andersen, walked in and said, "Your current grades as they stand are written on your exam sheet. If you don't want to take this final, you can walk out right now and keep that grade. To me it's important that you studied for the exam, not that you take it."

What a baller move.

During college, I didn't go home for vacations much, since we couldn't afford it. I stayed on campus and found work and things to fill my mind. One winter I did an "economic analysis of the theater industry." I convinced Andersen that I could come up with an equation that would predict the success or failure of a theatrical production. He knew it was bullshit and couldn't be done, but I'd be a fucking billionaire today if I could have done it. Even so, he got me a two-thousand-dollar grant to go up to Chicago every weekend and watch plays. I never wrote the paper. I still believe America, while having maybe the worst high school system in the world, has the best undergraduate system in the world. It's a system that makes you believe anything is possible.

Besides partying and hooking up with Tiger and Teresa, I actually did focus on school. I got on the dean's list after my first semester, so my parents were thrilled and felt like I'd finally done something with my life. My heart wasn't in econ, but I kept at it because of the promise I'd made to my parents. I figured I would finish college, then go back to India and maybe join my dad's business one day. During my second semester, though, I took an acting class on a lark, and that was the beginning of the end of econ for me.

I love drama class. I love how utterly terrible and amateur everyone is. You're able to do fifty monologues in a semester, and there are centuries of texts waiting for you to read and perform. There are also professors *encouraging* you to do this. It isn't some illegal thing you are doing while you're supposed to be studying political science and the role of the judiciary as it evolved during the 1960s with sociopolitical shifts and a changing global attitude toward communism. In drama class, you can be different people. You can be evil like Richard III, rage like Stanley from *A Streetcar Named Desire*, plot like Aaron from *Titus Andronicus*, all by 10:30 in the morning. You can stand up and say, "I felt vulnerable, but the anger wasn't coming, so I had to think about what happened to my dog when I was three, and then I found myself getting angry. My inner monologue changed, and I found the strength to call him a bitch." At 9:00 a.m. on a Tuesday? Get the fuck out!

I aced drama class. I lived for drama class. All I wanted to do from then on was drama class. One main reason I loved it was a professor named Ivan.

For some reason, Professor Ivan Davidson saw promise in me. One afternoon toward the end of the semester, he called me in to talk to him. Was I in trouble? Was he going to pull out a hockey stick and beat my ass? This was America though. Corporal punishment wasn't a sport like it had been at my boarding school. Ivan was a sixty-year-old, pipe-smoking professor with floor-to-ceiling shelves filled with old theater books and biographies of Laurence Olivier and Sarah Bernhardt. In other words, he leaned way into every archetype of academia.

"Hello, Vir. Come in and sit down," he said while I stood in the doorway to his musty collegiate office.

I sat.

"How's your day?"

"Day's good, sir. How's yours?"

"Can't complain. So, Vir. You've been in my class for a while, right?"

"Right."

"Right. I've been watching your progress, and I'm going to tell you something that I say to maybe one kid every seven or eight years."

I sat there, blinking. I had no idea what he was going to say. Maybe that I needed to focus on my economics classes and never step foot on a stage again?

"Vir, you're meant to do this. You're meant to be a performer. So, I want you to do me a favor."

"Okay, sir?"

"I can turn you into an actor, but you have to shut up and take every course I tell you to take."

He meant this in the nicest possible way.

"Thank you, sir, but I can't do that. I took a chunk of money from my parents and promised them I would get an economics degree. They would kill me."

Ivan sat back in his chair and looked me over. Of course, I *wanted* to take all the drama courses and forget about econ, but I also didn't want to get beaten by a slipper the next time I visited India.

"I'll tell you what," he said. "Take spring break to think about it, and then get back to me."

That sounded reasonable enough. I knew the minute I walked out of his office what I wanted to do though.

Four days into spring break, Ivan called me.

"Vir?"

"Yes, sir?"

"I'm giving you the second lead in *War and Peace* after spring break. I want you to seriously consider it. The whole theater department thinks I'm insane for doing this without you even auditioning, but just give me this one semester, and then you can decide for yourself. If it doesn't work out, you never have to act again in your life."

So I would be playing a Russian prince named Andrei who fights in the Battle of Borodino? Why not?

For a small college, Knox had a pretty big theater department. This play would be six hours long, and run over the course of two nights. It was ambitious. I returned from spring break and walked into a very pissed off theater department, since this teacher had just gone out on a limb for a random Indian kid. During the first few weeks, I got snapped at by drama majors and other teachers, but eventually they came around. This kid Ben Meyers was like the Al Pacino of Knox College, and since he was playing the lead, we started doing scene work with each other. Eventually, I got Ben's endorsement, and everyone else in the department fell in line.

I loved the theater. I did movement work and hung lights. I rehearsed scenes and helped build sets. To this day, I love the smell of an old theater. I love backstage and greenrooms and lighting grids. The whole thing is like a massively intoxicating drug. I helped build a comedy scene in India, and often we would be performing in old theaters and sweeping the stage before we headlined. There is an honor to a theater stage. You clean it before you headline it.

I never imagined I would go from the Harbach Theatre in Galesburg (capacity 500) to Carnegie Hall (capacity 2,804) or the Sydney Opera House (capacity 2,679). Back then, that five-hundred-seat theater at Knox may as well have been an arena.

We did something called rep term during *War and Peace*, where the entire theater department turned into a repertory company. You wake up in the morning and do acting class, writing class, reading, set building, rehearsals, and then you go to bed. It's 8:00 a.m. to 9:00 p.m. Your body is broken, and it's fucking paradise. Then at the end of the term, the play goes up.

I waited an entire year to tell my parents that I was focusing on drama. They were not happy, but they were too far away to do anything except grunt their displeasure over the phone. I don't think they knew it was a full-time thing, just their kid's new obsession, his new phase to be outgrown. I studied acting, learned the lines of whatever play I was in, and did some economics work when I had to. I got a job at a gas station owned by a Sikh man, and since I couldn't afford the school meal plan beyond the first semester, he gave me the leftover hot dogs and donuts that he'd have to throw out at the end of the day, so that kept me going. The place was called Quick Stop One. My boss spoke very little English, and he and his family lived in an apartment at the back of the gas station. We were like two constructs of the American dream, this privileged college kid and then this guy with a very real immigration story, working his ass off for a better life. We'd both smoke cigarettes at dawn before I headed off to class and his wife took over for him, because it was safer for her to work during the day.

You know that sound a cigarette makes? That crispy sound you hear from tobacco leaves burning when the lead character takes a drag? That sound is beautiful when it's dawn in Galesburg and minus 6 degrees and you're surrounded by snow.

From the day I was cast as Andrei until the day I graduated, I was one of the leads in every production at Knox. Ivan found every emotional barrier I had and broke it down in scene work. For example: I'm not a violent person, so he cast me as Stanley Kowalski in *A Streetcar Named Desire*, a guy who epitomized primal macho aggression. I did musicals, dramas, and comedies. I played a redneck from the Ozarks. I played an Italian guy with a Brooklyn accent, a Jewish guy, and a naked dude in *Equus*, the play that's famous mainly because a post–*Harry Potter* Daniel Radcliffe played the lead, buck naked on Broadway. When I played the lead, a character who is a teenager who murders six horses with a metal spike, I had a major issue. It wasn't really that I had to stand onstage in front of the entire department in my underwear. That I could handle. It was that my equipment, or the character's equipment, was not supposed to work when he was trying to make out with the girl he liked because the images of the horses in the barn were fucking him up. My issue was that there were no actual horses, and I had been making out with the girl playing opposite me in real life. So my equipment was very much hard-wired to work. It was the most terrifying thing that had ever happened to me, besides being beaten with hockey sticks.

I pulled Ivan aside and told him my issue.

"Vir, you just need to focus on your inner monologue."

"Sir. You have no idea what my inner monologue is saying right now. It has nothing to do with *Equus* whatsoever."

Instead of focusing on my inner monologue, which was telling me to hook up with my scene partner, I asked her to do something gross, say something creepy or mean that would give me the ick so I would definitely not want to do the deed. We rehearsed like hell, the ick set in, I got new wiring. It's funny how much of this shit is just mental wiring.

Acting exercises and the like, all sound a little foo-foo to an outsider, until you start to mess with your own internal systems and discover truly how much your brain affects your biology. Mostly, I think that experience made me a better comedian. There's nothing as humbling as being in your underwear onstage in front of a class. If you can't laugh at yourself and crack jokes to lighten the tension in that situation, you're doomed. These experiences also made me totally unprepared for the real world that awaited me. At Knox, I could be and do anything. I could play that guy with an Ozark accent, I could do Shakespeare and Tolstoy. I went into the world thinking these roles would be possible for me, but the world gave me Arab #7 and Indian #75. I had a lot to learn. Along the way, though, Ivan kept saying, "You're not Knox-talented. You're *talented*." It was an important thing to hear, even if the real world wasn't going to be as welcoming.

Ivan and the truly wonderful professors Liz Carlin Metz and Bob Whitlatch were three theater instructors who didn't treat us like students. They critiqued us like adults, which I believe is important for acting students: to sometimes hear that what you're doing sucks, and that's okay, because it won't suck forever, you just have to keep at it. I also think the average theater professor has to create a sense of community and deal with more emotions than the average calculus or philosophy professor. Everyone who walks into a theater department as a student is some kind of social reject, or narcissist, or both, coming in with all of their feelings splayed open. A theater becomes this safe space largely because of the professors that imbue it with a sense of acceptance. Think about it from their perspective. Here's this brown kid from India. A country that sends twelve students a year to Knox, and 99 percent of them are in computer science, premed, economics, and other serious majors. He's got a strong Indian accent when he is offstage, but he can thankfully do an American accent onstage. His English is not as good as the American students', so he struggles to read Shakespeare even though he's playing Leontes in *The Winter's Tale* this semester. He's one of the leads in every play he auditions for. This is not going to be the case when he gets out of here. He's also not used to being this open about feelings and background and trauma. It's not a part of his culture as much as it is over here, so he struggles with finding real depth as an actor. He's also close to failing most of his economics classes, which is what the idiot came here for. He has a 2.4 GPA in econ, so it's clearly not his calling. He's constantly unfocused, heartbroken, and in some sort of long-distance relationship.

I needed a safe space, and they gave me one.

During my time at Knox, I also spent time with my host "parents," Pinky and Gene Gibbons. Let me explain. When an international student comes to town, they are given local "parents," just a local couple who volunteer to take care of students and act as guides to American culture. You meet your host parents once every two weeks for a lunch on Sunday. And no matter who their host parents were, eventually all of the students would wind up at the house of Pinky and Gene Gibbons. Honorary host parents to almost every foreign kid, as declared by other foreign kids. They both rode Harley-Davidsons, and we loved them. Pinky worked in the cafeteria of the Gizmo bar cafeteria on campus. Their house was like a hub for international students, and they always treated the international kids as their own. They introduced us to the Galesburg community. I once rode on the back of Pinky's Harley, looking like a small brown stowaway. Pinky and Gene were (and are) decent, kind, hardworking people. They took care of kids from all over the world, worked to pay their bills, watched *The Bachelor*, and went to bed.

Because of them, I've always had an aversion to comedy that patronizes, demonizes, and shits on "real America." I've had a different experience, and I know that ignorance isn't the same as evil; it doesn't always equate to malice. You know, the year 2002, the year after 9/11, when I graduated from college, wasn't the best time to be a brown guy in Middle America. Pinky and Gene, and most everyone in the town, never treated me with anything but respect. They didn't scream, "Osama!" at me (that would happen later, when I was innocently riding a bicycle in Alabama). When I went back to Knox in 2018 to give a commencement speech that I called "Be Stupid," Pinky and Gene were sitting right up front. We took a selfie with my now honorary PhD. I haven't ever had the gumption to say that out loud. But I did change my Twitter profile for twenty-four hours, just to piss a few friends off.

I know not *every* small town in America would have welcomed me with open arms, especially at that time, but being in that place, for those three years, was really the first time I enjoyed how unique I was. I was the brown kid in the play, the first Indian to join a frat, the first Indian acting TA. I dated a stripper for a few weeks! I did feel like an alien in that small town, and in my previous life, that would have stressed me out, but instead it made me appreciate the things that made me stand out. It made me lean into those things, instead of trying to hide them.

That place, and those people, gave me the confidence to think that I could be a comedian. If I could do a hillbilly accent in a drama and *not* cause people to laugh, then surely I could be myself and *make* people laugh.

Right?

During my last semester at Knox, I was writing a paper in the Seymour Library and something insane happened. I decided I was going to be a comedian. It is hard to describe, but it was a flow state. Pure flow. It's happened to me maybe ten times since. I'd been watching a bunch of stand-ups, people like Richard Pryor, Eddie Izzard, and Eddie Murphy, so maybe I was inspired. Or maybe I just needed a way to procrastinate and not write that paper. Or maybe this was my final rebellion against my econ degree. Whatever the reason, I got on the computer and created a flyer for a show called *Brown Men Can't Hump*, a riff on the 1992 classic movie *White Men Can't Jump* starring Woody Harrelson and Wesley Snipes. For some reason, and I still cannot tell you why, I just made a poster. I needed a venue, so I booked a seven-hundred-seat auditorium on campus. I used the copy machine code from the Career Center and printed out one hundred posters, then went all over campus at two in the morning plastering them on buildings and bulletin boards. Once the posters were up, I had no choice but to follow through. That's still the way I work today. Book the venue, announce the thing, and then make it happen. Somehow.

The next morning, people on campus were like, "What the fuck is this?"

I gave myself six weeks to write an hour of stand-up, which is ridiculous. But I did it. The auditorium was packed, and for sixty whole minutes, I killed it. Maybe Ivan was a genius. Maybe I *was* meant for this. Maybe I was a brown George Carlin! I wasn't. It was inside jokes for many friends, and I can see in retrospect it was terrible craft and writing. But it gave me a freedom I had never experienced onstage. That night at Knox, performing *Brown Men Can't Hump*, I knew that my destiny did not involve becoming a credit analyst or a portfolio manager. My destiny was to become a comedian, to perform.

A SHORT DOSE OF GROUNDING

I drove a Hero Puch to school every day in Noida. A Hero Puch looks like a bicycle fucked a moped. It's this tiny motorbike that does a maximum of thirty miles an hour. Once, on a particularly cold and foggy day, I was crossing a narrow bridge on a back road to school near Sector 18, Noida, and I found a dude standing in the middle of the bridge. I took a sharp left, fell off my bike, and slammed chest first into the side of a cow. I lay there wheezing with the wind knocked out of me while the cow looked at me nonchalantly. It then shat on me for twenty seconds. It was a cold winter day, and that shit was warm.

CHAPTER SEVEN

ALABAMA DETOUR

Vir's show, Not for Members Only, *at the India Habitat Centre, New Delhi.*

*I*t's gonna be huge . . .
   It's gonna take everything . . .
   We're probably going to have to build it ourselves . . .
   I've always taken umbrage with people who complain about their success. If you have the ability to be successful in any goddamn part of the arts, given the utterly ridiculous odds that you are up against, and you then begrudge that success, you are an ungrateful asshole. You don't deserve to even attempt to participate in your chosen art form. Basically, you're the absolute worst.
   Having said that, if you're young and in the early days of your success, complain away.
   Early success is a bitch because there is such a minuscule group of people who understand what makes them successful at a young age. Being good at something takes a while, but receiving acclaim or applause can come super-duper early. Like, way before you deserve it, and before you even understand what it is that *makes* you good. And yes, I'm including the Leo DiCaprios and Timothée Chalamets and Eddie Murphys of

the world, who somehow know exactly what their artistic voice is at seventeen years old and lean the fuck in. They didn't stumble into early success—they earned it.

At twenty-two years old, I did not have a goddamn clue what I was doing onstage, what made me good onstage, and—most important—why people were sitting in the audience. In retrospect, I think my early success was built upon pure braggadocious ego mixed with ignorance. But even at that age, being onstage just felt like home. Ever since I was four years old and played that tree in the school play, as I stood onstage and waved my arms from side to side in my best palm-tree impression, I remember thinking, "Oh man, the view is way better from up here."

I wish everyone in the world could see what I see from a stage. A mix of warm golden orbs shine from the stage lights, forming a filmic lens flare in front of your eyes. Who says real life isn't a movie? Wooden floorboards shake under your feet. Tiny particles of dust float through each light beam, causing you to wonder how long each one of those particles has lived in that theater. The heat of the stage lights causes a single trickle of sweat to drip down your neck, and a cool draft from the old building drifts from a backstage wing, where everyone from worried agents to excited viewers has witnessed the electricity of a live show. And when you hear a crowd? My god, is that a hard sound to describe. The sound of four thousand people laughing, their feet moving, their hands clapping. Even better—the sound of four thousand people *not* moving, *not* laughing, *not* shaking. Just sitting there in pure silence. It's truly magic, as if, for a brief moment in time, you're actually, truly connected to every single person in the audience.

Like I said, I know all of this *now*. At twenty-two, all I knew was that I had written and performed a show about brown men (not) humping, in which I'd said "fuck" about seven thousand times and then received a standing ovation. I'd also received some very generous sex after the show, turning it into a very ironic evening.

I thought I killed it on that stage at Knox College. I felt totally and utterly confident, knowing deep in my bones that comedy was what I was meant to do. Praise was heaped on me by friends, professors, and my host parents. Turns out the joke was on me, because a few months after graduation, when I came down from my onstage high, I found myself washing dishes at a Grand Lux Cafe in Chicago during the day, and getting booed off every open-mic stage I stepped onto at night. It's tougher to impress twenty cynical comedy lovers in the third largest city in America than it is to wow six hundred friendly people in Galesburg. Maybe that's not a big surprise to you, but it was to me.

If you graduate from the protective bubble of a leftist liberal arts college and go to a city where you don't have citizenship and the only thing you do have is a theater major, you're in for some surprises. First, no one gives a shit how amazing you were in *War and Peace* as Andrei. Second, food is a lot more expensive, the public transport you take everywhere seems to feature people who look as unhappy as you do (only much older), and you start to wonder if things will ever get better. Third, you start to realize that you are utterly unemployable in your chosen art form.

The year I finished college started off great because I finally got to go to Harvard. Well, around Harvard. Call it Harvard-adjacent. I auditioned for drama graduate school while I was still in my final year at Knox College and got into a short program at the American Repertory Theater at Harvard, which was run in conjunction with the Moscow Art Theatre. The Moscow Art Theatre teachers are disciples of the great acting teacher/guru Konstantin Stanislavski. These people basically invented method acting, and once every few years they do a ten-week program where they take fifteen kids and teach them to act.

In Boston, I rented an apartment on Tremont Street in Southie, which is the part of town where Ben Affleck lives in every single Boston movie he's in. Keep in mind this was 2002, so I found the apartment on Craigslist. If I did that today I would have been found chopped up in a basement, but in 2002 we did shit like that. I'd wake up at six in the morning, take two buses to Cambridge, sit in Harvard Square with my guitar case open for tips, and sing for an hour while the rich kids walked to class and bought coffee at the co-op. I'd sing Nirvana, Pearl Jam, Bob Dylan, some Leonard Cohen. Just the kind of cheery, sunny music people want to hear first thing in the morning. Like a stripped-down Bad Attitude, if you will. Mild attitude. Some attitude. My somber repertoire earned me about $4.50, which was enough for breakfast and bus money for the next day. I'd go to Punjab Palace, where they sold a single samosa for fifty cents. I'd buy four, and that became breakfast and lunch. Then I'd spend all day doing theater with old Russians who taught me more about acting in two months than I had learned in three years at Knox (no offense to Ivan Davidson). We studied body work, movement work, voice work, reading, rehearsals, and most important . . . Truth.

On the first day of my Stanislavski Summer, the artistic director of the Moscow Arts Theatre stood up in front of the entire Harvard theater faculty, plus fifteen clueless theater students, and in a heavy Russian accent said, "Acting . . . uh . . . very simple. Read script. Believe script. Do what the fuck you like." Huh.

I had just spent $21,000 on three years studying at Knox only to find myself learning "Do what the fuck you like." Because of how little English they spoke, if you weren't honest in your performance, these instructors felt it. The words mattered less than the feelings you conveyed. They didn't give you flowery feedback or overintellectualized theater jargon. They'd just go "good" or "shit." God bless Russian bluntness.

After classes, at around five in the evening, I'd head to Harvard Square again and sing for another hour while kids caught up after class and smoked in the square. I'd usually make less busking in the evenings, so I'd clock about $2.50 on a bad day, but take the two buses home to Southie smiling from ear to ear. On weekends I'd walk around Boston until I was hungry enough to go home and warm up some Campbell's chicken noodle tins. I count that summer as one of the best of my life. I had no money, but I was studying acting, which I loved, and later that summer I discovered my comedic voice as well.

Harvard in the summer with no one around is kind of a vibe. It is very white, everyone is intelligent, everyone is reading a book, and everyone looks vaguely rich. There's lots of linen, people play chess in the sun in the park, and no one pays attention to a shabby Indian kid. I remember once I snuck into the Harvard Stadium and smoked a joint in the empty arena. I climbed over a gate and then through a small space, and suddenly I was in the stands. I sat there in a space meant for 25,884 people and looked at an empty American football field. Strangely enough, I thought of home and of Noida. Some evenings I'd walk around Southie and stumble into bars. Again, it was very white, and I immediately knew if I was welcome or very much not welcome. A few years later, I watched *The Departed* in the cinema and I swear so many of those Southie bars looked like the ones Jack Nicholson and his gang hung out in, with some very ominous-looking regulars.

I didn't make it back to Harvard until 2019. I was asked to headline the Harvard India Conference, which is sort of a superelite think fest where politicians, writers, filmmakers, and intellectuals from India get on a plane to Cambridge in February and give lectures to young, impressionable grad students. It was the first time I saw political members of the ruling party and the opposition abroad. When they are outside the country, they chill, smoke, drink, and hang together. Then they get back to India and toe the party line while trying to burn each other's houses down. I remember on the flight there, a young politician (from the party I would soon piss off to the highest degree) and I shared a beer together. I was flying first class, which I had forced Harvard to pay for. It was weird to see a politician in the traditional pajama kurta there with me. It went against the simple chaste positioning they project. We actually hung out for a few hours. He was my age and could not have been more chill. Liberal, even. The following year, he went on to make some of the most Islamophobic speeches I've ever heard. It's at moments like that that you realize it's all a game and none of them believe a word they are saying. They just follow a script they didn't write. Maybe that's why they hate actors so much. It's the same job, just less stress and bigger perks (sometimes). When I opened my set at Harvard that year, I made sure to let them know they had paid a lot of money and bought a first-class ticket for the kid who used to busk in the square.

Back to the end of that magical summer spent studying with some of the greats, when the Russians called me into their office and told me they thought I was talented, and if I was willing to learn Russian, they'd like to offer me a position at their theater school in Moscow. I sometimes think about what would've happened if I had said yes. I would've moved to Moscow, and lived my life under Putin? I guess that would've made for a pretty interesting book. I was twenty-two. I was already lonely, and Moscow seemed so far away and so cold, with so many prisons. I refused and went somewhere only slightly warmer. I went to Chicago.

When you graduate with a student visa in the U.S., they give you one year to get a job that will sponsor a work visa. I had burnt through half of that time with the Russians who told me to do what the fuck I liked, and then I did the opposite. I ran through four jobs that paid me illegally, in cash. I was an unpaid theater intern, a volunteer at an after-school program for inner-city kids, a banquet bartender, a dishwasher and, eventually, a door escort at the Grand Lux Cafe (which paid me legally). You can tell a lot about a person by what they leave on their plate. If the plate is full of carbs but the protein is gone, they're having sex. If it's all there, they didn't like the food, a date went horribly wrong, or someone died. If the plate is completely empty, they're immigrants. I loved being in the kitchen. We'd make fun of white people all day. I had a friend called Andrew who would just laugh about how my parents had spent all this money to send me to college and yet I was making the same amount of money as a high school dropout. Andrew was right to laugh, but actually, I love washing dishes. Yes, in America they give you a hair net and gloves and a fancy high-powered spray faucet, but to this day, if I'm stressed, I do the dishes. The mindlessness of it relaxes me.

Just a quick tangent: I think the biggest conversation in the world right now might be immigration. Who do we let into our countries? That single conversation changes the outcome of American elections. It's incredibly ironic that none of the people who are having that conversation seem to have worked in the world of the undocumented. At my dishwasher job, at my after-school program, at my banquet job, 80 percent of the people I worked with were undocumented. They are some of the most talented, hardworking, and funny people I know doing a job that I promise you no white person wants to do anyway for a wage that none of them would accept.

Every time I see that rhetoric of "foreigners taking our jobs, illegals being brought in to take jobs," all I can think is: You fucking try it. Try existing in the cash-only world as we did. Paying your rent in cash, paying for the train in cash, paying for cigarettes in cash, keeping your rent under your mattress and rolled up into socks that are then stuffed into the toes of your shoes so that your roommates or robbers can't find it when you're at work. Try going into banks and being told you don't have the documentation to even open an account. Try selling everything at pawn shops for 50 percent of what it should go for because you don't have enough in your bank account to set up eBay. Try going to your landlord's every month and dropping eight hundred dollars in bundles of ones and fives, which you have evenly split among your jacket pocket, pants pocket, bag compartment, and shoes, because you're worried you're going to get mugged on the Brown Line train. These are the people you want to kick out of your country?

I'd respect people more if they just said they were insecure and scared of what they don't understand. Immigrants experience America relative to something, and are not just taking it for granted. They know what they have left behind, they know what the alternative is. Why be upset at *them*?

But back to Chicago.

When I wasn't getting laughed at or scrubbing crusty macaroni and cheese off plates, I was doing open mics in Chicago. I was bombing at open mics on the South Side. I'm gonna say something that sounds racist, but it's not. And I know that's usually what people say before they say something racist. So here it goes: I don't think there's a tougher crowd than a Black crowd, and winning over a crowd never feels better than when it's a Black crowd. They will let you know how shitty you are and how funny you are quicker than any other crowd on the planet. So there I was in rooms on the South Side, bombing because I was doing some trite shit about cockroaches, while a crowd looked at me with hostility that almost made me feel . . . white? Can I say that? I said it. The problem was that at the time, my material was impersonal. It said nothing authentic about who I was, in front of what's probably the most authentic, self-aware community of people in America. My first real laugh in those rooms came not because I was being clever but because I was being honest.

It was a Tuesday. I was comedian number 18 in the lineup. We each got three minutes, which doesn't seem like a lot, but it is an eternity when you're as bad as I was and have thirty disgruntled people staring at you in utter silence (and not because they're utterly stunned by your talent). After about six weeks of death stares, I'd had enough. I was done reasoning with these crowds. I was just going to confront them and never show up again. I don't remember exactly what the joke was, but I know it had alliteration, and I know it got a laugh. I remember the sound of that laugh like it was yesterday. I think I said something like, "The fuck do you know about Indians? You think you're so cool. NONE of you appreciate Indian people. WE are cool. We are the quickie mart owners who sell you food, we are the doctors who check out your wife's pussy and make sure it's good to go. We drive your taxis, we sell you newspapers, we teach you math and science. Without Indians you'd be starving, stranded, sexless, sterile, and stupid!"

It wasn't Shakespeare, but it worked.

It was an average joke told at a shitty bar on a Tuesday night. But suddenly—lights, lens flare, warmth, laughter. Not everyone in the room laughed, but it was just enough people to let me know it was real. They probably weren't even laughing at the material; they were probably laughing at how tired and frustrated this tiny Indian man looked. I was honest, just like the Russians told me to be. The laughter felt amazing, but then I was out of material because I forgot the rest of my set. I thanked them and got offstage. I had done thirty-four seconds of my three minutes, but it was enough. I got a real laugh, from a real crowd. I was hooked.

Somehow, no matter how broke you are in your twenties, there's always enough money for booze and cigarettes. In Chicago I lived with a six-foot-four white linebacker from Wisconsin named Josh Hart. I'd met him at Knox College through Nalini (they eventually married). I made extra cash bartending banquets for rich WASPs, getting the gigs via a staffing company that made you buy your own tuxedo. I found a 1970s tux for twelve bucks from the Salvation Army. Picture an Indian kid with gelled hair, wearing pants with a too-tight crotch and huge bell bottoms pouring your chardonnay at the annual fundraiser. That was me.

Despite my biggish laugh that one night at the club, I eventually left Chicago. It was just too cold for my equatorial bones. I remember a night when I was trying to get home from the Grand Lux Cafe, which meant taking the Red Line AND the Brown Line. Now if your train pass has a low balance or has to be renewed and you haven't gotten paid yet, you gotta come up with options. You could walk home. In Chicago? At night? Kind of a "let's see if a stranger or the cold kills me first" contest. Fuck that.

So once in a while, I had to ride the Red Line in a loop for hours until it was warm enough to walk home in the morning. At that time of night the train was full of people on drugs, many of them without a home, some with guns or bulges that you hoped were weapons and not something else, some talking to themselves, plus one petrified Indian kid. I tried to distract myself by playing music on my headphones, which were hidden under my hood. I didn't want to be caught with a Discman. Kids, if you don't know what that is, it's a portable CD player. If you don't know what a CD player is . . . google it and wish me luck as an elder. So you put the music on, put your backpack on backward, over your stomach, zip your jacket up above your bag so you look pregnant, and then put your head against the window, maybe rehearse a monologue for an audition to keep your mind occupied. Then at about 6:05 a.m., the train will come out of a tunnel that feels like it gets longer each time you pass through it at night, and sunlight will hit your face. Golden light, warm cheeks, like the universe letting you know you made it, it's time to get off the train.

In February every single grad school in America takes over the Palmer House Hilton in downtown Chicago and thousands of kids audition to get into MFA programs for acting. A master of fine arts. I'd been through the process once and wound up not making it anywhere but to Boston. But this time I had Russian perspective on bullshit, and many hours of practice on the Red Line train. I picked two monologues. Aaron from *Titus Andronicus* and Pip from *Three Days of Rain*. I think when life beats you up a little, you get better as an actor. That's why young actors fresh out of college suck so much. You have NO tangible experience with what the character is feeling. But when Aaron says, "And so you must resolve, that what you cannot as you would achieve, you must perforce accomplish as you may," he's a horrible man; spend a few nights on the Red Line and you understand what "horrible" means a little better. When I was done auditioning for the second time for grad schools, I knew I was gonna get in somewhere. I just felt it.

I went home for a bit. Saved for a ticket, took five hundred dollars, which I knew would go a long way in Noida, and took a month off.

When I was back in India and the University of Alabama emailed and said they would pay me to come to grad school, a place that's warm and doesn't have a Red Line, I said: FUCK YES.

I knew nothing about Alabama, so I jumped at the chance. I would be at the Alabama Shakespeare Festival, in a beautiful theater by a lake. The festival is in Montgomery, and it is affiliated with the University in Tuscaloosa. I could get an MFA in Shakespeare. I could be a college professor, I wouldn't have to work in the cold, *and* I could stay in America. I conjured up this fantasy in my head where I would grow old like my professor Ivan Davidson, working in a cozy office with floor-to-ceiling books. Maybe I'd even change an Indian kid's life one day. Also, did I mention that this program said *they* would pay *me* to attend?

I was on holiday in India when I got the email from them. Once again, I got to walk into my parents' room and tell them I got into school, but this time I didn't need any money from them. I was three thousand dollars in debt because of my Discover card. I had an entire life in Chicago, but I called my roommates and told them I was never coming back. I also told them they could keep my stuff. I was done.

Last year, I sold out the Chicago Theatre. The one you see in all the movies? The big CHICAGO sign? That one. I went back to all my old neighborhoods. One of the people who employed me for cash was a wonderful lady named Lucy, who ran Lucy's Event Staffing. She had a tiny office by the train station, and one day when I was walking home I popped in and said, "I REALLY need work. I'm educated, I learn fast, but I'm not a citizen." She hired me as a banquet busboy. She came to the Chicago Theatre last year and brought one of my old paychecks. She said, "You left so suddenly, I still owe you like, a hundred and eighty dollars."

Having a professional degree and becoming a distinguished *anything* was good enough for my parents. It was better (in their minds) than telling people their only son was writing jokes about smoking pot for a living, and barely making enough to eat. Instead, their son would be a college educator. He would teach eager young students about Shakespeare and Chekhov, two white guys who never had to wash Buffalo Chicken Bites and Mini Chimichangas off dishes at a Grand Lux. I wouldn't be *me* if I didn't disappoint my parents a little, though, and so a few things happened that caused me to detour from getting an MFA in Alabama to starting a comedy scene from scratch in India. One was that I met Swara, whom I would later propose to, another was that I found myself onstage again, with an eager audience that—unlike the people in Chicago—had been totally deprived of stand-up comedy.

When I was back in India in March 2002, getting ready to return to Alabama in September, the premiere theater venue in Delhi was and is a place called the India Habitat Centre. It's posh, it's snooty, it's the kind of place where people say "theatuh" as if they're British royalty circa 1840. That theater called to me. I wanted to tell dick jokes on that posh stage. It's a 430-seater auditorium with incredible acoustics. On any given weekend you could watch everything from Hindi plays to *Hamlet*. One afternoon, my mother and I walked into the office of the artistic director, Vidyun Singh. She was this beautiful, sixty-year-old woman smoking a cigarette and smiling at us while she watched a videotape of my *Brown Men Can't Hump* show on the stage of Knox College. She watched about five minutes before pausing the video. She took a long drag of her cigarette.

"Vir?"

"Yes?"

I was sure she was about to shame me for insulting her intelligence by forcing her to watch such trash. Maybe she'd tell me never to set foot in the *theatuh* again.

"I'll give you a Friday evening show."

I figured she meant in a small room that would hold about ninety people. But she offered us the Stein Auditorium. I could not believe it. I also did not believe anyone would show up. I was a complete unknown, and the Habitat was famous for having this upper-crust, Delhi-high-society socialite membership that was not exactly my target audience—or so I thought. I had to get the word out to younger people. The date was set for eight weeks later, in January 2003. A poster was made, and flyers were printed. Vidyun told me to make sure the show had an eye-catching title, so I called it *Not for Members Only*. When I told her the title, she just stared at me. I imagine she was thinking, "Look at this arrogant twenty-year-old nothing who thinks he can rebel against the storied institution that I basically built with my bare hands." Whatever she was thinking, she still went for it.

I put up posters all over town:

Habitat presents

VIR DAS

NOT FOR MEMBERS ONLY
An evening of stand-up comedy
At the India Habitat Centre

We sold out in ten days. Word got around that the bastion of theater poshness was opening its doors to lesser mortals. Young people who would never have thought to come to the Habitat showed up. Not long after, I did another show there. Delhi showed up, and we sold out again. It was the first-ever public English stand-up show in a theater in Delhi.

I worked hard on my material. Open mics and the Russian theater teachers had taught me a little about honesty, so I just tried to stay as true as I could to who I was and what I was about. I talked about Lagos, about women, about Galesburg, about my brief time in Boston. I remember being so nervous that I covered the entire bottom of the stage in cue sheets, which we hid behind flowerpots. People in the audience were probably thinking, "Is he re-creating a garden up there? Is this a forest motif?" It wasn't subtle, but it worked.

So, again: lens flare, laughter, and then . . . a standing ovation?

Sahil and Nikhil were both backstage panicking while I did my set. When I walked off after the show, they stared at me in disbelief. We sat there in silence. What the hell had just happened? It was an amazing moment, but after realizing you've found your calling, you've got to then do something else that *doesn't* feel right, so you can go back to doing what *does*. At least that's how it works for me. I need to get on a flight to see the wrong person, to realize I love the other, right person. I love stand-up comedy from the bottom of my heart, but to realize that fact I had to leave India, leave that Habitat show, and fly all the way to Montgomery, Alabama.

Don't get me wrong, Alabama is beautiful. It really is like the movie *Forrest Gump*, if you just add a brown guy from India to the cast. There were so few Indians and Asians in Montgomery that I remember the one time, in the parking lot of a Chinese restaurant, that I saw another brown guy. We collided as if we were the world's last two pandas. I spoke Hindi, he spoke Arabic, which limited our bonding. We wished each other well, knowing that this being two years after 9/11, most people in Alabama would probably assume we spoke the same language and were planning to detonate a bomb, even though we came from different worlds and the most dangerous weapons we had access to were kitchen knives.

Believe it or not, the Alabama Shakespeare Festival might be one of the most beautiful theater complexes I have ever seen. There are massive, sprawling manicured lawns, a lake with ducks and geese, and an opulent building that relies on the contributions of rich trustees. But a college it was not. I was the youngest person in this program by a mile. These were actors who had all done community and regional theater, many of them were married and in their thirties. I was twenty-three and didn't give a flying fuck about lawns and geese. I thought I was going to grad school, not *To Kill a Mockingbird* with a bunch of older, regional dinner theater stars. I was living near a gas station, which is where I did my grocery shopping. I could not afford a car or much furniture. Turns out nine hundred bucks a month doesn't buy you a whole lot in Montgomery. I paid $590 for rent, and had $100 for groceries, electricity, internet, calls home, and clothes. I was broke by the third week of the month.

I thought grad school would be different. Back home, when my parents told their friends I was going to get a master's and become a professor, their reactions led me to believe I'd be respected, like a scholar. Instead, I was cycling three miles to the Alabama Shakespeare Festival on State Route 95 while people screamed racist shit at me. I was coming back to an apartment where the living room consisted of a mattress on the floor with an ethnic Indian bedcover. It wasn't like my magical summer in Boston at all. I felt lonely, out of place, immature. Forgotten.

Self-pity aside, here's what *also* happened. I had fallen in love with stand-up comedy *and* with a girl. Swara, the girl I would later propose to, had visited me in Chicago when I was a dishwasher. We fell in love and had this romantic summer in Delhi. She planned to move from New Delhi to Alabama and find a job so we could be together. The minute I got there, though, I knew I couldn't do that to her. Would we have been content? Sure. Would she have gotten a job and made a home? Sure. Would it have been a massive compromise? Yup. We could have created a pretty good life, and I think she would have been happy, but I had experienced a real gig with a paying audience at the India Habitat Centre. There was no going back from that.

But there I was, drenched in sweat in a theater in Alabama talking about *Titus Andronicus* and cycling home to a dingy apartment. It was a window into what my future in America might look like: scrounging for theater gigs, struggling to make ends meet, feeling resentful. Oh, and having racist shit yelled at me from the windows of jacked-up pickup trucks. So many of the actors at the festival had come in from New York or L.A.—cities that had chewed them up and spit them out. That's why they decided to get into academia. I know that the whole "those who can't do, teach" saying is cruel, but it isn't always untrue. I hadn't been chewed up yet. I hadn't been spit out. I had been cheered on. I felt . . . special. I know that sounds arrogant. But sometimes in my profession you have to be. It's the only way to counter the mountain of rejection you inevitably contend with. I remember once looking at myself in the mirror and saying, "The first time I tried comedy I was good at it. I sold out the Habitat. Twice. Maybe I AM meant for more."

I remember the final straw that broke Alabama for me. If you're as poor as I was, studying so hard that there wasn't time for a second or a third job, you become a Michelin-star chef on a minuscule budget. I took whatever was left in my kitchen at the end of each month, when the money ran out, and combined the ingredients to create new dishes. First, it was cereal for breakfast and lunch. Thank god for American cereal and the level at which this processed cardboard loaded with sugar fills your stomach. One night, I got home from the theater more tired than usual. I had cycled home for lunch that day so the internet guy could come fix my modem. I was exhausted. I was worried that my Indian accent was getting in the way of my performance.

A fellow student would keep asking me to repeat what I said in a scene, just to be a dick. Every time I'd do a line, she'd go, "Sorry, what was that?" It took every bit of restraint I had to not tell her that I spoke Shakespeare in an accent closer to the intended dialect than any American actor could. Learn how to say "lord" without rolling your r's first, madam. But at Knox, at Harvard, at the Habitat, my accent never really got in the way, and neither did my skin. As cultural beacons go, Montgomery isn't a great barometer for the real world, but for me at that moment, it was all too real. So I got home cranky and tired that night. There were two things in my fridge: Costco cut ham from the gas station and Dabur mango pickle from India. Chef Das headed to the kitchen, got a frying pan, and did what had to be done.

After frying/sautéing my mango pickle ham medley, I sat down on my dining table, a.k.a. the mattress on the floor with the ethnic Indian bedcover. As I ate my concoction and thought about my life, I had an epiphany that was both terrifying and thrilling: I needed to drop out of grad school.

If you come from an Indian family, you know that dropping out of school equals shame. We're talking "immediate family, extended family, and the entire nation shaking their heads in pity" type of shame. Did you hear about the Das family boy? Dropped out. Couldn't hack it in America.

Couldn't hack it in America.

America won. I was done. Well played, Alabama.

I packed my clothes and my ethnic Indian bedcover. I told my parents a lie about how the certification of the Alabama Shakespeare Festival had come under question and I might not be able to teach if I graduated from there. For those of you reading this, the Alabama Shakespeare Festival was, and is, a fully accredited institution with an amazing faculty, and anyone who studies there will be qualified to teach at the end of their MFA. It just wasn't for me. I told the people at the University of Alabama I had a family emergency and would have to go home. They were so nice they told me that they would be able to defer my admission to the following year. I had only been there seven weeks. I said I'd let them know, never intending to return.

Before I left, I walked to the gas station and said goodbye to the lady who owned it. She gave me a bottle of wine as a parting gift. I don't drink white wine, but it was my last night in America, so I drank the whole bloody thing, and the next morning I caught a bus to Atlanta, a flight to New York, and then a long Air India flight to Delhi.

When I landed back in Delhi, no one met me at the airport. Instead, a driver was sent to get me. When I was a kid, and I would watch people coming and going from airports, it never dawned on me that some of the travelers I saw might be deboarding a plane feeling like utter failures. I put them on a pedestal and envied them so much, I never assumed that someone coming or going at an airport might be questioning their life decisions, feeling totally lost and terrified about the future. Now I was one of those people, and maybe some awkward kid was watching me, with no clue that I'd just left a FREE education in America, a place I had dreamed of escaping to. Or maybe they could tell I had no clue where I was headed just by looking at me.

The next year of my life was tough. I was staying at home with my parents, but taking every chance I could to escape to see my girlfriend, Swara. I wrote another show for the India Habitat Centre and called it *Who Let the DAS Out?* Trisha hand-designed the poster. It was my head emerging out of a suitcase. Pretty fucking apt. You didn't know if I was coming or going. Just that I was trapped, somehow on wheels, and full of baggage. We put posters up at the venue, and I did interviews with local papers to market the shows. And we sold out. Again. Maybe my decision to leave Alabama wasn't so shameful, after all?

Socialites and the press started to come to my shows, which led to word of mouth spreading, and more people buying tickets. I was working hard, but I was also getting swept up by the Delhi party culture. Rich socialites were inviting me over because I was this young, novel thing. One night Trisha and I headed over to a socialite's house. Let's call her Anamika. It was an opulent Delhi party where, at some point after dinner, the hostess stopped the music and gathered everyone in her living room. I had no clue what was going on. She announced, "We have a stand-up comedian in our midst, and I think he can be persuaded to do a few jokes for us." She said it like I was a strange, speckled bird from the Amazon that she had captured and brought in for people to gawk at. Anamika moved a table to the side so I could stand in the center of the seating area. I remember making eye contact with Trisha and both of us realizing, without words, that this wasn't, and would never be, our world. But I was a grad school dropout, so instead of protesting I obliged and did fifteen minutes of material for free in this woman's living room while bloated, chain-smoking rich people guzzled vodka between fake bouts of laughter.

I bombed.

There was a polite smattering of applause at the end of my "set." The socialites looked at each other, and at Anamika, rolling their eyes as if to say, "What is all the buzz about with this guy?" I felt used, like I needed to go straight home and take a shower, like they do in movies after something shameful happens. Trisha and I didn't talk about the party on the drive home. I dropped Trisha at our parents' house and headed to see Swara. I walked in and told her, "I have to get out of here. I can't just keep doing one show every four months at the Habitat. There's no future in that."

We'd never talked about moving to Mumbai, but both of us, almost simultaneously, said, "What about Mumbai?"

Mumbai was the city of movie stars and Bollywood. It was where Shah Rukh Khan had gone with one suitcase from Delhi and become the biggest star in the world. I could barely get through ten lines of Hindi, let alone act in Hindi. Mumbai seemed like it was for bigger things and bigger people. Going from Alabama to Mumbai was a little bit crazy, so the conversation ended and we kept on living our lives in Delhi. I had no plan, no idea how I would make something out of my life.

Four weeks later, a lady named Sabina Sehgal Saikia called me to her office at *The Times of India*. She was the editor of the *Delhi Times*, the city supplement of *The Times of India* newspaper, and a very big deal. One of India's foremost food and restaurant critics, she was this boisterous, tobacco-chewing, chain-smoking, deep-voiced, thick-bespectacled force of nature who scared the shit out of you. She told it straight and could destroy your restaurant or your life with one review. She had been to both of my shows at the Habitat, and she had also happened to see me at Anamika's house. Once I settled into her office, she said, "Delhi people are utter bollocks." I loved that she used that word, "bollocks." The editor of the *Delhi Times* was writing off her entire readership. "You belong in

Mumbai. There's a show coming up called the Times Food and Nightlife Awards in Mumbai, and *everyone* will be there. You're going to emcee."

So I did as she said. At that one show, unlike that night at the socialite's house, I killed. The morning after that gig I decided with Swara to move to Mumbai in seven days. I quickly landed my first TV gig. About a year later, when I went to visit Sabina, she hugged me and claimed all the credit for my success, and for making me a full-time Mumbaikar. I've been a proud Mumbaikar ever since.

Three years after I moved to Mumbai, India was attacked. It was November 26, 2008. Terrorist gunmen went from room to room at the Taj Mahal Hotel next to the Gateway of India, shooting strangers in cold blood. It was one of the worst terror attacks on Indian soil. In one of the rooms in the Taj was Sabina Sehgal Saikia. I remember watching the news and learning that she was trapped inside the hotel during the four-day siege. I messaged her and told her I was praying for her. A few hours later, her husband confirmed her death on the news in a live interview with NDTV.

If she'd made it out, this is what I would have said to her:

Thank you, Sabina. In a moment when no one, including myself, thought anything of me, you did. You were a force. Your intelligence and grace were contagious. Much better than the bollocks.

The fact that I went from dishwashing in Chicago, to headlining shows in Delhi, to cycling along a highway in Alabama, to hosting a major show in Mumbai in the span of a year, right? It was pure luck, propelled by the kindness of strangers like Sabina.

Things were going well, but Mumbai wasn't exactly easy. The comedy scene was nonexistent. I had been slapped around a little by life by that point, and I'd had a few run-ins with kismet, so I firmly believed one thing: There wasn't a comedy scene, but there *could* be one.

I'd just have to build it, with other idiots like myself, whom I would have to find.

A SHORT DOSE OF GROUNDING

I read comments all the time. And I never respond. And I regret it every single time. I'm not at the stage yet where I've stopped reading the comments. I'm trying. My favorite comment is "Go to Pakistan!" Part banishing, part questioning of patriotism, part wanderlust. Used to happen more frequently but has died down a bit in recent years. I always wondered how Pakistanis felt about that comment. For a hot minute, thousands of angry Indian trolls were effectively Pakistani travel agents.

CHAPTER EIGHT

ONLY IN MUMBAI

The day Vir moved to Mumbai.

It is incredibly ironic that as I write this, the first rain of the monsoon season has just hit Mumbai. There's classical music playing in my study, and the world outside my window is an endless sea of gray. Gray and green. This rain comes hard and thunders for forty hours as it washes Mumbai clean, until the clouds disperse and we all feel alive again. This city that chews up and spits out the best of us (myself twice during an eighteen-year career) actually looks livable. We forget about our homes and apartments that are the size of matchboxes. We hear birds instead of traffic. People go outside, taking morning and evening walks. Stray dogs frolic in the streets. There's a sense of hope. That hope lasts for about two days, until the city becomes a brown puddle of dirty water during four months of what feels like a relentless stream of god's piss raining down on you. No matter which god you believe in, in Mumbai, that god will piss on you for four months.

If you've never experienced Mumbai, imagine that New York and London had a baby, and then the baby grew up to be a troubled child with tattoos and an anger problem. On the worst days, there is no worse place to be. But when this city decides to embrace you, as it eventually did me, there is no better place in the world. Almost every single Mumbaikar is accused of romanticizing the city, just like New Yorkers do theirs. But trust me, if you come here, you'll understand its allure within five seconds. And if you don't get it, you shouldn't stay.

It's a city where everyone looks at each other with a common understanding: This shit is hard, we've got bills to pay, careers and families to take care of, so (unlike New Yorkers) we should smile at each other, we should live, we should drink, we should dance, and we should acknowledge that none of us may be on this planet for long. Anything can happen. That's the promise of Mumbai.

Shah Rukh Khan, the biggest star in the world, has done countless interviews where he's said he showed up in Mumbai with one suitcase. He stared out at the sea and promised himself that one day he would run this city. He now owns a house that overlooks that very sea. Thousands of people flock to his gates every Sunday to wave at him. A mass of people stand on the road to catch a glimpse of a man who is the living embodiment of dreams coming true, and as they wave, they hope their shot at the dream is next. This man has an elevated platform built on a corner of one of the walls in his house so that he can stand on it and wave at people.

He helps them believe that anything can happen.

Johny Lever is arguably the most famous Hindi comedic actor in India. He has played the comedic relief in literally hundreds of movies. Before he got famous, he showed up in Mumbai with nothing and stayed in Dharavi, which was the setting of the movie *Slumdog Millionaire*, except he was in the real Dharavi, without all the fancy cinema lighting. He went from living in a slum to becoming an actor. He doesn't have traditional good-looking-actor–type features, and he probably has logged more screen time than Robert De Niro at this point.

It's Mumbai. Anything can happen.

This city is full of people who came here with nothing. You don't judge each other for not having made it yet. You just drink chai, sit on the floor, have a cigarette, and bitch about someone who has made it, until it's your turn and then people get to bitch about *you*. And then some of you do make it, and some of you don't, and some of you make something that never quite amounts to the "it" you wanted. That, in my opinion, is the most dangerous Mumbaikar of any sort, the one who thinks they haven't gotten their due. They can pollute a film set and a comedy club with this sort of cynicism, which is contagious and brings everyone down. I've worked in four different industries—TV, film, comedy, and music. There's one cynic in every studio, set, club, and concert. Stay the ever-loving fuck away from that person, because they will kill what is most innocent in you. Maybe this is why I like outsiders. We don't assume anything is due to us.

The best kind of Mumbaikar is the one who believes it's going to happen tomorrow, that they're right around the corner from IT, even though maybe they've felt that way for twenty-five years. Even better than that person is the one who something just happened for. They just got a gig, a gig that has a 19 percent chance of working out, but fuck it, it's something. To them, like Kate Hudson in *Almost Famous*, that means it's all happening. I love that person. They sit there wide-eyed in the greenroom of a club because they just got to watch a headliner they had only ever seen on Netflix, and they're trying desperately to play it cool and not ask for an autograph. Or they're on a film set with that director they've been dying to work with, and maybe their part is only five days, and maybe they did it for little or no money, but they try to be around the monitor to see how this magic is made. They are like a kid in a candy store. They're in a backstage area with rockers who just made people cry with a guitar solo or a falsetto and then casually walked off and lit a joint while ten thousand people still linger in the remnants of their starlight. They offer you a drag, which you take hoping desperately not to cough—god forbid the virtuoso should discover you're an amateur. I love that guy too. I am that guy. Much of Mumbai is that guy.

What I love most about this city is that you learn to live next to people you may not agree with when it comes to politics or music or life choices, people you do not understand but you're forced to walk across the same brown puddle of rain beside them, in matching rubber slippers, under the same relentless shower. In Mumbai, like in New York or Paris, you will see a heavily pierced graphic designer covered in tattoos sitting on the train next to a clean-shaven struggling actor who is sitting next to an accountant, a doctor in training, an admin clerk, a poet, and a driver. They're all on the same train to work, squashed into the same compartment, all in each other's personal space—with zero judgment. They all have an umbrella, and a pair of shoes in their bag that they will put on when they get to work. Everyone is sweaty and in slippers, and no one can understand the train announcement. If you don't know which station is next, are you really even from here? Learn that shit. We're Mumbaikars.

I now live in a very privileged part of Mumbai called Bandra. It's arguably where the artists and the creative people who have "made it" live. A few suburbs down is Andheri, where the artists who haven't yet made it live. Moving from Andheri to Bandra is kind of like the Queens to the West Village dream. Sure, you can stay in Queens, and many people do. But the Village is the Village. I use this word begrudgingly because of how much it has been bastardized and overused on the internet, but in Bandra there is a vibe. When I first came to Mumbai I had no clue about the vibe. I somehow just found myself in Bandra.

When Sabina Sehgal Saikia got me to do the awards show in Mumbai before I moved there, I was put up at the *Times of India* guesthouse in Pali Hill in Bandra, probably the third most expensive area in Mumbai, although you wouldn't know it from the apartment I stayed in. It was a two-bedroom that I shared with an accountant from *The Times of India*. The bathroom we shared was so small, if you took a shower you flooded the pot. For the awards show I wore the same suit I wore for my graduation at Knox College, which I'd bought for seventy-six dollars at JCPenney in Galesburg, Illinois. Fuck these Bollywood people with their designer clothes. I didn't need to impress them.

The first celebrity who came onstage to hand out an award was Aishwarya Rai, who at the time was literally the most beautiful Indian person on the planet, an actual Miss World–title holder. When I saw her, in an instant I forgot all about artistic outsider conviction. ALL I wanted to do was impress her, and all those Bollywood people in their designer clothes.

It's hard to describe how Aishwarya Rai, in person, looked to a kid in his twenties who had never been around a woman *that* gorgeous. It was like watching magic walk. It's one of those moments where you fully accept that god created this upper echelon of beautiful human beings and you do not belong with them. Your best bet is to offer to get them chai. She gave the award to the lucky restaurant winner, and I've never wanted to be a North Indian restaurant chef more in my life. And then, on that stage, in front of the entire Indian film industry, and in front of many chefs who were hungry for more than food, she said, "Vir, you're really funny!" And she walked offstage.

This was probably her being polite, but it was a gigantic deal to me. I sometimes wonder if insiders are aware of the effect they can have on people. How seemingly meaningless interactions with them can change a person's life. I wonder if it makes them more empathetic. I've seen very little proof so far. This is why I now know in retrospect, her kindness was a rare thing.

She had just been in a massive Bollywood movie called *Umrao Jaan*. I was in a seventy-six-dollar suit. We were on the same stage. In Mumbai. Let's. Fucking. Go.

I've met Aishwarya Rai a few times since that awards ceremony, and I've seen her be as polite to others as she was to me that night. I saw no reason to think there was something special about me. But that night, I took it to mean I was undeniable, and she was giving me the thumbs-up. Also, she later married Abhishek Bachchan, who is a legit funny star, so maybe she gets funny.

This is going to sound pretentious, so bear with me. There are moments in the life of an artist when the universe will let you know that it expects you to be undeniable. Not good, not great—undeniable. With no knowledge of consequence, no plan, it requires you to put everything you have into your performance, and trust that the universe will do the rest. You perform like you have nothing to lose, like the whole room is waiting for you to show up and leave people feeling amazed or moved or exhausted from laughing. It's what you feel when a prima ballerina walks onto the stage, or when Merry Clayton, the woman who does the duet with Mick Jagger on "Gimme Shelter," hits that high note.

That night at the awards show was my high-note moment. And it's because I had literally nothing to lose, so I was unafraid. Celebrities and powerful people are used to people being afraid of them. If you're reading this and you're in the business, and you're maybe going to interact with a celebrity, have zero arrogance, but also zero pandering, and zero fear. You'll pop in the room.

The next day I had an evening flight back to Delhi, a city where I was just considered a grad school dropout, not a guy that Aishwarya Rai thought was funny. When that show went well, I was asked to go to a meeting at Vineet Jain's office in Mumbai. He's a media mogul in India, the owner of *The Times of India.* His office was on the fifth floor of a heritage building, and was full of what I assume were priceless antiques. When I sat down with him, Jain didn't ask me to host another show.

"We want you to be a VJ on a channel we are launching called Zoom. It's like the Indian version of MTV."

I tried to play it cool. I had no clue how to be a VJ.

"That sounds interesting, but . . ."

"I'll pay you one hundred thousand rupees a month."

Calm down. That's about two thousand U.S. dollars, which was *still* a ton to me at the time.

"I'm going to think about it and let you know, if that's all right?"

"You need to be here in three weeks."

This man in his fancy office just assumed I was going to take the job on the spot and give up everything I was doing, because of this one meeting.

And he was right.

So that was it. I had to figure out this next, unexpected phase of my career, starting with what the fuck a VJ was. In case you're clueless like I was, it's a video jockey, like Martha Quinn or Downtown Julie Brown on old-school MTV. Think of it as an on-air host who interviews people, introduces video clips, and tries to act cool as shit even if they are, as I was, definitely not.

When I said goodbye to Jain and left the office, I walked to Marine Drive, which snakes along the sea. It was drizzling, and I smoked a cigarette while I walked next to the water, wondering what this next part of my life might be like if I left Delhi, left my family, and my gigs at the Habitat Centre. I also still had a serious girlfriend in Delhi. How could I not take the job though? I could finally tell my parents that their son was no longer a broke, unemployed joke cracker. I would be earning a living, and not just that, but 100,000 rupees. A MONTH.

There's an energy in Mumbai. I know that sounds like a fucking Instagram post or the start of a commercial made by a Mumbai travel agency, but it's true. And when it enters you, you discover a new gear that you never knew you possessed—I'll call it the drive to hustle. I think it entered me that day on Marine Drive. After I smoked that cigarette and stared out at the sea, I called up my friend Yamini. She was Swara's cousin, and we'd met in the U.S. once. I said, "I'm moving to Mumbai. I need an apartment!"

She asked me where I planned to live.

I said, "The guesthouse in Bandra is pretty nice, so maybe around there?" She laughed and called her broker to see if they would help me. This would be like someone from Des Moines with no savings and no trust fund walking around New York and saying, "I think SoHo is the place for me!"

Two hours after I called Yamini, a broker named Imtiaz, in a traditional taqiyah cap, showed up to help me find a new home. I got on the back of his motorcycle, and off we went.

I was driven to the house of Dr. Russell Pinto, in Bandra. I took the 230-square-foot spare room in the back of that doctor's house on the spot. It had a bed, a gas stove, a television, air conditioner, and a refrigerator—all crammed together on one wall, right next to the front door. The perk was that I could make dinner, piss, watch a bad sitcom, and turn up the AC, all without leaving my bed. It was affordable, yet extremely hazardous. You had to turn the gas off before you turned the AC on because we were always afraid that a spark from the AC would blow up the house. But it had a little balcony where I could smoke, and St. Paul Road was quiet. It was a ground-floor room, which I later learned meant I would have to swim to my apartment three days a week during the monsoons. But on that day a Muslim, a Christian, and a Hindu stood on a twenty-square-foot balcony and locked in a deal for six thousand rupees per month for rent. Mumbai.

I told Dr. Pinto I would be back in two weeks with all my things. But who was I kidding? I had no things.

Swara moved to Mumbai with me, and we made a little (literally little) life there in the rented, cramped spare room. Her father worked for Air India and had a three-bedroom five minutes away. She was allowed to stay with me three nights a week.

Look, I still don't know what a VJ does. I didn't take the job because it was my life's dream; I took it because when I told people that I wanted to be a comedian *as a job*, they typically laughed for an uncomfortable amount of time, making me think that a job with steady pay might be a good idea, even if I had no idea what it was or how to do it.

I remember one night, Yamini, who was dating a VJ, organized a dinner for me and some VJs at a VJ's house. So I walk into the room and VJ Purab, VJ Gaurav, VJ Nikhil, VJ Salil, and VJ Cyrus S. were all having dinner with each other. They were these tall, gorgeous, extremely eloquent, kinda fashionable man-boys. I remember thinking, "Are they required to live together? Like a VJ barracks kind of thing? They wake up in the morning and share hair gel and go off to battle bad music?" It was kind of like an enthusiasm-off tournament that night. That's the main thing VJs really have going for them: enthusiasm. So they kept out-enthusing each other. Like a *Twilight Zone*–*Stepford Wives*–meets-brown-*Zoolanders* kind of evening.

At some point one of them sat me down and said, "So you wanna be a VJ?"

"Not really. I really wanna be a stand-up comedian," I said.

"Oh fuck, bro. You should leave. Stand-up comedy in India? No future, bro."

Thanks, VJ Yoda! Did they teach you that at the tight jeans fitting? Trust a VJ to be so enthusiastic about VJing that they think no other profession is possible. But in his defense, there *was* no comedy scene in India at that time.

Despite the handful of shows I'd done in Delhi, it wasn't like Jon Stewart was knocking down my door, asking me to work with him. Once I started the job, I learned very quickly that being a VJ is not an easy gig, especially not for a comedian. As a VJ, you're supposed to be upbeat and enthusiastic about whatever song or topic you're told to discuss, whereas most comedians are natural skeptics who are born to question, call out bullshit, and make people laugh by *not* being positive and upbeat about stupid crap. "Guys! The next song is totally awesome and I love listening to it when I shower! Oh my god, I'm *so* pumped about it!" Being a VJ was like being an influencer without influence. It was like having a mental disorder called Overly Enthusiastic Syndrome. Think about it, you're in a tiny room in front of a green screen screaming your guts out to a single camera. This, while a producer who went to film school and a cameraman who wants to make movies both look like they want to kill themselves. You announce a song, rave about a song, pay homage to the song . . . and then the song doesn't play . . . you pause for three seconds and then react to the song that didn't play. It's insanity.

But there I was, standing in a tiny television studio looking into a camera, with no audience to ramp up the energy. They made me wear a sleeveless shirt even though I had zero muscle definition, which is a physical failing that producers have pointed out to me in front of film crews on numerous occasions throughout my career. A producer actually arranged for fake temporary tattoos to cover up my arms and make me look cool, to which my response was "JUST GIVE ME A SHIRT WITH SLEEVES!!! HOW ABOUT THAT???"

I was terrified and very clearly not good at the gig. Also, why was there so much gel in my hair? I could cut glass with each spike.

The show was called *Ek Rahin Vir*, which loosely translates to *There Once Was a Vir*. Even my supposed future was titled in past tense. It was a bad sign.

I faked it every single day, which is probably why they fired me after four months of pretending to love "Hey Shona" from the movie *Ta Ra Rum Pum* or "Ain't No Other Man" by Christina Aguilera. So there I was, back in my 230-square-foot hovel, my room with no view. Now I was not just an unemployed grad school dropout, I was an unemployed grad school dropout who'd just been fired from a fucking VJ job.

Mumbai gives you opportunities, but they may not always be the right ones. Tim Robbins had to wade through the shit pipe to get to the cleansing rain in *The Shawshank Redemption*, and this was very clearly *my* shit pipe. I also learned that I'd signed a shit contract.

Kids, listen to Uncle Vir for a second. Hopefully you move to Mumbai or New York or Los Angeles and someone offers you a dream job. But when they do . . . READ YOUR FUCKING CONTRACT. With a magnifying glass. And lawyers. And a red marker to circle the shit parts.

I had signed an exclusive noncompete contract with *The Times of India* where they owned me for *five years*, during which they would pay me each month. But if I quit that contract early, I owed them about $53,000 USD.

If I ever quit, they owned me, my jokes, my blood, my organs, my firstborn child, and the birthmark on my right ass cheek. So I was fired, but not exactly. The boss told me, "We're gonna continue to pay you, but put you on ice for eight months until we can figure out what to do with you." When I protested, he reminded me of my contract. Dick!

I had been in Mumbai long enough to know that eight months "on ice" meant artistic death. The VJ show was crap, and thankfully no one had really seen it, since I didn't last very long and the channel was new. Maybe if I went back to washing dishes for another sixty-seven years I could pay off the money I owed them and finally be free!

I lamented this to Swara. She said, "Even if they give you another show, it's not going to be funny. They don't know funny!"

And she was right.

I asked the boss for a meeting the next day.

I sat in this powerful, fifty-four-year-old man's office and said, "Look, I can be on ice for as long as you like. I'll take the money. But when I come back, I may not be funny. It's possible I've forgotten how to be funny. Maybe everything you have me do is deliberately unfunny. Maybe it sucks. Maybe I just can't figure out how to make it good. Maybe I've lost my talent by the time you put me back on TV."

The smile that came across his face very clearly stated: "Well played, young Das." He knew exactly what I meant. Don't waste money on me. I'm not gonna play ball. Let me go.

He hugged me, and then he officially fired me. I was unemployed, free of my contract, and thrilled.

There's a lesson here for all artists: As long as you hold the talent, you hold the power. The best they can do is try to bottle your talent, to get it out there. But only *you* can make that happen, and they know that, which means you ALWAYS have leverage when it comes to your art. Don't forget that. Don't get put on ice.

So what could I do next? Where the fuck did I belong? It sure as hell wasn't on a show where I sported fake tattoos and spiked hair and went home to camp VJ. Also, no disrespect to Christina Aguilera, but no amount of Shakespearean training or Russian method acting coaches could make me good enough to seem genuine and honest about loving that song.

I loved Jon Stewart (still do), and this was at the height of his reign at *The Daily Show*. I figured, I like to tell jokes, I'm politically engaged-ish, so why not try to be the Jon Stewart of India? And how did I accomplish this? With a Handycam, of course.

While I was VJing, I was still doing stand-up in Mumbai at night, so I had some material. I took my Handycam and went to my old debating partner, Ruksh's, house. He was now a journalist working in Mumbai. Ruksh from DPS Noida, the most principled man I knew, fellow debater who had listened to my bullshit for years, married Karishma from DPS Noida, my other closest friend from high school. The head boy of DPS Noida married the head girl of DPS Noida. Achievement married achievement, and all these years later, they were still dealing with their clueless friend's bullshit. We used his dining table, rented two lights, and made a cardboard cutout of a show background, which I called *The Indian Excess*. I put the camera on a tripod, turned it on, sat down at the kitchen table, and shot an episode of my pretend *Daily Show*–esque pilot. We spent all night editing it. It looked like a home video, but we thought it was the shit. I took that pilot into the office of every news editor who would see me, and I hit play. Some had seen me at the *Times* Food Awards, so they knew I could deliver. Out of those meetings, a lady called Vandana Malik gave me a shot. What was it with powerful Indian women taking chances on me? I owe them my career, I swear. I was offered a job on CNBC in India, doing two minutes of jokes every night on a television show that was watched by the entire country, including the prime minister. I was twenty-five.

My first TV gig was four months of obsolescence, and my next was four years of prime time.

I had gone from an outsider washing dishes, to an outsider in Alabama, to an outsider inside a tiny studio with one camera, to a lonely comedian in a newsroom with five hundred journalists running and screaming and shouting at each other to make the 9:00 p.m. show happen. A newsroom is the most electric, chaotic atmosphere you can imagine. Where else will you find five hundred people running around passionately screaming about their country?

"The textile minister just announced!!!"

"The attack has been claimed by . . ."

"Arjun is having an affair with . . ."

"There's an additional tax levied on . . ."

VJ Yoda's head would explode in that room.

Even as the joke man, I had to work with urgency. We would film my segment at 4:00 in the afternoon, which gave them enough time to edit it and then slap it on the 9:00 p.m. bulletin. Every night at exactly 9:56, after a commercial break, the anchor would say, "And to close the night off here's Vir Das with 'News on the Loose' . . ." and my segment would play. Working in that environment, I learned what news truly means to people, what an anchor really does, how they have to pivot live, how they deal with brand-new, sometimes tragic, information. I was sitting in a studio waiting to do jokes when India won World Cups, when terrorists attacked Mumbai trains, when politicians resigned, when actors died by suicide. I heard all of it with the same earpiece, from the same control room as the anchor.

One day Swara left her office in Churchgate and told me she would meet me at home in Bandra after my filming. I knew she took the train. I was doing my segment when Savio in the control room got in my ear and said, "Vir, there's been a terror attack. Stay in the studio, we will do your segment later."

Two anchors rushed in and started doing the news with what little information they had. I was in a corner and couldn't cross cameras to get out. Bombs had gone off on the train that Swara was supposed to be on. I remember listening to the control room as a producer said, "Gaurav, there's one more blast . . ." Then he'd anchor some more. "Gaurav, stand by. One more blast . . ." I watched this man masterfully take information in and deliver it in a way that wasn't stressed or disrespectful. When they cut to some full-screen footage, I was able to dash across the studio and call Swara. She hadn't left her office yet, but the train that had blown up was the one she took every single day. The next day after the attack, we still did the jokes. My producers Suresh, Venkat, and Natasha told me it was important to make people laugh in the face of tragedy. Good lesson. It was an incredible place to work. I was like their odd adopted child, and I learned so much from the anchors about professionalism, integrity, and the fact that even in dark times, the show goes on.

When the music for my segment played, I would appear on camera sitting at what looked like a child's desk in the corner of the news studio. I would be drawing circles on a piece of paper, which was something I blatantly stole from Jon Stewart. I'd open by saying, "Welcome to News on the Loose, my name is Vir Das . . . and that's the bad news." And then two minutes and twenty-five seconds of jokes until it was time for five seconds of closing music. Basically, it was an open-mic set, with new material every day, watched by millions, five nights a week. It was exhilarating.

The segment was a huge hit. It finally felt like my work meant something. It got to the point where businessmen and politicians would call up the channel and ask us to do jokes about them to soften their reputations. It also meant that my audience was old as balls. None of my fellow twenty-five-year-olds were watching CNBC at night; they were getting high and enjoying Mumbai. Since the show was watched by every businessman in the country, I started getting booked to tell jokes at corporate gigs. Money was coming in, so my attitude became: Is there anyone else out there who likes watching Pryor? Carlin? *SNL?* Thinks that jokes can be made about more than onion prices and GDPs? Maybe jokes about dicks and VJs? They had to be out there. I knew there was an audience. I had seen that in Delhi, but in Mumbai I was cut off from them.

The disparity between my on-screen act at CNBC and the jokes about my life that I was doing live couldn't have been larger. I remember once I was in Kolkata at a car launch doing thirty-five minutes for automotive journalists. In the middle of their afterparty, in a nightclub with blaring music, they stopped the music and threw me onstage to tell jokes. I bombed hard, worse than the car that was discontinued a year later. A lady in the middle of my set screamed, "*Why?* Why are you doing this?"

I stopped and responded, "Uh, madam? I'm being paid to do thirty-five minutes."

"No, I mean comedy. In general, in life." She got a solid laugh. That made one of us. I knew I had to find a young audience, and soon.

So much of those early years was people not knowing where to put me or what to do with me. I remember my first foreign gig. I got booked to play in Dubai for 22,000 rupees, so about $275. I was going to do comedy at a Daler Mehndi concert. In case you're not aware, Daler Mehndi is a massively popular Punjabi singer. Bhangra is the fastest-paced music in India. Punjabis are the most violent, passionate dancers in India. You dance with a heart rate of 230 with every part of your body. None of this lends itself to thoughtful pauses and witty jokes.

I needed to buy a laptop, and I was told they were cheap in Dubai, so off I went. We were at a huge outdoor venue in Dubai, packed with twelve thousand people. I was to do five minutes in the middle of each of Daler's kurta changes, of which there were six. I was also to bring on three "item girls," who were beautiful women that would dance to pop songs. One of them was Negar Khan. This is what led to my first-ever appearance in a Mumbai newspaper.

I bring Negar Khan onstage, and she is dancing (as "item girls" do) with a hint of disinterest. Maybe her thoughts are also focused on the laptop she possibly wants to buy in Dubai. Then a sweet engineer-looking kid climbs up onstage and starts to dance three feet away from her. Dubai security is notorious for running on some vicious cocktail of anger, protein, and steroids, and they slapped the kid twice and chucked him back into the crowd. The crowd lost their goddamn minds. I was then sent out to calm them down. Because that's what an angry Punjabi crowd that has been drinking since dawn on concert day wants most—a terrified comedian with hacky, unpolished material.

I came out and yelled, "Hey, guys, what is up with airline food?"

And twelve thousand people yelled, "FUCK YOU!!! WE WILL CUT YOU UP, BASTARD!!!"

"Er... You ever notice the curtain between first and business class?"

And twelve thousand people screamed, "FUCK YOUR MOTHER!!! SEND OUT DALER!!!!"

Now I was starting to tear up slightly. "You ever notice how women talk too much and guys don't listen?"

And twelve thousand people raged, "MEET US OUTSIDE, BASTARD, WE'RE GONNA KILL YOU!"

Eventually I gave up and just said, "Ladies and gentlemen, welcome back Daler Mehndi."

I was escorted out of the venue, put back in my hotel, and didn't get paid. I arrived in Mumbai to a headline in the city tabloid that read, NEGAR KHAN GROPED BY FANS IN DUBAI BECAUSE EMCEE VIR DAS FAILED TO CONTROL THE CROWD. THEY WERE RESCUED BY DALER MEHNDI.

Once again it struck me. I needed to find my own audience. Soon.

I needed to find other crazy people who were my age, not wearing suits and talking about the budget deficit but wearing jeans and sneakers and talking about balls and heartbreak. It would take me two and a half more years, a flop movie called *Mumbai Salsa*, being in the background of another movie called *Love Aaj Kal*, quitting my job at CNBC, and finally getting cast in a very big movie, *Delhi Belly*, to start my own company with some comedy friends, in a city that was hungry for a laugh.

We called the company Weirdass Comedy, because that's how Americans pronounce my name. Vir Das becomes Weirdass in America. I'm proud to say it was India's first-ever comedy company, as far as I know. It was a collection of pure idiots, potheads, and rejects who thought there had to be something funnier out there than some of the shit we were being subjected to on TV and film. I had just been cast in two movies, one being *Delhi Belly*. In the middle of making *Delhi Belly*, I called to the set the only two funny people I knew in Mumbai: Kavi Shastri, who is still my creative partner today, and Sorabh Pant, a young writer I knew on *News on the Loose*. Kavi and I had met as background extras on a movie called *Love Aaj Kal*, and Sorabh and I had been in the trenches together at CNBC. The day I called them to the *Delhi Belly* set, I had been shaved bald and dunked in cement.

The three of us stood in the heat inside a tent at the Film City studio complex (think the Warner Bros. lot on steroids), and I said, "Let's start finding other funny people. Let's do an open mic like I used to do in Chicago. I'm done doing jokes for old uncles." And then I went back on set and got dunked in cement again.

When *Delhi Belly* eventually wrapped up, we did Mumbai's first English-language open-mic comedy event. We called it the Weirdass Hamateur Night, and it was at a spot called the Blue Frog. The Blue Frog was THE indie music club in Mumbai. They typically had rock shows, until I came along. The owners gave us a Monday night, as you do with shitty gigs that are expected to attract no one.

The first night, ten comedians showed up to perform. If you've ever been to an open-mic comedy night in L.A. or Chicago, you'll know you might get twenty audience members, nineteen of whom are dating or related to one of the unknown comics. On our first night, 350 people showed up. That's how novel stand-up comedy was in Mumbai. I'd learned a few things since that show in Delhi where I used flowerpots to hide my cue cards, but I was still an amateur. We all were. For example, we had no concept of how *actual* comedy clubs notified a performer when their set was about to be over.

Usually there is some system where a light is flashed, so you can panic while thinking to yourself, "Oh fuck, I have two minutes and I've only gotten through half my set." Instead, I used the stopwatch on my phone to keep track of each person's set, and when time was almost up I took a metal spoon and banged it on a steel plate, like some DIY gong from hell. It was the least subtle system you can imagine. I would ring the gong/plate and unintentionally scare the shit out of each comedian. We did that for six months before we realized there were better, gentler, less startling ways to run a comedy show.

The way the shows worked was that each comedian would have about two and a half minutes for their set, and since I was the "headliner," I did my forty-five-minute set and tried to include new material each time I did. If that sounds like a power grab, you should know that the other comedians got two and a half minutes because that's all the material they had. I was on TV and was known around town, so I wasn't headlining as some demented ego trip; I just had enough recognition to bring people in (people I was not sleeping with). Completely by accident, I basically put these comedians through every horrible thing you can do to a new performer: the gong, two and a half minutes to make people laugh, a crowd that had to stand the whole time as if they were in a frozen mosh pit (there were no seats), and, worst of all, celebrities in the audience. Imran Khan—the Bollywood actor and my costar in *Delhi Belly*, not the former prime minister of Pakistan—came to one of our shows. If that doesn't sound impressive to you, it would be like Ryan Gosling randomly showing up to an amateur comedy open-mic night at a small rock club where one slightly known and several totally unknown comedians were performing. Maybe Ryan Gosling spends his Monday nights this way, but I doubt it. He's married to Eva Mendes.

Pretty quickly, our buzz went through the roof.

A lot of the people who showed up to tell jokes at the Blue Frog were hobby comics, guys who worked in advertising who thought they should be famous because they were the funniest people at their conference room tables. Many of them never came back after their first attempt, but of the comedians that did, at least ten or fifteen are now huge comics in India. These were careers that, like mine, were forged in fire. Forged at the Blue Frog, in between gong strikes. By the way, the worst audience member in the world is that advertising guy who feels like he's funnier than the comics onstage and is sitting there thinking, "Yeah, I can do this shit. How hard can it be?" Those guys got eaten alive onstage every time they performed.

I paid for all of the Blue Frog shows, and I lost money every single night. But I loved it. I was dating Shivani by this time, so she did our event management. We had massive fights before each gig, and crazy sex after. It worked for us.

The shows allowed me to hone my material and introduced me to a small group of comics who became longtime collaborators. We got an office and made Weirdass Comedy official. I had some money from my CNBC gig, so that helped me pay for the office. We were like the cool pothead kids with eight thousand ideas, so we started writing sketches. It's not easy to motivate a bunch of potheads, but somehow, we churned out a ton of material. Some material was so terrible it should have been sent off to sea after being lit on fire like at a Viking funeral, but some of it was pretty great. It felt like punk rock.

We wrote all the time. Sketches, comedy, rock songs. We did improv. Within six months, we had enough material to put on India's first sketch comedy show, with new material every month. Unless someone was doing improv in a small rural village somewhere with no internet, I'm pretty sure we actually were the first. Our shows turned into a scene. When I look back at it, I realize that my comedy then was pretty vulgar and borderline sexist. I call that time my "Look at Me, I'm Bill Burr Phase," which is a phase I'm pretty sure every wannabe male comedian goes through. I wanted to be edgy, but it's hard to create alternative comedy when there is no existing scene to be an alternative to. In your twenties, you also usually don't have enough life experience to back up any edginess you're trying to put out there.

But what an environment like that does is make you ready for literally any crowd. I've done some pretty terrifying gigs, but nothing could compare to the sheer unbridled fear of a Weirdass Hamateur night.

Five Hamateur nights in, models and celebrities and DJs were coming to our shows, possibly because they'd heard about *Delhi Belly* . . .

About that.

Because I was doing comedy all over town, managers, agents, and filmmakers started paying attention. I'd landed a major part in *Delhi Belly* alongside Bollywood stars like Imran Khan (a.k.a. Ryan Gosling of Bollywood). *Delhi Belly* was produced by Aamir Khan, who is just a cinematic icon and perhaps our most credible film producer to date. This man is single-handedly responsible for elevating the intelligence in Hindi cinema, and *Delhi Belly* was his gamble on a young, fun, vulgar caper. If you ever get the chance to be around someone who works at his level, fucking take it. My work ethic today comes from having been around people who work at the top and seen the hours it takes.

I had already shot the movie when Weirdass Comedy was taking off, but for whatever reason the movie sat on the shelf, as they say, for a Long-Ass Time. But because Imran was in it, people in the film industry knew about it, and by association, they started to know about me. In case you don't know about *Delhi Belly*, it finally came out in 2011 and was a hit. It was kind of like the Indian version of *Lock, Stock and Two Smoking Barrels* or *Snatch*, a Guy Ritchie action comedy peppered with over-the-top violence and crazy, ridiculous shit going down at every turn. I made my big movie debut wearing a curly black wig and glasses, which you really should google if you haven't already. So there I was, this short Indian comedian acting alongside the Ryan Gosling of Bollywood. I felt totally out of place, but I loved it, which is the story of my life.

So at this point life is pretty good. Shivani and I have moved in together. I'm getting enough corporate work to tide me over and make rent, and then I made *Delhi Belly*. I got to be where magic is created from nothing, a film set where kids from small towns show up to be part of someone else's madness until hopefully, someone is dumb enough to fund their own madness. It's hard to describe how addictive that is. When I quit/lost my job at CNBC because I was too busy juggling it with film work and a global recession was coming down, film was all I wanted to do.

While we waited for *Delhi Belly* to come out, Imran and Ranbir Kapoor, who may still be the top actor in India today, were set to host the Filmfare Awards. The Filmfares are like our Oscars, with like 98,000 more sponsors and 7,000 percent more attitude. They had been struggling with a scriptwriter who had been around for about twenty years and was writing jokes as if he had been around for twenty years. By the way, as I write this, I realize I've been around for close to twenty years, and now I am having an existential crisis about my own age and writing. And so it goes.

The Weirdass gang was called in on a Hail Mary to see if we would write some segments and sketches. We did, and it went great. It was possibly the most stressful writing gig I've ever experienced. Very little time to work, rushed deadlines, total pressure.

Then the following year, 2010, we got a call to write for Shah Rukh Khan. Yup. That one. Mumbai-suitcase-by-the-sea-balcony-platform-six-thousand-people-on-Sunday-waving Shah Rukh Khan. I was invited to Mannat, his dream house by the sea. Imagine George Clooney mixed with Marlon Brando inviting you to his 27,000-square-foot mansion.

You know someone has achieved an otherworldly level of wealth and fame when even their house has a name that literally translates into "Dreams."

So welcome to one of the most terrifying experiences of my life. This was the first time I was exposed to true fame. People who are as famous as he is can call meetings at strange hours, because *who would question him*? He's Shah Rukh Khan. I arrived at the appointed time—11:00 p.m.—and was met at the door by a security guard, who politely asked, "Where have you come from?" I was so nervous I replied, "Myself. I'm Vir Das. I've come from myself." I was there to get hired as a writer, and my first conversation out of the gate was a total failure and made zero sense.

The guard led me into the grand study lined with grand bookshelves. I waited there for *three hours*, alongside a few other mere mortals who were called to hold court with Khan. It was me, a doctor, a politician, and a few event organizers all waiting around. To ease my nerves, I gorged on his fancy food and looked at his books while we waited.

Then he arrived. Court began. All I remember is that he walked in followed by roughly seventeen people, who moved like they were extra parts of his body. You got the distinct impression that this was someone who was NEVER alone. Which made me fascinated by what he possibly did or thought about when he *was* alone.

He smoked a cigarette and said, "You read the script?"

The room was utterly quiet as he and his posse waited for my reply.

"Sir . . ."

"And?"

"I don't think it's funny."

More silence while everyone exchanged looks that very clearly telegraphed the thought "This dumb punk kid is getting tossed off the balcony and into the sea."

Khan stood up and walked closer to where I sat. "All right," he said. "Let's see what you've got." Translation: "Bring it, young blood."

So the kid who got kicked out of boarding school, the one who snuck porno magazines onto a Lagos rooftop and got left behind by a Carnival Cruise ship, was writing jokes for an icon who was worshipped by millions. If I fucked this up, I was pretty sure I was done. I would have to leave India and start a comedy scene somewhere else, somewhere remote and humorless, like Siberia, or maybe I'd just go back to my boarding school, as a teacher.

I pitched jokes for five hours, got some laughs, and changed some punch lines while he smoked and drank black coffee. We wrapped at about 7:00 a.m. I could see the sun starting to come up over the ocean through the antique-looking and yet somehow entirely automated electronic wooden blinds.

"Go home and rest up, and come back later," said Khan. "We'll start again then."

I basically moved into his study in Mannat for four days to work on his jokes. I was in my twenties and he was forty-something, so I'm sure some of the material I came up with was immature, but he was never patronizing, and always kind. People say you shouldn't meet your heroes, but Khan was an exception. Hanging around him was unlike anything I've ever experienced. If you've ever seen someone walk into a room and felt the energy shift, that's what it was like. When he walked into a room I could feel the *ground* move, and I mean this in the literal sense. When he walked onstage at the Filmfare Awards, thousands of people shifted in their seats, I swear. I've played large crowds myself, but I have never experienced anything like that. It's another level. You can't manufacture that kind of magic or charisma or whatever the hell you want to call it. He just had *it*.

Here's the thing: Being a writer is heartbreaking business. You write words that you fall in love with and then you have to watch someone butcher them. Weirdass Comedy wrote almost every major award ceremony in India for the next three years, for almost every single major Bollywood star as a host. Khan is the only person I've seen take a line, make it entirely his own, and then somehow make it better.

Khan has met millions of people, and each one of those meetings likely meant way more to the person than it probably did to him. Do you know how many writers for movies, books, articles, ads, and more he meets a year? Probably thousands. But somehow, he makes you feel like you are the only person in the room, and that your voice is being heard. He also makes sure you are fed when you're in his house—and that's very, very Delhi. For that brief moment he spends with you, he finds a way to be kind and entirely present. It's something I have tried to learn, a feeling I try to conjure up each time I go onstage. I try to make my audience feel the way he made me feel. I haven't always succeeded, but it's a noble goal to make someone feel entirely seen, heard, and like they're part of your story. That's when fame truly means something beautiful.

We love Khan because he is the king, and yet he is the perpetual epitome of an outsider. The Delhi boy who showed up with a suitcase, no contacts, no family backing, and built a house by the sea. If it's possible for him, it's possible for us.

I've toured the world, I've made movies, I've become a part of show business, I've crashed and burned, been canceled, been investigated, made my way back. I now have a global audience, bigger than the Blue Frog. I am, by many people's yardstick, a success. But I know only two things for sure: I've been audacious, and I connect with people. Whether it's moving to Mumbai, putting flowerpots down onstage, deciding to be in the movies, heading to Alabama, going on prime time, or starting a company. I have never believed something I do is going to be small. In my mind, it's going to be huge, and it's going to require everything I have. There is no other way.

I've usually been wrong, but when I've been right, boy, have I been right.

I think that's really the only upside of fame. You can believe that something is *going* to happen. Khan or Dave Chappelle can wake up in the morning and think of something and know that it is probably going to be believed in, funded, listened to, and seen. The amount of time that passes between them having an idea and that idea reaching a green light is down to the minimum. I've woken up with eighty ideas in my head every single morning since I was eighteen, and fame to me means reducing that time span between having an idea and having someone green-light that idea. That span is still far from short enough.

I recognize that even though the person on the stage is literally elevated, the audience members are the ones on a pedestal. I learned that from being in the room with greatness when I was very young. Most truly famous people, most truly great artists, understand how humbling the experience of being in front of an audience can be. Fandom is fickle. But attention and respect, hopefully, last a long, long time.

I wrote the Filmfare Awards later that year. Twelve years later, I had just turned my phone on again after going underground after having performed at the Kennedy Center, which got me canceled and which you'll read more about soon. After that debacle, I came back to Mumbai and was keeping a low profile, editing a show I had just starred in that we all were convinced no one would buy. "Starring the terrorist Vir Das, here's a show for kids!" Everyone, from my management, to my family, to the press, to the industry had written me off.

I was taking a cigarette break at the edit suite when I got a call from an unknown number. I answered.

"Vir. Shah Rukh."

I froze.

"Khan?"

He said yes and laughed, as if we talked every single day. I had never spoken to this man on the phone in my life. He had just heard something I had said about him on Whitney Cummings's podcast the year before. I have too much respect for him to share exactly what he said. I won't talk about what he and his family had been through that year. But let's just say he was kind, during an extremely rough year in my life.

I will share that he ended with "This is my number. Now you have it if you need me for any help."

Courage from a king is worth more than gold. That's when fame, or stardom, or artistry, is truly beautiful. When it inspires, connects, and makes you brave. I finished my cigarette and went back in to edit.

I knew I wasn't done.

That was three years ago. I went from being at a complete low to co-directing a movie, acting in three, winning an Emmy, and working on a new special. I finished my first solo director's gig, starred in a show. Only in Mumbai.

Whatever comes next, I know this: It's gonna be huge. It's gonna take everything. We're probably going to have to build it ourselves.

A SHORT DOSE OF GROUNDING

I once walked into an audition for Gabriel Iglesias's sitcom, *Mr. Iglegias*. I think they saw my headshot and thought I was Mexican. I walked into the hallway and saw about fifty Mexican guys there. Then I went into the audition and told them I was Indian. They politely asked if I could do a Mexican accent. I had never done a Mexican accent in my life. So I did an audition in some sort of a racist Cheech & Chong rip-off accent. I said "amigo" five times in three sentences. I would give anything to get my hands on that tape.

CHAPTER NINE

BOLLYWOOD ANTIHERO

Vir having some fried chicken before hosting the International Emmy Awards.

Is there some kind of unwritten rule that says if you write a chapter about a certain industry, you have to have actually succeeded in that industry? Because if that's the case, I have no business writing this. Here's why: I have been in eighteen movies. Five of them were successes. I'm told that's a pretty good ratio. Now consider that I've been the lead in four movies, and *none* of them was a success.

So why am I writing this? Because I want you to understand Bollywood.

In case you don't know, Bollywood is a big, flashy word that is supposed to encompass the entire Hindi film industry. First of all, you should know that most Indians in the industry *detest* the term "Bollywood." It's reductive and crude. It's the equivalent of calling Hollywood "Marvel Town." Even though I have not succeeded as a leading man (as I write this), and by all popular accounts I have kind of crashed and burned out of the film industry, I now head to an editing room every morning to finish the edit of a film called *Happy Patel*, which, if all goes according to plan, will be my first Hindi release in eight years. *Don't call it a comeback, I've been here for years*, as LL Cool J says. But yeah, it will hopefully be called a comeback, if you consider the middle of the celebrity ladder an exciting place to come back to. I do. But we'll get back to *Happy Patel* much later.

Just like in Hollywood, manifestation and delusion are the two things that you need to succeed in the Hindi movie industry. You have to have an undeniable level of confidence mixed with an undeniable level of luck mixed with—if you're *really* lucky—an undeniable family tree. And even then, on any given Friday you could be rejected by the audience. Why? Because the movie wasn't good enough, because you were not tall enough, because the role you were playing didn't suit you enough, because your voice wasn't deep enough. Who knows? But the audience somehow, collectively, decides how they feel about you, and they usually are in complete agreement. There are *very* few actors that an Indian audience is divided about. They either love you, or they fucking hate you. All of us. It's pretty unifying, and also utterly heartbreaking if you're on the receiving end of the latter.

Before I actually got cast in a film, I *never* thought I would be in the movies or act in India. I just wanted to tell jokes, make people laugh, and do the occasional serious role onstage. If I could have a world tour and play Titus Andronicus in a play that ran for eight weeks, hell yes! That's a good life. The first time I saw a Bollywood movie (yes, we hate the term, but I'm using it anyway, as it's the easiest shorthand) in the theaters it was a Shah Rukh Khan movie called *Kabhi Haan Kabhi Naa*, which means "Sometimes Yes, Sometimes No." That title also perfectly describes the audience–artist relationship. I was twelve years old in a theater in Patna, Bihar, and I saw people climbing over each other to get tickets to the Friday, the opening day, show. In the theater, they danced during the musical numbers, and when Khan, who wasn't even that big of a star back then, showed up onscreen, the roar in the theater meant that the gods had chosen a few special people for a certain kind of stardom and hero worship, and he was one of them.

I never thought I could be a hero like Shah Rukh Khan, or Aamir Khan, or Salman Khan, but as I spent more time in Mumbai doing stand-up, I kept asking myself, "Where is our Adam Sandler? Our Ben Stiller? Our Mel Brooks? Our Robin Williams?" Where is our comedic leading man? And then, I guess you could say I *did* start dreaming about it. I didn't think my fate was ordained by the gods, but I guess I thought maybe I could make people laugh onscreen, just like I did onstage.

Would the audiences accept that? Would they cheer?

If you want to truly experience and understand Bollywood cinema, go to Gaiety Galaxy at 8:00 a.m. on a Friday. It's a massive multiplex in Mumbai, and it's where the stars of whatever film is opening that weekend sneak in to see if their movie works. In most American theaters, movies don't even start playing until 10:00 in the morning, so if you're ever wondering which audiences are more devoted, a Bollywood fan could take down a Hollywood fan any day of the week. They're that serious.

The real Bollywood audience piles into the theater as if it were a pilgrimage. There is no "shushing" happening. This is not a quiet, safe space. The audience talks, laughs, whistles, dances, yells, and claps during the movie, which is why if you want to know if your movie is good, you go to Gaiety Galaxy on Friday morning. If it's bad nobody will be there because they'll walk out, and word of mouth will spread like wildfire. If it's good, you'll need earplugs.

The entertainment industry in India moves fast. In Hollywood it can take years to put together a TV show or film, but in India a project can be conceived of, shot, and released in a year. That makes the audience in India very unforgiving, since we release three to seven movies a weekend. There's always something new, so why waste time on a bad film? For the Bollywood audience, each week's film releases become their big outing. That's what I love about Bollywood—the average person in India gets one outing per week where they sit down with their family in a theater. Whether you're a tailor in a small town, a father of four who works at a bank in a big city, a woman who runs her own business, a laborer, a student, privileged, middle class, or struggling, you can watch a movie.

There is nothing more unifying than the darkness of a cinema. There's no religion, class structure, or discrimination in the dark. The one weekly outing we all have in common is the new movie that released that weekend. It's religion, it's escape, it's equality, and—most important—for many of us, it is the only time we will enjoy ourselves until seven days in the future, when we will do it all again. So the movie had better be good. That begs an important question: What the hell is "good" for everyone? It means our movies have to be magnanimous and escapist. If you show a hardworking man or woman and their family *Spotlight* (a drama about uncovering child molestation in the Catholic Church), they're going to jump off a bridge.

Which is not to say that we don't have our share of dramatic cinema, story-driven dramas, gangland epics, violent action films, mainstream comedies, and even slacker and stoner movies. But for a movie to be a pan-Indian hit, it has to be patriotic, entertaining, or—preferably—both. You need to show big dreams, family dynamics, bright colors, amazing musical numbers, and a fair amount of slow motion. What *The Avengers* did for America, Bollywood has been doing for India for years. That's all Marvel is, by the way—America's Bollywood. Bold costumes, massive set pieces, insane action, revenge stories, unabashed enjoyment, thin plotlines. On any given Friday, every Indian hero is Iron Man.

In 2006, I decided that I wanted in. I had been working at CNBC for a while, stand-up was going great, I was making bank, my girl loved me, I could not complain about much at all. Which is usually the time I decide to shake shit up and attempt the impossible. I wanted in for the same reason that anyone wants in: I watched a movie that blew me away, and opened up my perception of what (and who) could be onscreen.

The film was called *Rang De Basanti*. Aamir Khan is a star who brings people to the theater, but really this was a bittersweet ensemble movie about four college kids who went up against the system. Aamir was the reckless lead guy, there was a strong, silent type in Kunal Kapoor, and then . . . there were two other guys, Sharman Joshi and Siddharth. One was a warmhearted utter buffoon, and the other was a thoughtful, chain-smoking, melancholic dreamer. I saw myself in both of those characters. They didn't look like leading men. They weren't particularly well built; they looked like everyday people. Because of this, I realized that I could have played either of them. There they were, standing next to a superstar, holding their own, not because they were ripped and six feet tall but because their acting was solid. This was an ensemble film, with realism and strong character arcs, and yet it had all the excitement of a Hindi movie. I was hooked. I walked out of Gaiety Galaxy on a Saturday afternoon and told Swara, "I haven't acted in about six years, and I miss it. Look at those two guys. I think there might be a place for me in Bollywood."

We both laughed. She was leaving for Rotterdam to do her MBA soon, so we shrugged off my comment like it was this distant dream, like "I wanna own a bar someday," or "Maybe I'll start my own record label." Eight months after she left, though, I was on set starring in a Bollywood movie.

Here's how I did it . . .

By Bollywood standards, I am not meant to be a leading man (I don't have a god-given six-pack, for starters). So I asked a bunch of men who *looked* like leading men where men who looked like leading men went to become the leading men they looked like. All of these men pointed me in the direction of Aram Nagar, an area of Mumbai where the casting directors of the industry all had offices. My mission was to try to get meetings with them and see if they thought I had "star power." Back then, no one gave a shit if you were good for a certain type of role or if you had particular strengths. You just had to be captivating the second you walked into the room. So these casting directors were the gatekeepers of the industry. Anyone who is not from a Bollywood family and has made it to the movies (which is like 20 percent of the industry, to be honest) came in through a casting director who believed they were the next big thing.

The first day I went to Aram Nagar, I found my five-eightish self auditioning and waiting for a meeting alongside nine hundred boys who were all ripped and tall, with jawlines and cheekbones. They all looked like leading men, they all had acting training, they were all built like gods, and *I* certainly believed at least 70 percent of them were quite captivating. Sitting there waiting for my turn, I realized that I was never going to make it to the front of this line, and this was not the path for me. It was so clear the second I walked in, not only because of my build but also because of my background. My Hindi was all right, but the fact that I was an English-speaking comedian was always going to be a problem in the minds of casting directors. It's a perception problem I still struggle with.

Instead of walking away and giving up, I figured that if stand-up was in my way, maybe stand-up could *be* the way.

Just like I had xeroxed two hundred flyers back in Galesburg, I spent my (small) life savings on a DVD that showcased my stand-up. I called Vidyun Singh at the India Habitat Centre and said I wanted Stein Auditorium to shoot a show. We did it with five cameras. It was basically a ninety-minute audition reel. I found a DVD designer in Lokhandwala Market called Kapil to design the hell out of the cover so it would look legit sitting on a shelf next to actually legit movies like *Magnolia* and *Fight Club*. Then on a Sunday, I went to every video store where I knew Bollywood directors went to rent movies. Yes, some owners put my DIY stand-up special, which I called *VIRagra*, on the shelf. I told them I was a famous American comedian (What? The one show at Knox doesn't count?) and gave them ten DVDs that looked professional, free of charge. I spent about three minutes max giving this pitch to each DVD store employee, and it worked.

It was an utter shot in the dark, and it changed my life.

By this time, I had a manager called Vivek, and he had started getting me auditions for the comedic sidekick roles. I met Vivek when I was waiting for a three-minute audition for a TV show called *The Great Indian Comedy Show*. Look, it was TV comedy. Not quite as edgy as the things we were doing live, kind of sanitized and safe, but it got a mammoth number of eyeballs and was actually funny sometimes. If they knew you were a live comic, though, they didn't trust you to be clean, to be able to act; at best they wanted you to write for them. The producer, who didn't like me, gave me, at the behest of his younger team, an audition slot, then made me sit on a chair outside the studio for three straight days, waiting for my three-minute audition. In walked this actor who was part of the cast. His name was Ashwin Mushran. I remember watching him walk in like it was in slow motion, not because of his innate charisma but because he had the new iPod. I found myself thinking, "Now that's a working actor. He has an iPod." I could afford the damn thing myself, but it felt like he *deserved* it.

He had seen me sit on that chair outside the studio for about thirty-four hours, and he eventually came up and said, "What's happening to you isn't professional." Then he handed me his agent's business card! "This is my agent, Vivek. I've heard of you, and so has he. Give him a call. He will make sure shit like this doesn't happen again." Who does that? Vivek signed me on our first meeting. He even got me my first professional international acting gig in *The Curse of King Tut's Tomb*, a B movie shot in India with Casper Van Dien. I played the part of Jabari, a character with one line: "I'm sorry, sir, I broke the emerald tablet."

Stardom, here we fucking come!

So ever since that day, in anything I have ever produced or directed, there is a role written for and offered to Ashwin Mushran.

Because of my *VIRagra* DVD and the kindness of Mushran, I got an audition for the third lead in a movie called *Mumbai Salsa*. It was a *Friends*-like movie about three guys and three girls who meet at a local salsa club three nights a week. I was auditioning for the comedic relief alongside a brooding, well-built, captivating hero. The producer was Vikram Bhatt. He had made a couple of big movies and had just gone out on his own with his own production company called ASA Productions and Enterprises. He was known to be pretty hands-on, and he did the auditioning himself. I got in at 2:30 p.m. and did the reading. On the way out, I told Vikram, "I do stand-up. If you ever have some free time and want to have a laugh, here's my DVD." I dropped *VIRagra* on the desk and caught a rickshaw home.

It's thirty minutes from Andheri, where his office was, to Bandra, where I lived. When I got out of the rickshaw, I had a message from Vivek that said, "Vikram wants to talk. He's at this number." I called him from the street outside my apartment complex, and he offered me the lead in his movie. He said, "You're my hero. You've got something. I saw your DVD, watched fifteen minutes, and called Vivek." Me? A Bollywood hero? I was still doing my nightly bit on the news. I still took rickshaws. I still lived in a tiny box.

Sometimes artists tell a story about the person who said, "Don't quit your day job, kid!" That's exactly what everyone said to me at this moment. DO NOT QUIT THE NEWS CHANNEL FOR A VIKRAM BHATT MOVIE! Turned out, it was pretty good advice. I didn't quit the job. Somehow, while working nights, I managed to star in a Bollywood movie during my free time. I bought a motorcycle, and when I was done shooting in Film City at 8:00 p.m., I would bolt over to the news studio, shoot jokes by 11:00 p.m., and then get home by 1:00 a.m. to get some sleep and be back at the film studio by 6:00. It may sound insane, but it was a blast. I loved everyone in that movie. It was so unapologetically small and try-hard. Several months later, I invited all my friends and CNBC colleagues to a screening of *Mumbai Salsa* the week before it came out in theaters.

A film screening is an interesting psychological experiment, where a bunch of people get together in a room and innovate with the process of lying straight to your face. There is nothing worse than watching a bad movie and wondering what you are going to tell the director/star who is DESPERATE for feedback and approval.

Two things you need to know in this situation:

1. If you're on the receiving end of feedback: If they come out talking about the story or the acting and their head moves up and down while they tell you about it, you made something good. If they come out talking about the cinematography and the costumes and their head moves casually from side to side . . . sorry, you made dog shit.

2. If you are on the giving end: Here are two methods I use after watching a shit film. I look the director straight in the eye and emphatically say, "Congrats! You've done it again!" Then I exit as quickly as possible. *Or* I confidently point to the screen and say, "Now THAT was a movie!" And I exit as quickly as possible. Both statements are technically true, and very useful.

After the first screening of *Mumbai Salsa*, many people came up and told me about the costumes.

Now, if you google "*Mumbai Salsa* review," you will find two reviews online. The third link is for an actual Salsa Club, and the fourth is for a Mexican restaurant. *The Times of India* said, "Watch out for Vir Das trying to be Woody Allen," which is not a sentence I'm comfortable with, knowing what we all now know about old Woody.

IndiaGlitz said, "Vir and Manjari [Fadnis] are candidates for more films. Wonder why there was no prerelease buzz around them?" If you add up those two journalists, plus the people who acted in and made *Mumbai Salsa*, plus their immediate families—that is how many people in total saw *Mumbai Salsa* in a theater. To say it was a flop is to pay it the compliment of being on the radar. It came and went. I have so many friends who went to a theater and were told by the owner that the show was canceled because no one showed up. That's a phone call you don't really want to get from your buddies, I promise.

So it was back to "Stick to stand-up." I hear that advice about once a week, even today. "Stick to stand-up." The people telling me that are basically saying, "Know your limits. Don't reach. Don't think you deserve more than what you were built for." To which I always think (but never say out loud), "No one thought I deserved stand-up either." If I lived my life according to what other people or the market thought I deserved, I'd be back to washing dishes.

I worked at CNBC as if *Mumbai Salsa* never happened. My parents weren't upset, because I had a job and a girl I loved. From the outside, it probably looked like I was doing pretty well. But I had spent three months on a film set. I got to see people come to Mumbai from all over the place to make magic, because that's what I believe movies truly are—magic. I had seen rough days that turned into good scenes, and great days that got cut out of the final reel. I'd experienced the collective madness of moviemaking.

Going back to CNBC after Film City was like going back to academia in Alabama after tasting the professional stage at the Habitat. Which is to say, I could not do it.

Much to the dismay of everyone I knew, I left CNBC and the cushy gig. I was going to be a full-time actor. How that would happen, I had no idea.

Things move fast in Bollywood, but it took me one year and eight auditions to land a colead role in *Delhi Belly*, the movie that would push my career to another level. That audition came about because an assistant to the assistant of the assistant director (AD) actually watched *VIRagra* and showed it to a producer. They changed directors on the movie twice during preproduction, so it took time for them to cast it and start shooting. During the year that I waited to hear if I'd landed the part, I got a job as a background character in *Love Aaj Kal*, a movie that was shot in London. One of my creative partners, Kavi, got a background role too, so we were two young guys staying at the Berjaya Eden Park Hotel, praying that if we danced hard enough in the background, maybe the director would notice. They did notice, but not in the way we were hoping. I think we danced a little *too* well (or too enthusiastically) on the first day, because on the second day the AD asked us to take five steps back, *away* from the camera. On the third day, he asked us to take twenty steps back. Eventually they just stopped lighting us, and my friend and I were convinced we were going to be out of focus the whole movie. One day, I looked at him and said, "We're getting fucked, man!" So we just kept scooting back, kept dancing . . . but then everything changed.

One night back at the Berjaya Eden Park Hotel, the phone in my room rang at 3:00 a.m.

"Hello?"

"Vir?" It was my agent. "You got the part. You got *Delhi Belly*."

I screamed so loud the Queen probably heard me from three miles away at Buckingham Palace.

"Congratulations, man. I'm going to negotiate so hard for you."

Usually you *want* an agent to say this. It means they want to get you the most money and the best deal possible, but that is not at all what I wanted to hear.

"Please do *not* negotiate, at all. Whatever the fuck they are willing to pay me, we will go for that."

I knew how good the *Delhi Belly* script was, and I was not going to lose this role by asking for a crazy sum of money. I'd never been in a big movie before, so I did not want to make the first impression that I was a "complete asshole."

The next day I walked onto that London set with a little bit of an attitude, like, "I don't need you guys, I just booked *DELHI BELLY*."

My two costars in *Delhi Belly* were Imran Khan and Kunaal Roy Kapur, who played a stoner-slacker guy. Imran, if you remember, is the guy who looks like India's answer to Ryan Gosling, whereas I look like . . . me. But there we were, together, on film. We didn't make a ton of money, but it was still worth it. That's how good the script was, and how much we wanted to be in this film. I played Arup, this angry, eccentric, bottled-up guy chain-smoking his way through a heartbreak. I'd just been cheated on by Swara, so I could very much relate. I started the movie with this curly afro-type wig glued to my head every morning. Even worse, since the character shaves his head halfway through the film, they shaved my head. Like I said before, I'd recently slept with my future wife at that point, so "suddenly bald" was not an ideal look. Imran had become a superstar, so everywhere we went there were four thousand women screaming his name. I remember thinking, "This is it, this is the goal," completely forgetting that four thousand women were not going to scream for me, no matter what I did with my hair. We shared a trailer, and every time Imran opened the door you'd just hear "AAAAAAAAH-HHHHHHHHHHHHHHHHHHHHH" from the screaming posse of girls outside. Then I'd walk out with a shaved head covered in cement (a ceiling collapses on my character, covering him in cement), and they'd all go "Huh? maybe he's the villain." Pretty grounding stuff.

This wasn't a typical Bollywood experience in that it was more of an indie, so the three of us were always together and smoked a lot of weed at night after we had finished shooting for sixteen hours. It was like being at boot camp, so we really got to know each other. Imran was grappling with stardom, I was grappling with heartbreak, and Kunaal was grappling with a sandwich. This was a massive learning curve for me. It was nothing like the theater work I'd done at Knox, because acting for the camera is not the same as acting onstage. Onstage, you have to *be* spontaneous, and on camera, you have to *appear* spontaneous. It was like being at Disneyland, just this wild, insane group of people from all over the country coming together to make this thing we all believed in.

It wasn't always romantic. The only time I've ever walked off a set in anger happened on *Delhi Belly*. There's a scene where I'm riding on the back of a scooter with my hands tied behind my back, and my necktie is flapping in the wind. A goon was supposed to pull my necktie, so for safety reasons, they had a tie that fastened with Velcro, to keep me from dying before the age of thirty. We shot that scene about six times, but the Velcro kept coming apart. One of the stunt directors was this old alpha male Bollywood guy, and without telling me, he went to the costume department and ordered them to stitch up the tie. So on the seventh take, they placed the tie back around my neck, I got into character, the scooter took off, the goon grabbed the tie . . . and I nearly got choked to death—for thirty feet. When the scene ended, I didn't go into a rage, but I did quietly walk off the set. The director and everyone else knew I was pissed. I had every right to be pissed. No one wants their cause of death to be "strangulation on the set of a Bollywood comedy."

It felt good to stand my ground, but then I experienced a panic that had become familiar to me on the London shoot: *I'm going to be out of focus this whole fucking movie.*

Luckily that didn't happen. Overall, this was a pretty wonderful phase of my life. I was heartbroken, but I got all the shit any heartbroken guy with cash to burn would get: a nice car, a big-ass TV, a stereo system that could blow your hearing. I also had a movie set to go to, and on the days when I wasn't being murdered or yelled at (which was most days), it was amazing. I was also single enough that I could fall in love with making movies. For part of the shoot, Imran, Kunaal, and I stayed at the Dolphin Hotel, which was the kind of place that had three lights in each room: one was red, another green, and the third was yellow. There's an 85 percent chance that pornos were shot there. We didn't care. We were kids having a good time. We'd smoke weed at night, get three hours of sleep, wake up at four in the morning and go make a film.

Once you're in an Aamir Khan–produced movie, buzz gets around. I started getting other movie offers. I didn't study film, so I had no idea what to look for in a script; I just knew when something felt like good writing. I was cast in a zombie comedy called *Go Goa Gone*, which eventually became a cult hit. Suddenly I went from that comedy guy doing two and a half minutes each night on CNBC to the guy who had just starred in two of the coolest movies to come out of Bollywood. *Delhi Belly* became a phenomenon. And yes, we went to Gaiety Galaxy on a Friday to watch it. We were told that the 8:00 a.m. show was sold out, so we got there at 7:45 a.m. It's a strange experience watching seven hundred people roar at the screen when you're dancing or singing or doing something outrageous. You fully understand how it gets to some stars' heads. You're seeing hardworking people who woke up before dawn, spent a good chunk of their weekly pay, and traveled who knows how far to watch you on a massive screen.

Kind of like in that mythical idea of Hollywood, Bollywood can be a place of mind-boggling excess. Women who look like living goddesses, men who are more perfect-looking than an AI version of the "most handsome male in India." I spent time awkwardly nursing a drink at parties with movie stars, and going to events where the worst dressed person was probably in a designer suit that was two years old. Stars don't recycle clothing, they are draped in the new for a short amount of time until it isn't new anymore; they don't clean their own homes; and some of them, as I learned, don't like the color red. I worked with one actress who refused to allow anyone on set to wear red. If a gaffer or an intern had on a red shirt or pants or shoes, she would have them sent away. She said the color messed with her head, and she felt entitled enough to yell, "Get off the set!" if anyone had on crimson, maroon, or burgundy clothing. When someone is a star, people accommodate any level of crazy.

Another example. I once had a meeting with a major director—think of the Indian Spielberg. One of the first things he did after saying hello was to tell me my hair was "all wrong." He then asked his assistant to fix my hair, so the assistant did as they were told and moved my hair from one side to the other until the director was satisfied. We were not meeting about my hair though. We were meeting because I had written a script that the director had read and supposedly loved.

"Your script spoke to my soul," he said. "It made me cry. It was magnificent . . ."

I got excited, until he looked at his assistant and—referring to me, the guy whose ego he'd just blown up—said, "But look at this guy. He's a clown, a sidekick, a joke man, a fool."

He rearranged my hair again, this time with his own hands, and added, "You are one of the most beautiful artists I've ever met."

And then I never heard from him again.

I witnessed one of the more shocking levels of this insanity while in the middle of a lake, on a boat. I was filming a scene with another famous actress. Out on the shore, hundreds of people stood waving at her. Maybe ten of them were waving at me, so I did what most human beings would do. I waved back.

"Don't wave at them," said the actress.

"What? Why not?"

"If you want to be a star, you must never reciprocate their love. Have an aura of mystery about you."

"But isn't that rude?"

"If you give them love back, they will see you as accessible and will no longer love you," she said as she ignored her madly waving fans on the shore. "So bask in their love, but never ever give it back."

My god, the fact that she even thought about that and formed a plan was fucking terrifying. It also goes against everything I am as a comic. I struggle with how to manage my awkwardness, but Bollywood stars can handle fame because they feel like they're entitled to stardom. When people fawn over them, they expect it, whereas I am always startled by it. Stand-up is about relating to people. I want to stand for something or mean something to the audience on an emotional level. I do the exact opposite of ignoring their love. If I was a passenger on the *Titanic* and we had just hit the iceberg, I would still have been more comfortable than I was on that fluorescent plastic boat with some sort of shit cartoon character painted on the side. I'm not saying she was wrong—chances are she was spot-on. But I knew inherently it was something I would never be able to do. Putting myself out there 900 percent is the only way I know how to do it. I'm not on the pedestal; you, the audience, is on the pedestal. And if that means I'll never be as famous as the lady in the boat . . . that's fine. Fame wavers, funny lasts. That's what makes stand-up good—its accessibility.

As I write this chapter, I am in Sydney. I have this tour manager named Vince. He is a balding British man with some remnants of his long hair still streaming down his back. Vince loves Ozzy Osbourne, and he's done all the drugs in the world. He has the best stories. When I finished the Melbourne show yesterday, there were fans waiting at the stage door, and he was supposed to help get me into the car safely. There was this sweet kid, maybe twenty years old, who came up to me and said, "You don't think you impact people, but I want you to know you do. Can I give you a hug?"

Now, the Bollywood actress would have told me to swiftly turn away and ignore this person. Instead, I gave her a hug . . . and she burst into tears. Because I am awkward with these things, I didn't know how to handle it, so I stood there hugging her for two or three minutes, which is an eternity for a hug. I remember thinking, "Should I let her go? Am I making her cry harder?" Vince was no help, so eventually we unhugged and parted ways. When Vince and I got into the car, he said, "That kind of thing happens a lot, but most people don't stay and hold the person. They move on."

I am not most people, I guess. I'm as scared as the person I'm holding. Unlike the major stars who wave from their balconies or shun hundreds of adoring fans (who then apparently grow to adore them even more), I have no clue how to engage with fame. So I hug strangers.

Back when I *was* still trying to fit into Bollywood, *Go Goa Gone* came out right after *Delhi Belly*, and both were huge hits. Imagine an actor who is largely unknown suddenly starring in two *Hangover*-like comedies in a row. Since I wasn't the heartthrob type, I had tried to Adam Sandler my way into the movies in a country where the majority didn't really know who Adam Sandler was. Sandler never tries to be the hero, unless he's a goofy comedic hero, or an oddball antihero in an indie movie. There is no way to predict whether a movie will be any good, so I came up with a plan to try to branch out, so I wouldn't always get cast as the eccentric comedic weirdo guy. My plan was this: I had two hit comedies, so next I would do an art film to prove I could act. Then I would do an action movie, followed by a big mainstream sex comedy. I thought I could engineer my career so that I would become a gargantuan Bollywood phenomenon. I would become the funny guy who can also act, be a romantic lead, and leap off tall buildings. It was a genius plan.

Or so I thought.

I had zero control over when each movie would come out. I figured they would come out as they were shot, but the movies came out in reverse order. So the big sex comedy, *Mastizaade*, which was supposed to be last, came out before the others, and it was unwatchable. I guarantee you the audience at the Gaiety Galaxy filed out early from that one. I went from being the guy in two of the coolest movies of the decade to the guy in this shitty sex comedy, so those unforgiving audiences were like, "Fuck you, we're done. Next!" Then, once they decided that they weren't going to pay to see me in an action movie, it was clear that they *definitely* weren't going to spend their week's wages on the art film. *Delhi Belly* came out in 2011, and by 2015, I was done in Bollywood. I told you things move quickly there. I just didn't expect it to be my career, speeding at full force in the wrong direction. That's a quick turnaround when it comes to crashing and burning. One minute I was driving around in my Range Rover, going from magazine shoots to brand shoots to my bachelor pad with the giant TV. And then I was over.

At least, I thought I was over. As I write this, I'm getting set to do three movies. The thing I have learned, very much the hard way, is that an audience can smell inauthenticity. And inauthenticity, from a comedian, is intolerable. The thing comedians have going against them is that they have a very strong image offscreen. You don't know what Tom Holland is like on a weekly basis once he is done being Spider-Man. But you do have a sense of what Bill Burr and Dave Chappelle are like. So when they play a character, and that character or genre goes against their voice, a voice you love them for, it's hard to reconcile. When the comedian who does reasonably progressive routines about women does the most regressive movie of the year, you can smell the greed, and it's distracting.

I'm arguably having a comeback as this chapter is written. I'm starring in projects that I now get to bring a sizable comedy audience to. No matter what the character is, the lesson is: Be in stuff that you would watch. Even better, make it yourself.

At the time, *HuffPost India* came out with a story called something like "When Is Vir Das Going to Realize That His Movie Career Is Over?" Thank you, editor of *HuffPost India*, for hammering the last nail into my press coffin. It was all slipping away. I would wind up in one of those "where are they now" stories, where they'd film me washing dishes back at a Grand Lux somewhere, reminiscing about my glory days.

But fuck that.

Since no one in Bollywood knew what to do with me, I decided to do what I'd always done: Make my own shit.

In 2016, after my movie career crashed and burned, I took a trip to America. I had meetings in Los Angeles, and since I'd been away from stand-up for a while, I decided to get onstage at the Laugh Factory, a famous comedy club on Sunset Boulevard, and do a seven-minute set. During those seven minutes, I fell back in love with stand-up. Unlike in Bollywood, I fit. No one was trying to change my hair or tell me not to wave back at people. It was just me, on a stage, relating to people. I loved it.

What my first foray into Bollywood showed me was that fame is dangerous for me. You know how some people are allergic to almonds or aspirin? Fame creates a bad reaction, chemically, in my body. I either get obsessed with it or retreat from it, or I get nervous and hug someone for three minutes. I've learned to pare things down to protect myself from becoming an entitled nightmare of a human being. I'm allergic to excess: I travel alone. I have no entourage. I work with local tour managers in each place instead of having one tour manager who coddles me everywhere we travel. I'm a minimalist. I own maybe sixteen shirts and two pairs of pants, and I take pride in not giving a fuck about what car I drive or what car drives me. I guess my vibe is antifamous. If I'm in an ivory tower, what am I going to write about as a comic? How pretty the view is?

I've come to believe that success is the amount of time between you having an idea and somebody saying, "Let's make that idea!" The goal is for that time to get shorter, but you have to fail a few times to arrive at that place. When you're young, success is how much money you're getting or who is around you or what you're driving. I'm a minimalist now, but when I started making money in my twenties, I had an entourage of like seven people. I would go to a meeting with a makeup and hair person, an assistant, a publicist, and a few friends. I desperately wanted to be one of the beautiful people, and I don't mean that as a metaphor. But Bollywood stars are like another breed of human beings. Remember when Brad Pitt and Angelina Jolie were cast in *Mr. and Mrs. Smith* together and everyone thought, *Of course they're going to fuck.* It's just evolution. It's two superior beings coming together. I get that he was married to Jennifer Aniston, but the Pitt-Jolie union (at the time) was meant to be, for about thirteen years.

If you let success or money or fame get to your head, then you think you can reach that upper echelon of humanity, the Brad Pitt and Angelina Jolie level. It took me going into Bollywood and then getting booted from Bollywood to figure out that I am not in that upper echelon, and that's not a bad thing. I'm good where I'm at now. The reason Adam Sandler is so successful is that he always plays the underdog. He knows how people perceive him and that he'll never be the sex symbol. He can get fit and build biceps and a six-pack, but he'll still be Adam Sandler. For me, for a hot minute, I was like, "No, I'm an action star and a rom-com hero!" It took many episodes of failing at that shit to discover that I can be the best golden retriever in the world, but I should stop trying to belong in a world of Alsatians.

Ben Stiller is another great example. You will never find a movie where horrible shit doesn't happen to Ben Stiller. Even when he's playing a vain male model in *Zoolander*. When he's a leading man, terrible things happen to his character so often and so hard that you feel for him. For a while, I thought I was the same as the guy in *Entourage*—the handsome superstar with the latest sports car and fifty gorgeous women following him around. I was deluded. The audacity of thinking I could compete in a theater with a star like Shah Rukh Khan was absurd. For you to be a Bollywood star, people have to LOVE you, not just like you. I will never have that type of fan base or wave from my balcony, but I hope I'll always have an audience. Fans will drop you, but an audience will have your back.

Speaking of which, I have been waiting for this audience for a long, long time. This young audience has spent too much time being the main characters on their own social media. They know that looking good and having great music play behind you while you emote is something they are good at because they do it every day on the Gram. So their whole concept of fame has changed, and it's killing the idea of stardom for anyone below the upper echelon. They crave, support, and rally behind authenticity. They expect the star to stand for something, speak up, and be real. They detest performative interviews, and they love podcasts. They don't care if the celebrity is wearing LV, but they want to know if they came out against Diddy. They're not awed by movie marketing, because eventually a movie is an equal-size box on Netflix right next to the documentary they like and the comedy special. Think about that for a second! Tom Cruise, Akshay Kumar, and Vir Das all have the same-size box on Netflix, and all we are competing for is your attention. What a glorious democracy.

Sure, Bollywood is a crazy place full of loud characters and handsome men in silk shirts dancing with gorgeous women on a beach as massive fans blow their hair around. It's about exaggeration and excess, but mostly it's about that family who saves enough money to go to Gaiety Galaxy on a Friday to see something magical.

The stardust is changing, but the magic is still very real.

A SHORT DOSE OF GROUNDING

In Chicago, when I was totally broke, I lived with Josh and another roommate named Adam. I would steal orange juice and shampoo from them because I couldn't afford my own. I'd have to measure the last level their juice or shampoo was at, make a mental note, and then fill it up with water to get it to the starting point. One day, Josh bought me shampoo. He said he'd rather do that than wash his own hair with soap water.

CHAPTER TEN

THE DEVIL HANDS YOU A MICROPHONE

LEFT: *Vir at the Kennedy Center.*
RIGHT: *Vir performing outdoors during the pandemic in Goa.*

When you're feeling like everything is going amazingly well, that your career is blowing up, and that nothing can stop you and all your dreams are on the verge of coming true—that's usually the moment the devil comes for you. Apparently, this is what Denzel whispered in Will Smith's ear during the commercial break at the Oscars when Will Smith had just asked Chris Rock to keep his wife's name out of his fucking mouth and slapped him in front of an audience of millions. The problem with this is that Denzel only appears after you fuck up, and I think we all need a Denzel to show up *before* we fuck up. Hindsight is Denzel-20.

I got slapped in front of millions of people, metaphorically. This has happened a few times.

The first time was 2016. I was touring around America because Bollywood was over for me. I had just crashed and burned with a massive studio sex comedy called *Mastizaade*. I think I was so ashamed in my own mind that I convinced myself the rest of the world felt the movie was awful too. To most people, a movie comes and goes, and if an actor does a shit movie, it's not an unforgivable offense. But the actor has to be able to forgive themselves, which is hard to do in my case.

I had decided maybe American entertainment shores were worth exploring because I had legitimately fallen in love with stand-up again. Here's how that happened. I spent five years doing movies and shooting during the week and doing maybe one stand-up show on the weekend. The show was called *History of India VIR'itten*. It was a chronicling of Indian history through stand-up. It was a great show, with a massive run. The problem was, history doesn't change, and so my material didn't change for five years either. The young people came and went, the journalists came and went, the hipsters came and went, the comedy crowd came and went. I was just performing for rich old people. At my two hundredth show I remember looking out at the crowd and realizing there wasn't one person below fifty. Every single comedian who worked for Weirdass was doing edgy solo material, they were in a comedy collective, or they were YouTube stars. I had become *Cats the Musical*. I was the guy who made jokes about history, and therefore soon would be.

I was signed by an American agency that saw a YouTube clip of *History of India VIR'itten*. I was in L.A. taking meetings, and I happened to do a spot at the Laugh Factory on a Tuesday night. My friend Raj Sharma, an amazing second-generation American Indian comic, hooked it up. He'd done my comedy festival in India a couple times and crushed. I remember watching comedians talk about shit that happened that morning in the news with an edge that I was wholly missing. I recognized that edge. I used to have that edge, and I had just let it fucking slip to do jokes about Mountbatten for five goddamn years. Shame on me for ignoring the stage, giving it up for trailers and the back of an SUV, for phoning it in when I could've been doing this.

I deserved to bomb that night, but I didn't. I went up between Whitney Cummings and Dane Cook. I did seven minutes. I killed with utterly shit material. I improvised something about the new *Twilight* movie. There were 180 people, sweat down my back, nervousness in my entire body, lens flare, stage dust. I realized how much I missed it. It was like making out with an old lover. We just knew each other's moves. The owner of the Laugh Factory, Jamie Masada, took me outside after he saw my spot and said, "Buddy, buddy. You got it, buddy. You're gonna be a star, buddy. I wanna sign you, buddy, and manage you." I smoked a cigarette in front of the marquee thinking, "If he only knew I wasn't going to *be* a star." I was a fallen one. He offered me three more spots that week. When I came back the next night, my name was on the marquee. My second spot, on my second night in American comedy, and I was on the marquee. Some comics at the Factory were supremely pissed at that.

But in the tradition of how my career has gone this whole time, I'd decided I was gonna try to make it in the U.S. and get good at comedy again. This would take being away from India, cutting my own celebrity ego down, really getting my feet wet, and learning what Americans found funny.

To do that I needed context and common ground. I couldn't go up to small crowds in America talking about Bollywood movies. So I resigned myself to being on the road in the U.S. for a few years. I was doing shows in places like Arlington, Texas, which was good practice as far as seeing if my humor would translate with an international audience. Also, I kind of liked the freedom that it offered from the trappings of Mumbai. If you're not careful, Mumbai can convince you that you need *more*. A stylist, PR, a manager, an agent, an acupuncturist, a social media manager. It was so good to be free of that. Once in a while my reps would call and say, "There's a movie . . . ," "You wanna do a shoot for this magazine?," "*GQ* best dressed wants you to . . ."

"Nope. I'm in Charlotte, North Carolina."

"Why the fuck are you in Charlotte, North Carolina?"

Because it's not Mumbai.

Sometimes even a largely Indian crowd would show up and look at me with the same confusion. "You're in Bollywood movies. Why the fuck are you in Arlington?" This was back when the only metric we Indians could comprehend for success in showbiz was Bollywood success. Thank god that changed.

On the road, I got to go grocery shopping, walk around, be anonymous, take a train ride. It started to feel like I was getting material from everyday life, like I did in the early days.

I have struggled in America twice in my life. This, the second time, I chose to, on my own terms, which is a different vibe. You squeeze every drop of juice you can. Now you've got a credit card. When the one-year America run was done, my manager, Reg, and my agency hooked up a solo showcase at the Hollywood Improv. That walk over from the Uber to the Improv is interesting. On your right is a brick wall with a massive mural that has Robin Williams, Pryor, Carlin, Jim Carrey, and more. The marquee says: "TONIGHT—VIR DAS—SOLD OUT."

The crowd was made up of Very Important People from Hulu, Netflix, and HBO, all trying to determine whether or not I was worth their time and money. There was a magical crowd that night who helped me through the set, and ironically, Imran Khan, who was visiting L.A. with his then wife, Avantika, was there. It was a great show. I remember finishing and meeting all the agents, and shaking a bunch of hands, and then I was by myself with all that adrenaline. One of the downsides to my profession is that you go from ten thousand people to utter silence and adrenaline that has no place to go. I remember calling Imran and Avantika and asking if they were still up. They had rented a small house near Melrose in West Hollywood. Their daughter was asleep and they were in their pajamas when I walked in, looking lost. Avantika warmed some pizza up for me and sat me down and said, "You don't get it. I saw the looks on their faces. Your life is about to change, and I am so happy for you." It was cold out. No one tells you L.A. gets freezing cold. The pizza was warm, though.

The next week Netflix offered me a comedy special.

It was the first project Netflix U.S. green-lit out of India. I remember every single representative I had saying, "Go into the meeting and take whatever they give you, whatever venue and budget, since it's your first."

I asked for a two-city special shot in a stadium in Delhi and a basement in New York. Basically triple the cost. Netflix said yes.

Cut to six months later and I am standing next to Conan O'Brien, who, if you're a comedy person, you know to idolize way more than any other late-night host. He's funnier, and has done more for underdog and unique comedians than anyone else on late night. The same week the special comes out, I get six minutes on Conan O'Brien's show, which actually gets me more attention than the special (no offense, Netflix). A late-night spot is a tricky thing. If it goes well, maybe your career will go well. If it doesn't, your career is definitely over. It's four minutes that you shoot at 4:00 p.m. and then agonize over until it comes out at 11:00 p.m. It all goes by in a flash, like an out-of-body experience.

I was subtly told that if it went well, Conan might walk over, and if it went really well, I might get invited to the couch to sit down. All I remember is this. They asked me if I wanted a hand-held mic, and I arrogantly said no. Because something about doing that felt like a club, not late night. Then I went up onstage and did four minutes like a blithering idiot who had an invisible microphone. If you look at my left hand, by force of habit it is miming holding a microphone that isn't there. Without the microphone my body language has a strangely 1940s German vibe to it, like I'm telling jokes but thinking of the Fatherland. I have no clue how the set goes, but I'm getting laughs, and then Conan O'Brien is walking toward me. As he gets closer I realize this man is six foot four. When he stands next to me, we look like a pencil and a sharpener inside a stationery box. I look like Frodo to his Gandalf. Then I am walking toward the couch because he has invited me over. I sit down, we cut to break, he shakes my hand and says, "That was great. I mean it. Really, really great." I got escorted back to my greenroom. I waited three hours in there for him to get off work so I could take a selfie. It was pure fanboy energy. Indians all over America were like, "Our guy made it!"

That kicked off about three years of touring and being welcome at most comedy clubs in the world, which turned into smaller theaters. I started enjoying it more and more. Which means I started focusing on India less and less. My material became less about India too. I kind of became this "outside guy" in Mumbai, where I had lived for more than a decade.

And then the pandemic sent me packing for home, and changed my voice completely.

During the pandemic my wife and I relocated to Goa. That move became our way of life, and it changed the tone of my comedy forever. No clubs were open for a while, and I felt like I had just found some sort of comedic momentum. You know that phase in the gym where your muscles have memory, you've done enough reps, you're seeing just a hint of a six-pack? I felt loose. So when the world shut down, I was not having it. Plus, my dog, Watson, who you will meet very soon, was not well and needed a change of scenery. We were these North Indian outsiders in a tiny village called Parra in Goa. I found a venue called Omaggio, where an Israeli-Indian dance troupe had a tiny stage in the forest. They used to do trapeze work from trees. I'm no trapeze artist, but I'll take the stage. I bought a mic and two speakers on Amazon. I would hike up in the forest with a speaker and do stand-up for small crowds, outdoors. Fifty people, socially distanced, who really just loved comedy enough to hike up a hill at 2:00 p.m. I filmed the shows and turned them into a series called *Ten on Ten*, with ten episodes that lasted ten minutes each, on ten different topics. All topics that were on people's minds in India.

We were in the middle of the pandemic, and India had the worst second wave anyone had ever seen. Death numbers were being faked, everyone was raging about vaccines, and everyone just had this open vulnerability to them. What was I going to do? Shallow jokes about dicks and going to the gym? We're on a hillside like some cult. This had to be real. My voice became more political, something I had been afraid to do so far in India. I'm not an idiot, and I read the news. Ask any Indian, and they will tell you this new government isn't a fan of comedians. I personally think that the benchmark of a truly secure leader is their ability to tolerate satire.

The government and I have a very clear difference of opinion on that. It's no secret that satire can get you into trouble in India. Even people who support the government treat it like a shortcoming they can live with. "Yeah, they're bad with comedy, great with policy. What can you do? Just play ball." But in a pandemic, where everyone is locked indoors and law enforcement is too busy to worry about jokes (as they should be), you don't necessarily have to play ball. I'm not a YouTube star. What I do know is that by being on Netflix you miss out on a massive young audience that loves comedy.

The Goa shows got younger people paying attention to my comedy. They changed my audience and my voice. I crowdsourced the topics, so there were episodes about cancel culture, religion, and freedom of speech. We talked about god, the government, patriotism, Covid, censorship, and more for a crowd that was sorely missing that kind of discussion. It felt good to say it, openly—literally out in the open. But there was no place to rehearse this material. It would go up online raw and unrehearsed. So there was an ease to it, and it never came off as performative. It had to be real and flawed. By this time, I was three Netflix specials in with *Abroad Understanding*, *Losing It*, and *For India*, and a few YouTube videos changed everything.

When the world opened up, tickets went faster than they ever had for me. Eighty percent of the audience was now between the ages of eighteen and thirty. I could fuck around, play, be loose. We announced a massive tour with flagship venues. It all sold out. And then, the devil came.

In 2021, when the world opened up and comedians were unleashed again, I went back on the road. I was high on a recent Emmy nomination for the Netflix special *For India*. I was in Hyde Park in London enjoying the September gray and we got tagged in this nomination for best comedy. A package arrived from Netflix CEO, Ted Sarandos, the next day with a two-hundred-dollar bottle of champagne and some accoutrements. We decided to play good karma and leave it under a park bench for college kids to find. I put a post up on Instagram and left. Our next stop was a sold-out show at the Kennedy Center in Washington, D.C. All of this is to say, I was feeling pretty good, pretty confident.

I was critically acclaimed, newly viral, and too cool for Ted's booze. Then . . . the devil came. Where were you, Denzel? Where were you?

Shivani and I headed to D.C. the night before the show and settled into the Watergate Hotel (maybe an ominous sign?). We did some monument tours during the day, and then headed back to the hotel to prepare for the show that night. On the day of a show, I typically nap in the late afternoon (this is part of my prep), but that day I only slept about thirty minutes. I don't usually write a show a few hours before, but I'd been thinking of a "Two Indias" riff for several months. The pandemic really brought the disparity in India into sharp relief: You had migrant workers and farmers dying and suffering, and then prominent families who were definitely not having that same experience. It was hard to ignore the privilege you had and what that meant relative to others. Now don't get me wrong, this is something that we are only too happy to ignore on a daily basis. Mumbai is a dichotomous city where people sleep on the street outside a nightclub and everyone seems to go about their lives like that isn't the case.

If nothing else, the pandemic was a time when people spoke up about how they felt about their country. Not just in India but globally. From farmers' protests to the Citizenship (Amendment) Act, 2019 to Black Lives Matter to Boris Johnson. People were talking, and people stuck at home were listening more than they ever had before. So you just walked around more conscious of where you lived, and maybe you walked around abroad feeling homesick. I'd been off tour and in India for two and a half years. Being on tour again was different. I missed my country, my dog, the hills, the forest. Groggy from my nap, with all of this on my mind, I wrote a set I decided to do after the show at the Kennedy Center in about twenty minutes, and called it "The Two Indias." It came out of me in a flow state, if you will.

When I read it out loud to Shivani, I asked her if I should actually do it. If you haven't watched the show, the format was "I come from an India that does *x*, but I *also* come from an India that does *y*." One aspect would be horrible, and the other would be redeeming. It was about the complexity of the country, but I also wanted to call out bullshit. In its purest intention, the show was designed to make us remember the light that we are capable of, that the positive flip side is still there, even though for over twelve months it had felt lost.

I thought of it as a love letter to India, an India that I felt was fading in the pandemic. I tried to end it on a positive note. "I know that India still lives . . ." I wanted a big ovation for India.

"Sure, you should do it," Shivani said. "What could go wrong?"

We headed to the Kennedy Center, ready to put on an amazing show. It wasn't the first time I'd done a show that questioned things about India or called out privilege. Despite what some people later came to believe—that I used an opportunity handed to me at a great American institution to disparage my country—it's still a regular theater that charges rent, and while they are very picky about their programming, you will find more than the occasional dick joke onstage at the Kennedy Center. It's not the United Nations. I hired a wedding photographer to film it, the only guy available on a Sunday in D.C., for four hundred bucks, so I could put it online later. It wasn't some vast conspiracy. It was just me, doing my work. Or so I thought.

Problem was, the Kennedy Center is not a forest.

The crowd that night was amazing. Based on the reaction in the room, they loved the show. Then we did the Two Indias piece. The Indians in the audience had been nodding along, laughing through the show. I figured, "Cool!" Then during the piece, which I read from a paper because it was brand-new material, they were silent. They chuckled a bit, and then their energy grew and grew and grew into something just massive. The last words of the set were "I know this is the Kennedy Center, but tonight this is our fucking house, so make some noise for India." There are no words to describe the ovation they gave. It was not for me but for something else.

It felt loose, like the forest.

Shivani and I went out to dinner with some friends after the show, and a few days after we left D.C., I posted the video online. When you post something potentially divisive on social media, it always goes well at the start. I woke up the next morning and saw that the post had about 800,000 views in twelve hours, which was a lot for my YouTube channel. I had talked about corruption, fake news, women's rights, farmers' rights, youth protests, patriotism, cricket, censorship, elections, religious equality, colonial hangovers, abuse of power, and more in a nearly seven-minute video. It was gonna track. Cool. Every comment seemed to be positive, and filled with love, or at the very least a disappointed nostalgia for an India we missed and felt could be brought back.

And then it happened. One editor from one news channel reposted a small part of the video on Twitter, and my world imploded.

The clip that this one editor posted had a fatal flaw, and it all comes down to grammar (believe me, when you get canceled and lose all your jobs, you have tons of time to overanalyze things). Like I said, the format was "I come from an India that does x, but I also come from an India that does y." Well, my mistake was in one single observation I forgot to say "also." Instead, I said, "I come from an India where we worship women during the day and gang-rape them at night." That one word, "also," would have changed the entire meaning. I wrote that line because several horrific gang rapes had happened in India. Now look, anyone with any level of basic intelligence knows the intention behind the piece is to celebrate our darkness as much as our light, and understands where the line fits in the whole piece. "I come from an India where men in skyscrapers are silent and where children in the comments section have courage" does NOT mean that men in skyscrapers are also children in the comments. "I come from an India where we laugh behind closed doors, but I come from an India where we break down the walls of a comedy club." This does not mean that the comedy audience are the same goons who vandalized two comedy venues that year. Most people get this when they see the piece, that this piece is about two very different, separate groups existing in the same country, but when you take a line and post it out of context, I come from an India where the shit hits the fan.

I guess the lesson is: Don't use the Kennedy Center as your open-mic night where you test out new material. Yes, the people who came after me would have found any reason to tear the monologue apart, but I do firmly believe that grammar is fucking important, and one fuckup can create an excuse to incite the mobs.

Once that post happened, people lost their minds. In both good ways and bad.

Here's the thing I've never spoken about. That single video got over 6 million views on YouTube and about 9.5 million on Instagram. Pretty unremarkable, not newsworthy.

That's NOT where it was shared the most. It got shared and sent around on WhatsApp as a download. That's where everyone saw it. Almost triple the online viewership. Indian people, we're smart. We knew this would be political wildfire, but we still believed that what was said needed to be heard, so we found a way.

Then my name started trending, and I was the number one trend on Twitter for a week. Then I was the subject of every prime-time bulletin. Politicians and news pundits on both sides were dissecting it on the news. I was being called a traitor, a terrorist. There were demands for my passport to be revoked, for my arrest the moment I landed back home. Then foreign news outlets started to pick it up. CNN, the BBC, *The Washington Post*, *The Guardian*, Al Jazeera, some random Brazilian portal. It became terrifying, an unexpected wildfire. It was a strange feeling being on the news constantly. I wasn't famous enough for that, but then all of a sudden I was, for all the wrong reasons. I had just come off a period of raising almost fifty thousand dollars for Covid relief in India by doing Zoom shows for charity. I was feeling an intense amount of national pride, but that doesn't mean I wasn't going to call out the things I didn't like about India. So I went from Emmy nominee to terrorist. Sorry again, Netflix.

I've always believed that people in power are busy, and therefore not scary. They have very real things to worry about. The people who are two to six degrees of separation away from those with power, looking to make an impression on the big boys? Those are the scariest people in the world. Fringe groups started filing complaints against us because doing so was a gateway to them getting on the news. I was banned from performing in two Indian states.

Then the death threats came. Now look, usually Indians are pretty passé about death threats. Comedians in India have dealt with any number of them. In my case, there were more than fifty thousand in the first two days, mostly on email and WhatsApp, very graphic, talking about death and rape. And then we switched our phones off. If they were just threatening *me*, it would have been one thing, but keyboard warriors were saying they would rape and murder my wife and my whole family. I was like, "This is a lot of rape, guys." How were they planning to manage it all?

One thing I said that night was that I come from an India that is not going to think this riff was funny, and I was right. If people would have blown me off, like, *This guy is just an idiot*, it would have been no big deal. Instead, I became a national terrorist because I was bad-mouthing the country, a villain that kept the news cycle churning. Once politicians started coming for me, it kind of proved what I'd been saying; India is a country that does not want to air its dirty laundry. I was a comic on a stage. It's not like I flew to Davos, Switzerland, to shit-talk India during the World Economic Forum.

More than anything else, I wasn't used to this level of attention. I was just a comedian. I DID NOT understand why I was on the news this much. An overreaction makes sense, but this level of overamplification seemed utterly bizarre. Maybe it was the Emmy nomination?

That video was posted on November 17, and the Emmy ceremony where I was nominated was less than ten days later. Talk about whiplash. At the beginning, I had friends and colleagues from the bottom of comedy to the top of Bollywood sending me messages of support.

"We're so proud" and "Thanks for saying something." But one by one I started noticing that those threads were being deleted. People were scared that my phone was hacked, and that they'd be implicated and canceled by association. No judgment, I get it. We've all got families to feed and bills to pay.

If you've experienced any level of online backlash, you probably know how tempting it is to respond.

When I spoke to my lawyer, she told me, "Please just shut up. A news cycle is typically a week. If you can just get through six days without responding, the cycle should die down and move on, so you might be okay. If you're still on the news on day eight . . . scream from the rooftops, because we're fucked." Her advice wasn't based on a scientific study of publicity tactics, but basically, she wanted me to let things calm down.

If you start screaming into a void, it gets worse. I knew I couldn't compete with the media machine, so I did what she said. I shut the fuck up.

That didn't keep every single media sponsor, every show, every gig from getting canceled. I was done. Career over. I remember a call from my management in India, "Vir . . . we think it's gonna be a while before ANYONE wants to work with you. They've all said they respect you massively, but they just can't do it anymore." That year, we lost income worth more than the last five years of my life in total.

And I had an Emmy nomination. I was not about to go on the news and cry and start apologizing. I wasn't going to weep on Oprah's shoulder to try to redeem my career. Also, she wasn't asking me to do that, so it wasn't an option.

Despite the whole "you'll never work in this town/nation/world again" thing, I flew to New York that November for the Emmy ceremony. Netflix had booked a hotel suite for press junkets and interviews, and I felt bad that they'd gone to all that trouble for a terrorist. One of the executives was like, "Why'd you do it, man?" I tried to explain that I never thought it would blow up and lead to death threats and (when I later tried to tour again) eventually people stomping on my poster for cameras and burning effigies in the streets. I kept my head down and did the interviews, and all the while I was being called the most wanted man in India. I had more than ten police complaints filed against me there, and the fear of actual jail time became real. But I had pre-Emmy interviews to do!

From a non-Indian perspective, it might be hard to understand why people were so upset with my Kennedy Center show, and how it could literally turn me into a guy who could be sent to jail for bad-mouthing the country. The angry mob thought I was being not just unpatriotic but treasonous. Is it rational? No. Did their anger feel very real to me? Hell yes. It took a little growing up to also realize that along with being angry, and hating me, they were hurt. True or not, what I'd said hurt their feelings. That's what still eats me up about it. I feel bad that I hurt someone's feelings. Still.

A few news channels had talked about income disparities during the pandemic, but to call out sexual violence or injustice was too much for some people. And I wasn't delivering the news. I was voicing some pretty strong opinions, on a very public (non-Indian) stage.

So picture this: Netflix agrees to take along five journalists to New York for the Emmys. They are given backstage access and guaranteed one-on-one interviews. They are there to celebrate you and be graceful if you lose. Now they are in New York with a guy who is not the sweet entertainment story but the top headline on their networks back home. This guy, who wants to go into hiding and have NOTHING to do with the press, has contractually guaranteed them interviews. There is no way they are gonna let me off the hook. So now I am in my hotel room rehearsing news interviews with my legal team. At some point the question comes up:

"Vir, a LOT of people will watch these interviews."

"I know."

"If you want to apologize, this would be the place to do it."

I think about it. How easy it would be. Make everything go away. This whole news cycle would end. Call it a misunderstanding. "I apologize for hurting people." I have seen that typed out on Twitter enough times to know it passes.

And then what? Never do stand-up again? Or do it with an audience looking at me and both of us knowing that I told the truth and then denied it? Isn't that technically a lie? Could I live with that? That inauthenticity? The thing that no one questions about that video? You can argue whether it was appropriate or not, funny or not, ill-timed or not, seditious or not. NO one ever argued about whether it was true.

Comedians have sometimes gotten into trouble for fabricating things to get on the news, to get sympathy, make it to the headlines. This would be the first time a comedian told a lie to get off the news. I wasn't doing that. I did not and do not think there is anything worse than begging for sympathy.

One journalist on the junket in New York was kind to me, though, compared to so many who were just out for blood. She said, "I hope you win." I'd gone from being called "the Priyanka Chopra of Indian comedy" to the most wanted man, but here was this one journalist, telling me she was rooting for me. Maybe I'd win the Emmy and redeem myself.

I didn't win the Emmy. It was a long shot at best. I lost to *Call My Agent!*, this French Netflix behemoth that was in its final season.

I got smashed at the after-party and headed back to the Beekman Hotel with Shivani. She wasn't upset that I didn't win an Emmy. At that point, we were both just worried about making it home. After she fell asleep, I went out on the balcony that overlooked the open foyer way down below. I remember looking down and thinking that if I jumped, I would make a lot of people extremely happy. If I jumped, I could avoid thinking about the fact that my career was very clearly over. Instead, I went back into the hotel room, stared at the ceiling unable to sleep, and headed back to India the next day because my O-1 visa was expiring in seventy-two hours. I had to go home, a place I wasn't sure I even belonged to anymore.

I remember making a video in the next room while Shivani slept. I looked dead into the camera and said, "If you're watching this I have been arrested." Then I transferred some money to my wife's account. The money was for her. My visa expired the following morning. Some people suggested that we just hide out in the U.S. for a bit, some people suggested I never come back to India. But we had to come back. It was home.

When I said goodbye to the Netflix executives, it didn't feel like a "Hey, loved working with you so let's get on a call soon about your next special" kind of goodbye. It was more like a "Have a nice life in obscurity" kind of farewell. When we boarded our Air India flight, I kept my head down. To my surprise, the pilot came out and said, "I don't know if I'll be allowed into Indian airspace with you on board." His joke (yes, it was a joke) made me feel like not everyone would greet me with torches and pickaxes when I returned. Later on, a few older Air India flight attendants, whom we call aunties, ushered me into the back of the cabin, poured me a drink, and said, "You're going to get drunk!" They were being kind, but I think they also may have expected that I'd be arrested as soon as we landed, so I'd better live it up while I could. One of the aunties told me, "I'm proud of what you did. If you go to jail, you stand up straight."

Again, it might seem strange that I would need actual protection after making jokes about my country, but in India anyone can walk into a police station and file a defamation or "hurting sentiments" claim, and if the police decide to investigate, and if you're found guilty, you can go to jail. It doesn't happen often, but it *has* happened. At one point, I had complaints filed against me in fourteen police stations. This means that any policeman who decides the matter is worthy of investigation will summon me and detain me. Would it go to trial? Probably. Would I get bail? Probably. Would that take a while, and possibly keep getting "delayed"? Possibly. Process is sometimes punishment.

It was a long flight.

I'm famous enough for the paparazzi to know my name should I happen to be in the place where they have gathered. I am not famous enough to organically gather a hundred of them at an airport. Fun fact: Most paparazzi are actually summoned by celebrity PR teams. The paparazzi are usually loud and annoying, yelling your name and asking ridiculous questions. When we landed and made our way through Mumbai airport, their silence was terrifying, like I was a dead man walking. It was a scary time. I met with lawyers, made sure I had money set aside for Shivani and my family in case anything happened to me, and got prepared in case I actually did get arrested. When we arrived home, we turned our phones off to news alerts and social media for six weeks.

After those six weeks, I turned my phone back on. No one was talking about hating me or arresting me. There were no more threats. As I write this, the Kennedy Center video on YouTube has 6.6 million views. It's probably 2.2 million people who liked it, 2.2 million who hated it, and 2.2 million who don't give a shit but just wanted to see what all the noise was about. I felt angry. Relieved not to be behind bars, but angry. There was only one thing to do: I announced a world tour and called it the Wanted Tour. I didn't have a single venue booked, but fuck it. As I've said before, my M.O. is to announce the thing, then make it happen. If forty-five publications tore me down, there were maybe eight that defended me. There were still supporters out there, but as in most situations, the angry masses are much louder than the people who have your back.

I made a promo saying we would visit every city in India, even though I was pretty sure no one would work with me. I used all the hate I'd gotten in the press, all the negative headlines, and turned it all on its head by matching it with positive press, like the Two Indias format. So if one headline said I was a terrorist and should be hanged, another said I was the bravest comic in India. I put both reviews in my promo. I put out the promo, scrambled to book venues, put tickets on sale, and cities sold out in hours. Like wildfire. Like never before in my career. There are moments in a career when you have to keep things in perspective. Look at the Chris Rock Oscar slap, how he took that like a pro, in such stride. Then he shut his mouth and hit the road. If you wanted to know what he had to say, you had to buy a ticket. What a great fucking road map. Silence, and when your mouth opens, it's jokes and jokes alone. I wasn't going to burst out, "See guys, I AM brave!" I wanted to just get to work, write the best material I could, and get back out there. I have yet to give a public interview about the Two Indias controversy. I have no intention of ever doing so. If you wanna hear my thoughts, you have to buy this book.

So we had a sold-out tour, massive amounts of intrigue and buzz, a made-up number of cities and countries we planned to hit. I had literally just put 40 percent of the city names up on a promo without venues booked and a "coming soon" tab on my site, and then it became my agent's job to make those cities happen. The ones we had booked, man, had they sold! Now all one needed was jokes. I started popping into Mumbai clubs to do trial shows.

At the first show I did after the canceling and the threats, there were maybe two hundred people in the audience. And hell yes, I was nervous. When I walked out, I said, "It's good to be back in the country. Actually, it's good to be *allowed* back in the country." It got a massive laugh that broke the tension so we could all collectively breathe. I was honest with the audience and told them I wasn't exactly sure how to talk about what had happened, but I was going to try. We were going to try. I did that in every city, and in almost every city there would be fringe groups outside the show protesting, burning effigies of me, calling for my arrest. People were breaking glass and acting crazy, making every single stop on the tour some twisted version of *This Is Spinal Tap* meets *Argo*. Ridiculous comedy mixed with real threats of violence. One night a police officer got roughed up by the crowd, and later he looked at me and asked, "What the fuck did you do?" It was absurd.

The hate started to get drowned out by the support. People would tell me they fought with family members over my Two Indias speech. They took a certain pride in me, and it felt heavy. Like I was undeserving. But strangely, it's the first time I have ever been claimed by an audience. *He's ours, and we don't care if you don't approve.* I'm not boasting here, just expressing gratitude. It didn't make me feel invincible, since there were still mobs stomping on posters with my face on them, but it did make me feel like there wasn't much else to lose. When you're writing with that kind of mindset, that's a different kind of writing. And then, in the midst of all this, something insane happened. Netflix called.

It was a lovely woman named Natalie, who was head of comedy for Netflix Asia Pacific. She asked me to do another special in the spring. Finally, after hiding out and fearing for my life and my family's lives throughout the winter, I had some work. And not just any work, a Netflix special. It was all coming together. Not that I was desperate (I was), but I kept bugging my manager, asking when the Netflix contract was coming. You have to understand what a lighthouse this was for me. It's one thing to be able to speak your peace live, but to do it on Netflix is an opportunity I had been 100 percent sure was never going to happen again.

Every week, I'd call the States and say, "Did they send the contract?"

Not yet.

"Did they send the contract?"

Business Affairs is working on it.

Note to the kids reading this: If you don't have a contract, it's not actually happening. I looked around at venues but didn't book anything, because I can be bold when it comes to my work, but not bold enough to book a venue for a Netflix special before the contract has been signed, in blood.

Then, it happened. Not the signing of the contract, the total negation of it. Natalie changed jobs, and they downsized the number of comedy specials they were making. Not just me, everyone. They said they were "moving away from comedy."

Lighthouse off.

When you truly have no work and nothing to lose, you either accept it, or blatantly bluff. It was time to bluff.

I called another Netflix executive named Tanya, whom I knew. I knew she was intelligent, and amazing, and that she had been supportive of my stuff. I said hello, and then said, "Tanya, I'm going to create a special that makes people feel amazing about India, one that no Indian comedian has ever done, and if you cancel on me . . . that's fine, I'll go with HBO (who had zero idea about my new tour). OR you and I can go get nominated for another Emmy together."

Sheer, unapologetic, desperate bullshit.

I wasn't trying to be a jerk; I was just trying to get my life back. Tanya was silent for a minute, no doubt wondering whether I was bluffing.

"Vir, give me two weeks."

Two weeks later, Tanya called.

"Let's do it," she said. "But I want to be clear," she added. Ah, shit. "We will control the release plan. And you have to take a pay cut."

Fine. Yes. A thousand times yes. Where do I sign? In blood!

This all happened while I was performing at the Edinburgh Festival Fringe that August, and as soon as I got off the phone with Tanya, I started writing the special. There's a certain kind of freedom you feel at a comedy festival, maybe from all the manic creative energy swirling around, but I buckled down and wrote my heart out. I had an idea. Two weeks into the Fringe, when I was walking up to a tiny cliff in the middle of Holyrood Park, it hit me. I knelt to the ground and started gathering some sand by the fistful and put it into my pockets. Then I walked home. That night I did the bit. When I walked out I gently sprinkled the sand on one half of the stage. Making nothing of it. Very nonchalant. Then three quarters into the show I revealed that since I was accused of having defamed India on foreign soil, I carried around actual Indian soil to each of the shows. So every time I did a joke about India, I was "technically" standing on Indian sand. The applause was gigantic. Like a magic trick. It became the show. Little did they know that was local Scottish soil.

That meant I had to time every bit of footwork to make sure that when I was talking about India, I was standing on the sprinkled soil. If you watch it now, you can see me maneuvering around so I could get the timing exactly right. I did not want to be called the most wanted man in India ever again.

Then in October we were set to film the show for Netflix at NYU. The week before we left, we went up to Juhu Beach in Mumbai and packed two zippered bags full of very Indian sand. I carried Indian sand to America terrified I might get caught. Each team member did the same. We got to NYU and built the set, and eight zippered bags full of Indian sand from Juhu Beach in Mumbai were sprinkled onto the stage. Commit to the bit.

We finished editing the special that fall and sent it to Netflix. We chatted about the title, and to their credit they never really got into the content. I think the team saw how personal it was for me. I'm eternally grateful for that respect shown to me. They did, however, release it the day after Christmas, when all government offices were shut and there was ZERO publicity. Smart.

I had a few shows left in my India tour before the special was to come out in December. Comedians always try to throw in a few last-minute shows before a special is out and the material is burnt forever. I tried to do so in India, but the fringe groups were getting out of control, to the point that a theater owner got beat up. They'd show up, burn effigies, scream my name, and just scare the shit out of us. One night after a show in Bengaluru I looked at my two tour managers and saw that they looked like they'd been through a war, like they'd aged ten years in two months. One of them said to me, "You're being used by these groups so they can get on TV. No one cares about the Two Indias video anymore. They're showing up to milk you for attention. Your special is a month away. If this keeps up, and you keep getting these headlines, Netflix will bail."

So we decided to cancel the tour dates, but to do that I faked an illness, and also faked that I had just signed a massive deal and had to immediately stop touring to work on this insane project. So there I am posting, "Hey guys, just signed on a big, secret, amazing project so I have to cancel shows!" And then people were congratulating me for this pretend project, which made me feel terrible. But I knew we had to keep a low profile so Netflix wouldn't get spooked.

It was a lie, and many people had bought tickets. I'm sorry we had to lie to you.

I was trying to keep my team and my special safe. In 2023 I did a massive India tour that went off without any hitches. Eventually the memory and the controversy faded away. I made sure to do the longest run that any comedian had ever done specifically in Bengaluru because I felt terrible about the lie. We canceled a show for 900 people; fourteen months later, we came back and performed for 32,000.

When the special, called *Landing*, came out, it was met not with pure hate, but with love. It was my fourth Netflix special, and the reaction it got kind of settled everything, in a way. It settled the chaos and the threats, it settled the accusations and the fear. My career wasn't over. It might never be the same, but it wasn't over. And it not being the same wasn't even necessarily a bad thing.

Seven months later . . .

I was walking around my house in a weighted vest, and my producer Akash was there. While I was walking around in that ridiculous vest, I got pinged that *Landing* had been nominated for an Emmy.

And then a few months after that, we won a fucking Emmy.

A few months after the nomination was announced, I went back to New York City for the event. Back to a place where I was last called a terrorist, but this time with new journalists who were pretending the last time never happened. Like their news editor didn't do five bulletins about me, calling me an antinational. Just casually, "Vir, how are you feeling to be here in New York?" I don't know, madam, do you guys archive footage?

I'm not going to describe the Emmy Award. It's a beautiful statue, so to describe it is tacky. I'm going to tell you how it feels, and about a cookie.

You never think you're going to win, but there's a small part of you that hopes. I checked into my suite at the Sofitel, and the Emmys had a wonderful spread of food waiting. The centerpiece was a Christmas cookie. About four inches in diameter, with white frosting that said "International Emmy Awards" with the logo. I put my bag down and ate some of the chocolate-covered strawberries. Keep in mind this was PTSD, nominee nervousness, and déja vù, all together in my system. So I was stress-eating beyond belief. I lifted up the cookie, about to dive in, and thought, "If I win, I'll eat it."

Now I'm getting ready and hoping to god my suit fits. I do this thing where I launch a new designer every time some publicity milestone happens in my life. Fuck it, I'm here because people in power took a punt on a kid—I'm doing that too. Both of my Emmy outfits and most of my red-carpet looks are brand-new, made by fashion students from small towns who get paid well, receive a big platform, and I'm proud to say, go on to design for much bigger celebrities than myself. Yes, A-list designers would happily dress you for free and send you something unimaginative and trite. But a kid, with underdog energy, will share your underdog energy, and combined underdog energy is a powerful thing. THAT's exposure.

Then it goes like this:

You put your suit on, then you're on the red carpet, then you're having a glass of champagne to calm the nerves, then you're rooting for your fellow Indian nominee, Shefali Shah, who is nominated for the Best Actress Award, then your category comes up. A guy who has a camera on his shoulder comes and sticks that camera in your face. You're nervous and crack some sort of stupid smile, trying not to blink too much because you feel like he's close enough for people to see every single eyelash move. They announce your nomination, the smile gets stupider. You feel your body and the bodies of every other person at the table around you tense. Like a rubber band stretching and stretching and stretching and stretching. You hear the presenter go "and the winner is . . ." And then . . . from the crowd two tables away, you hear a lady go, "Vir . . ." Just whispering it to the person next to her while they drink red wine. Just a random lady. I don't know why I noticed her; there is no way she could have known. She looked about sixty and like she was from Brazil. You're thinking, "Does Vir mean 'more wine' in Portuguese?" This silence feels forty-five minutes long. And then what happens next feels like one millisecond.

You hear your name. Everyone at your table explodes. You're on your feet and hugging people. You didn't smile, you didn't exclaim, you didn't cry, you're just kind of in a trance. Then you're walking up to the stage, and you have no idea how you even found the way there, you were so fucking far away. Now words are coming out of your mouth, even though you have no idea who you're actually addressing. You find yourself saying, "Thank you, namaste, salam alaikum, sat sri akal, good night." You have never uttered all those phrases from those religions together before in your life. Now there's an Emmy in your hand, it's heavy, and you carry it through an entire press junket where you're struggling to find any words because all you are thinking is "FUCK!!"

You meet a member of your team who assures you that you thanked your wife and Netflix, even though you do not remember any of it. Now you're in a Cadillac Escalade headed to an after-party. You're dancing. On the way to the party you're on the phone and people are crying. Your wife and your parents, you.

The first call I got after talking to my wife and parents was Netflix's Tanya, who said, "I cannot believe you called it."

"I was being arrogant!" I told her. "I can't believe I called it either."

The next morning, I realized they gave me the Emmy in a box with no handles. I had to go through JFK being a brown man with a beard carrying this pointy object in a nondescript black box. I stole the belts from two bathrobes at the Sofitel and fashioned myself a makeshift handle.

As I was leaving, there it was still, that cookie on the table. The one with the international Emmy logo, four inches wide, with white frosting. I took a bite, and it was stale. But there was strawberry icing under the white frosting, and I ate the whole damn thing.

I crashed on that flight like you wouldn't believe. Thank god for Air India. Here I was again, two years later, headed home on an Air India flight the morning after an Emmy ceremony. Slightly different circumstances. What a crazy goddamn circle. After they'd let me sleep for about ten hours, when I finally surfaced, two younger Air India air hostesses came up and said, "Sir, we heard about the Emmy. Can we see it?" They drew the curtains, and three of us stood there in first class at thirty thousand feet and unpacked it. It was the first time I had a second to just look at it. A gold lady with wings, on a brown Air India flight.

Then I ate aloo matar and three rotis. There were some paparazzi waiting at the airport when I landed, but way fewer than before. Thank God.

So now, I don't think I'll ever get to be shallow again in my career. There are some days when I just want to be lowbrow, but now I feel this expectation where the audience is thinking, "We kept you out of jail and fed your family. We are your audience. Don't you dare start complaining about cancel culture or do shallow dick jokes again." I hear you guys, and I'll try.

A SHORT DOSE OF GROUNDING

I hate showers. I grew up on bucket baths. I stay in the fanciest hotels in the world and wish I had a plastic bucket and a mug. If you have never felt the joy of squatting on both legs on a cold bathroom floor on a freezing Delhi winter morning and then pouring over yourself a hot mug of water from a bucket you perfectly monitored and mixed between a cold and a hot tap, have you really lived? I think not. Once a year I travel to Ladakh and spend a week or ten days staying in a tent by the river. The highlight is the hot bucket baths. Maybe I'm getting older, or I'm just indulging so much that the bath is taking too long, but my glutes hurt after every bucket bath. I don't know if I have the core strength anymore.

CHAPTER ELEVEN
A TALE OF TWO PASSPORTS

Vir performing a set on religion outdoors.

I didn't really want to write this book. I wanted to write a book, but not a memoir. This inherently felt like the wrong time to do it, and that's because I think you write a memoir at the end of it all. When there's not much left to do, no more choices to make. Writing it now felt like trying to build a dam while swimming in the middle of the river. I'm an artist, not a beaver. I haven't hit a bank yet. I don't know where I'm going to wind up, and when I say that, I mean both artistically and geographically.

Let's talk about controversy. In one of his many sublimely wise moments, one day my manager looked at me and said, "Your content may become controversial, but controversy should never become your content." That's a profound thought, ideologically speaking. It's also impossible to follow, comically speaking.

You don't know you're burning your career down until you've burnt it down, and usually even then you are completely blindsided. That's because in modern comedy the audience has a voice that is louder than the artist's, and for the first time in a long time words have very serious consequences. And none of those ideological thoughts apply when you're being milked for headlines, which is what controversy ends up being. You end up being this ratings machine. Anyone who wants to get their picture in the paper, their face on the news, their podcast to go viral, their article to get clicks finds themselves talking about you, or to you. It's fair game, until it isn't.

The only people in my life who were possibly actually happy that I was canceled in India after the Kennedy Center chaos were my managers in America. Not because they were cold-hearted, but because for years they have been asking me when I was going to make the move to America. I think they figured that, like many rational people, I would want to leave a place that had labeled me a terrorist and burned pictures of my face in the streets. To attain real success in America, you have to give America everything. You have to move there, like Arnold Schwarzenegger, Trevor Noah, and the dozens of Canadian comedians who crossed the border for *Saturday Night Live*. The problem is, it has always felt inherently unnatural to me to do that, to leave India for Los Angeles or New York. Maybe I'll never be able to fully leave for America because India has been stringing me along like a fickle lover. That doesn't mean I haven't thought about it, though.

I think about it in new terms now, as America goes through its great reclamation of stand-up comedy. I wonder if there's a place for an outside voice. In my more pessimistic moments, I think that the comedy pendulum swung from overly apologetic, woke, and lecture-ish to some sort of "dudebro edgelord saying r words, c words, f words, and really only avoiding the N word because edgelord doesn't want his ass whooped" phase that it's in now. Eventually it will swing back to a more nuanced, middle-ground place. Then on other days I think that comedy in America has gotten too attached to ideology, and maybe Americans need a blatant outsider to come in and show their country back to them? Someone with no dog in the race, no camp to impress, just someone who sees the things they don't. I could be that guy.

Don't get me wrong, it's not that I don't like spending time in the U.S. It's not that I don't want to be on American TV or in American movies. I've just always sort of resented the "you have to FULLY become us to play with us" aspect of it all. I'm just not sure what the future looks like. I leave India and live in Los Angeles and get one of those famous L.A. tans, which kind of already looks like my natural complexion. A hint of an American accent creeps into my voice more and more each year, until it sounds convincing enough for me to play a delivery guy who appears in one or two scenes in the new Nicole Kidman movie. The sassy but conservative Indian accountant who "tells it like it is" in that one scene. I see my family once a year on Diwali or New Year's. We get SUVs, a mortgage, and some sort of house with a pool in a cul de sac. I tour the U.S. on the weekends and tour the world when there is time, shop at Whole Foods, do yoga, head up to Big Sur on our two-week vacation; and I wait for the fifth lead role to turn into a fourth lead role, and so on. Maybe a movie I write gets made, maybe I star in it, and maybe, just maybe, I get nominated for an award. And then the next time I'm in Boise, Idaho, I sell two thousand tickets instead of five hundred, until I'm fifty-eight and no one in Boise wants to come see me anymore.

Other days I think about the U.K. Maybe I move, start doing the panel shows, start directing British cinema. Maybe do the occasional West End play, a BBC show, get a country house, do the Fringe festival every year. Get some dogs, sheep, a pub, a garden. The major appealing factor in both cases is freedom. The comedic freedom that you have to stand on a stage and say what you like. And the worst thing you would have to deal with is feedback.

For the last decade, at least once a day someone has looked at me and said, "Get out, bro, you belong where you have the freedom to say things." And yet, I've spent so much time in those other countries and never felt like I fully belonged. Not fully. I think most Indians abroad would admit that their breathing changes the second they land in India. Even if they are just visiting. It's not the pollution, it's the tasalli. "Tasalli" means ease, relaxation, chill. I got it from an Indian limo driver in San Jose who said, in Hindi, "America is great, but you can never FULLY be at ease." I don't think anyone has ever said it better. You'll settle in, but you may never fully belong. To get tasalli, you need to belong. Say what you will about Mumbai, on my worst day, and on my best day, I can go over to a friend's house for chai without calling first. The pau wallah comes at 7:00 a.m. My parents are close by, my rupee goes way further than their dollar, life is way more comfortable. I can live in an apartment I would have to be a gazillionaire to afford in New York, and I can walk onstage without having to address where I am or how I got there. If I commit a crime, I am in no more or less trouble than the other people standing next to me on the street. This is not the case if I commit a crime in New York City, Los Angeles, or London.

Then again, in these other, potential lives, I can say anything I want on a stage. What a cruel choice. Artistic freedom versus tasalli.

And, that green card application ... was something I thought about.

The problem with this plan, with getting a green card and moving to L.A., is that wouldn't I be turning my back on the people who held me up, who gave me a career in the first place? So much of my identity is rooted in being an Indian in the world. Meaning, I don't come to American comedy stages and talk about the big buildings and the five things white people know about India. I go onstage and say I'm from Mumbai, and whether you like it or not you're coming to Mumbai tonight. Don't get me wrong, it's a tougher road to take people out of their comfort zone, but it's the only way I know how.

It's a weird conflict and a Catch-22. Being too Indian for America and too Western for India. Maybe if I walked into an American audition room and said, "I'm from Naperville, Illinois, my parents own Ramada Inns, and my dad came there in 1982 looking for a better life!" and if I said it with the perfect American twang, I'd book the gig. I'd be just Indian enough to not threaten American sensibilities. I feel like I'd be half Indian if I went to live in America or the U.K., when my whole thing is being full Indian, even though I've never fully felt that way either. Basically, it's complicated.

Still, during that uncertain, scary time when I had no idea if someone might actually murder me onstage, I sat Shivani down one day and for the first time we talked about leaving India. You have to keep in mind these are two self-made Delhi people who came to Mumbai with nothing, and the city gave them everything. Being Mumbaikars is a big part of who we are. Still, we decided to apply, and see where fate led us.

To get the green card, we'd have to stay in America for eight months, so Shivani asked what our lives would be like if we picked up and left for New York. "It'll be like *When Harry Met Sally*," I told her. "We'll get a brownstone in the Village and we can rediscover ourselves and each other."

I pitched her the most Hollywood, romanticized version of life in New York. Fall leaves and baseball games, deli sandwiches and strolls in Central Park. She could go back to school, start an events company. Anything was possible in New York. Right? We'd both just had the shit kicked out of us by life and a seven-minute YouTube video; maybe we deserved a little time away from being ashamed, and the place that had shamed us. Even as I was saying all of this, I knew that what it would really look like would be me doing sets at the Comedy Cellar until two in the morning and then passing out from exhaustion to do it all again the next night.

About the Comedy Cellar. It is paradise, hell, and litmus test for emerging comedians, all existing in a tiny basement filled to the brim with legacy. It's one of the top two reasons I love New York City and would even think about living there. That and the coffee you get in the Village. If you're good, the Cellar lets you know. If you're shit, you're not at the Cellar. But if you're good and you're doing bad work, you will find out pretty quick on that basement stage. The place is legendary, but it's not about managers and agents. The owners would never talk to managers and agents. Every single show is sold out every night of the week. It's an institution on MacDougal Street in Greenwich Village. Jon Stewart,

Dave Chappelle, Amy Schumer, Robin Williams, Sarah Silverman, Jerry Seinfeld, and so many more have been on that stage. Getting time at the Comedy Cellar is like making it into a secret society. And you have to impress Estee.

Estee Adoram is the legendary booker of the Cellar. She started working there in the 1980s and eventually became feared and revered. No matter who you are, you have to first be recommended by New York City comics to even audition for Estee. And then you go in and get three minutes to impress this woman who has seen the best of the best for four decades. After two Netflix specials and three world tours, I got the chance to audition for Estee because Nimesh Patel, an awesome New York comic, recommended me.

When my three minutes were up, she took me upstairs to the Olive Tree Cafe and sat me down at a table. She said, "You're really good! Start sending me avails and I'll start booking you." I walked out into the early-November New York City cold and smoked a celebratory cigarette. I had gigs at the Comedy Cellar for about ten days before the Kennedy Center performance, and once that blew up, I left the U.S., and the Comedy Cellar, and went into hiding.

When I went back to New York in April 2022, several months after the Kennedy Center mess, Estee came up to me and said, "I want you to bring a photo in, you're going up on the wall." You cannot imagine what a big deal that is for a comedian. The Cellar wall is on either side of a staircase that leads to their basement space. On it is a photo or headshot of every single legendary comedian in the world thanking Estee and the Cellar for jump-starting their career. Seinfeld, Chappelle, Carlin, Stewart, Pryor, Burr . . . everyone. I hold that honor with as much pride as I hold any other achievement in my life. It actually made me feel . . . like I belonged.

The Cellar became my safe space. I spent nearly a year going onstage there when I was in New York, working out material that would end up being part of the *Landing* special. I could walk in and not be ashamed. I remember walking onstage at the Cellar and saying, "Uh . . . I'm being called a terrorist, and I'm charged with sedition complaints at police stations," and everyone just laughed. There was zero sympathy, just a laugh at how absurd that was, which is typical of a New York crowd. After that set I sat down at the comics' table at the café upstairs, and a Cellar regular came up to me and said, "You know what the worst thing is? They're calling you a poet! Yuck!"

It was the first time I laughed at the whole situation. The Cellar crowd got me.

Over time I went from being the Indian guy, to the visiting guy, to just being a Cellar guy. That's usually when the doorman and the staff know your name. I kept the Bollywood, Mumbai, Indian fame, and all of the other parts of my life in India a well-guarded secret at the club. I just wanted to be respected as a comic, nothing else. I was at the Cellar the week after the Kennedy Center show, so the place started to fill up with Indians, which led some white comics to open with lines like "Wow, there are a lot of brown people in here."

Great work, guys.

One night, Chris Rock came in, which bumped the entire lineup because . . . he's Chris Rock. I was supposed to do fifteen minutes in the middle of the show, but once Chris Rock came in, I figured I'd get bumped, so I planned to just sit back and check out his set. We call it "taking class," watching a legend, seeing if you can learn something. I did. He unflinchingly searches for material onstage. Walks around going "What else? What else?" confident that the crowd will follow as he figures it out. He may go up there with ten minutes, but he leaves with fifteen. He ended up doing about twenty-five minutes instead of forty-five, so Liz, the manager of the club, came over and asked me if I could go up and do a short set while the servers dropped the checks.

Fuck.

The check drop is the worst time to get onstage. It's the end of the night, people are tired, and then they look at their bills and get pissed because of the two-drink minimum charges they forgot about because they were wasted. So I went up after Chris fucking Rock, telling jokes while angry, drunk patrons focused on their bills. There is something about following a massive headliner. People think it's a tough thing to do, and that can be the case only if you try to pretend like what just happened didn't happen. People came into a club and for twelve bucks got to see Chris Rock—one of the best to ever do it—walk in the room and entertain them for twenty-five minutes. I figured the best approach would be to address it, and come out swinging. I made a joke about following Chris Rock, and for six minutes I managed to make the people paying their checks look up and laugh. Got offstage thanking god it had gone well.

For the next week I would come into the Cellar, watch Chris Rock annihilate, and then get so angry (in a healthy way) that I would attempt to annihilate too for six straight minutes. At the end of the week, every doorman and server knew my name. I wasn't the Indian guy anymore—I was Vir, the guy who followed Chris Rock. Closing the show out for him gave me confidence that I wasn't just India-good, maybe I was America-good too? After two Netflix specials and three world tours, it took a week at the Comedy Cellar to make me feel like I could take on pretty much any stage. It didn't make me want to move to America, though.

My *When Harry Met Sally* version of our lives in New York sounded nice, but performing at the same venue five nights a week and trudging home at three in the morning didn't sound like growth to me. New York isn't an easy place to live. I have enough sad shit in my head. I don't need freezing Manhattan at 3:00 a.m. on a Tuesday in December. I wanted Rockefeller Center at 8:00 p.m. with the Christmas tree lit up and a hot chocolate in my hand. I didn't want to get lost in a scene, trying to become something I wasn't. So I sat on the green card application and kept pushing it out as long as I could. I would tell my managers in America to give me five months; no, wait, give me another year . . . America had to make me an offer I couldn't refuse, like in *The Godfather*, but less violent. After high school, I could not wait to get to America, which is why I ended up at Knox. But things had changed. I had changed. My voice had changed.

Once I accepted the fact that my home is India but that I'm really a child of nowhere, and now more so than ever, it freed me up.

You can get angry at the mobs, you can get validation at the Cellar, but really what hurts the most is that your country, your place, isn't proud of you anymore. The next year of my life became this weird mental dance: I have this green card application, and if it eventually gets approved, all I have to do is stay in America for seven months in order to activate it. But can I? Would India have me back? My confidence as a performer took a huge hit because of the controversy. And would I get bored of New York? If I have a place in New York that makes me feel like I'm part of something, am I no longer part of Mumbai? WHERE DO I BELONG?

By this time I thought Shivani had given up on me and my indecision. She finally said, "When you fucking decide let me know and we will go from there, but be sure!" She didn't *want* to move to New York, but she would have so we could be together.

I wasn't ever sure.

I realize that there are people who think I'm unforgivably stupid to postpone the all-access American pass to the world. It just didn't add up for me. It felt like running away. So I was back in India, in limbo. And then, in the fall of 2022, a year after the Two Indias, Spoken Fest happened.

Spoken Fest is a two-day literature event in Mumbai every year with music, spoken-word poetry, and people getting onstage telling stories. In November 2022, they asked me to come do a fireside chat as part of the closing night. I wasn't telling jokes; I was going to simply talk and get out in front of a crowd for the first time in what felt like ten years. I was living in Goa and hadn't been in Mumbai since I was canceled, so it was a strange feeling stepping back into the throngs of the city that had once embraced me and then tossed me out. I had no idea how the crowds would react. Would they throw things at me? Heckle me? Love me? Hate me? I had no clue. But I knew I had to get back out there.

I walked onstage and saw thousands of faces staring back at me. I saw a mass of people that recognized that artists evolve, they experiment, and as long as there is truth at the center of what they are trying to do, they deserve kindness. So many people came up to me, put their hands on me, and said, "What happened to you was wrong, and every word you said was true."

It's a much different experience, being able to look someone in the eye, instead of seeing a mass of bodies out in an audience. The audience there didn't heckle or call me a terrorist; they were *proud* of me.

There are moments in life where you have to ask yourself: *What is my story? What's the truest version?* When the universe hijacks your narrative, you have to accept it on a certain level. The fact that "terrorist" will pop up when you google "Vir Das" is part of my story now. I can't control it, unless you know a way to erase years of Google searches. If so, please DM me immediately. I have to accept that, but I knew, that night at the festival, that I didn't want "he ran" to be part of my story. I didn't want to take the easy route. I'd spent time in America on and off over that year, but I hadn't actually moved. I hadn't left.

Around this time, my company Weirdass went bankrupt. It happens when a pandemic shuts the world down *and* you lose every single job because you unintentionally whipped up a political/cultural firestorm. I tried to keep eighteen of the employees on through the pandemic by not taking a salary so they could get paid, but we finally had to fold. Literally no one wanted to work with us. I had started this company with two friends in a tent in Film City while covered in cement from *Delhi Belly*'s ceiling-falling scene. This company that had helped build the comedy scene in India from nothing. This company that every single major comedian in India had passed through. This company had zero money. Our investors were offering us debt. We didn't have a single green-lit project to hope to pay that off. It was time.

In my mind I had been a terrible leader to the people there. I had never understood business, somehow landed us a major investment through sheer charm and luck, and then proceeded to fuck it all up because of perceived hubris. They all knew it was coming. They knew it was why I was coming back to Mumbai from Goa for a few days. They all knew I was thinking about leaving and would probably need to shut down the company if I did. And I think they all knew that my heart was broken.

Four days after Spoken Fest, I took the employees to a bar in Mumbai called Eddie's to have a drink one last time. Before we all got drunk, I asked them, "Would you rather I hadn't done it?" I meant what I said in the Two Indias piece. I wanted honest answers, not four-beers-in answers. Every one of them said I should have done it, that despite what was happening with the company, they were glad I spoke up. If they meant it, they were incredibly kind, and if they didn't, they were still incredibly kind. I'm not proud of everything I've ever done, but I was proud of having done the Two Indias, as painful as the aftermath had been. My co-workers saying that meant the world to me, and I can say that because they are all fully employed and thriving now, so I'm not walking around carrying a load of guilt. It was still heartbreaking though. To build something from nothing, and put so much passion into it, and then watch it end is brutal. I remember feeling like I'd failed, and talking to a friend who told me, "You're allowed to fail. Just because you had a public fuck-up, everything you do from now on doesn't have to be a success. Just get out there and fail."

I was free. There was no paperwork or company tying me to India anymore. I didn't have employees to monitor. I didn't have office hours. I could go wherever the hell I liked.

We filmed *Landing* under a new company name, Zazu Production. The company didn't have a bank account or a logo when we made the film. We did it in New York City so that I could work it out at the Cellar, and we could film a large crowd without a riot.

The day we filmed I think we all knew it was special. It was the culmination of all the confusion I had felt in the last year. How displaced I was. How hurt I was. How ashamed I was. And what it meant to love your country even when it didn't love you back.

Because Netflix did no publicity for the special, my American publicist, Pam, went into hyper mode, taking it to American outlets. Around this time my immigration attorney was calling constantly about the green card, asking if I had made up my mind about whether to apply. And then Pam lands what she calls "a big fish." A Very Important American Magazine (which I shall not name) asked to do a ten-thousand-word profile of me. This magazine is extremely highbrow and literary, so the idea of getting a massive profile had my managers in America practically throwing a parade in my honor. What a thing, to go from feeling like a complete failure to feeling like this American magazine wanted to hear all about me—in ten thousand words. I responded by saying, "I'm not sure," and everyone just kind of flips out, saying: "YOU FUCKING KIDDING ME? THIS IS THE ____ _____! THEY DON'T DO PROFILES ON JUST ANYONE!!!" So I decided to get on the phone with the magazine.

Now keep in mind, I'd gone on a few podcasts where people were asking about the threats and the police and the drama and how scared I was, and I was like, "Can we just talk about the jokes?"

When I got on the phone with the reporter, they did not want to talk about the jokes.

"Can I talk to the police?"

"Was your wife afraid?"

"Can I see the investigation papers?"

"Will your lawyer talk to me?"

"How powerful is this politician?"

"Will you be arrested anytime in the near future?"

"Can we be with you on release day in case you go to jail?"

To which I wanted to respond, "Yeah, but what did you think of the jokes? The lights? The sand?"

I think the final straw for me was interview number three, where the reporter was asking me about democracy and censorship. It just felt like my story was being fetishized and stolen from me. I didn't want to be another brown person being turned into a commodity. I distinctly remember thinking, "You want to write about what happened to me across the world, so you and your readers can feel better about where you live?"

There is something Conan O'Brien pointed out to me when I went on his podcast, and it didn't fully hit me until he said it out loud. He said, "What I love about this special is this: When celebrities have a horrible experience, some people go cry on *Oprah* or the equivalent, and you just write jokes."

Conan got it. So would my team if I told them I was not doing the Big Important Profile . . . right?

If you think calling your family and telling them your country thinks you're a terrorist is hard, try calling an American agent and telling them you want to pull out of a profile with the Very Important American Magazine. They tried their best to convince me to do it, but it just felt wrong to me. So I pulled out.

About four months later, they did the Big Important Story about another brown entertainer. They fact-checked his comedy routine and turned his own narrative of his own experience into something they used to make their readers feel virtuous. I felt like I'd dodged a bullet. I would love to be embraced by America, but it has to be me telling my story. I don't want some cheapened version of what I'm about or how I've lived or who I am.

Controversy is a short-term currency that helps you sell short-term tickets, but it doesn't help you fall asleep at night. I struggled with PTSD for a long time after the controversy. When I did shows, I was looking at the door every three seconds expecting someone to storm in, a mob to come rushing on to the stage. I finally told my therapist that if I didn't find a way to enjoy comedy again, they'd win. It took a while, but I finally started to enjoy it again. I stopped looking at the door.

Here's something I also know. I am an English comedian in India. Now don't get me wrong, we have one of the largest English-speaking audiences in the world. We actually have as large an English audience as America right now. But there is a competitive ceiling in India for an

English comedian. If you do comedy in Hindi, my lord, the world is your oyster. That gives way to TV, movies, writing, and an audience of close to a billion. But if you do comedy in English and you want to know if you're really good, you have to break that ceiling. It's not a financial ceiling, you can make a great living for the rest of your life as long as you can maintain relevance. It's an artistic ceiling. There aren't enough of us yet for you to truly know if you are undeniable. There is an entire world you can compete with. The only way to get good at tennis is to go to where the good tennis is.

Weird choice. I can stay and maybe plateau, or I can leave and my craft can rise along with my loneliness. Or I hope this world changes into a small enough digital space where I can do both? A truly global life? Die on a plane? Live in limbo before I head to it?

My friend and fellow comedian Zarna once frantically messaged me, "I know your heart is in India, but you need to bend your heart into submission and take the huge step that your art deserves. You are the only Indian positioned to reach those heights."

I do not agree with her second statement. But she got my heart right. It was torn.

To give you context, I started writing this chapter a year ago. I just finished it, twelve months later, with absolutely zero internal movement on the decision.

I've always admired people who can get up and go. Because leaving for a foreign shore means leaving their loved ones and their roots behind. For me it's more than that. I've left those behind at least six times in my life. For me it's leaving my perspective behind.

I look at Indians settled abroad, and they seem entirely out of touch with a country that is undeniably claiming its power in the future. We're on the precipice of unchallenged global greatness. With a perspective everyone will want to hear. If we get there, when we do, I don't want to be caught doing jokes about Gavin Newsom, emotional support animals, and rapper beefs.

Maybe I'll leave one day, maybe I'll find just the right balance. Or, at the peak of my career, with enough money, maybe I'll just fuck right off. And then one day, social media accounts gone, take my money and start a café in a tiny village in France where no one knows who I am. Shivani says I would go insane in three months, start a Hamateur night at the café, launch a French Weirdass, and build a comedy scene in the village.

Honestly, it doesn't sound half-bad.

For now, I'm still pushing it out another five months, another year. And when people ask where I am, where I belong, I just say I'm not anywhere. I'm everywhere.

I'm figuring it out.

A SHORT DOSE OF GROUNDING

Sometimes when I have writer's block, I like to go watch something. I was at a hotel near Lincoln Center in New York City feeling blocked while working on this book. So I called the concierge and asked him to get me tickets to the next jazz concert I could see. He booked me something at 8:00 p.m. An hour-long performance.

I sat down at this jazz club they have called Dizzy's, and a woman joins me at the table. She's American and about fifty-five. She says, "Which one's yours?"

"Excuse me?"

"Which kid is yours?"

Then thirty high school teenagers with acne come onto the stage. The concierge had booked me a high school jazz recital.

I say, "Uh . . . I'm just here to watch." Which is the WRONG fucking thing to say to a parent. I now realize that everyone in this club is a parent eagerly filming one member of the band on their phone, beaming with pride, except for a random bearded brown man with an Indian accent who just "showed up."

I now have to explain to this American lady that I'm not some shady creep who randomly shows up to watch other people's children play jazz. Eventually I wish her and her daughter luck with jazz school in Los Angeles, for which the kid auditions in two weeks. Also, why the fuck would the Lincoln Center ticket something like that, as if it's a regular jazz show? Which, by the way . . . was terrible! Only one of those kids had talent.

Take it from me, I was in Bad Attitude.

CHAPTER TWELVE

B.W.D.

LEFT TO RIGHT: *Lucy, Stupid, Watson.*

If you want to truly get to know me, you have to know Watson. I realize writing an entire chapter devoted to a dog might seem unusual, but this dog is (and was) the best part of me. If there was one being on earth around whom I felt totally, completely, and utterly myself, this damn dog was it. Caring for him, and losing him, is the toughest thing I've ever gone through.

So, yup, here's a chapter about a dog. Specifically, a British bulldog aptly named Dr. Watson.

As I write this, I'm at home in India, in a room decorated as if it's England circa 1840. It's a little weird to have British influences, since it's a culture I'm supposed to hate (colonialism, remember). But in my more egotistical moments, I fancy myself a Sherlock. And every Sherlock needs a Watson. I don't know why I gravitated toward the stories. As much as this sounds like a clichéd montage from a 1980s movie, I hid in the library through a lot of my boarding school bullying. I picked up Sir Arthur Conan Doyle's *Sherlock Holmes* collection there, and he quickly became my favorite fictional character. He was superintelligent, bad with people, more obsessed with what was in his brain than with the world around him. Something about that world drew me in, this foggy, chilly England where people wore overcoats, where principled thieves thrived in the shadows. There were lots of pipe smoke and messy parlors. I think those books were the reason I brought a British bulldog into humid Mumbai, a city dominated by muggy monsoons, insane heat, and tiny apartments.

We had dogs growing up, and for years I knew that one day I'd get a British bulldog and name him Dr. Watson. I also wanted to get a bloodhound and call it Toby, but I had no clue that highbred dogs are always five seconds away from death in Mumbai, no matter their age. The weather isn't conducive to their health. It's not cool and rainy like in Britain, it's hot as hell, and when it rains, it monsoons. But as you can probably tell by now, I'm a person who, if I decide to do something, I'll go all in. I'll buy all the tech, gather all the equipment, and then I'll probably suck at it, but I'm still going to try it, damn it. I'm that guy. Before I entered the minimalism phase of my life, I had fifteen guitars, even though my playing is not great. I had about nine sound cards for making music, and I never figured out how to operate the things. And don't get me started on martial arts equipment. I could probably get my ass beat by a thirteen-year-old, so no amount of equipment could save me.

Turns out not a lot of people in India had the same British bulldog obsession that I did. Lovers of these dogs form a very tight-knit community, and they all give you the same advice: Make sure your *first* dog is not a British bulldog. They are not for beginners. They are very tough to care for and require seasoned dog owners. But since when does Sherlock listen to the community?

In this case, though, the community had a point.

Have you met a bulldog? Let's break this down: They have toxic shit and toxic farts. When I say "toxic," I am not exaggerating in any way whatsoever. Consider the average human shit, then expose that to nuclear radiation, then put it in an oven full of masalas and gasoline, and that is what fresh British bulldog shit smells like. The average bulldog fart is released about twenty times a day, precariously and precisely in the direction of your nose. They love farting in your face. There is no graceful way to say it. Watson would do this thing where he would stick his bum into your armpit when you were sleeping, as if your chest was this little cave where he felt secure. Anyone who has had a dog knows that there is no better feeling than this. It's like a safety and love that you physically imprint on each other as your breathing syncs and you both fall asleep. Then, just as you're fading away, the fucker farts in your face and singes your nostril hair off. But you just keep cuddling with them.

Then there's the face. That iconic squishy Churchill face. You can never tell if they are angry or happy. The face comes with wrinkles that need to be maintained, wrinkles that smell almost as much as the anus that could create crop circles with a single gust. You have to clean these damn things thrice a day because they are covered in drool. Because bulldogs want to eat everything, and they eat it with their entire face, you also have to clean their eyeballs. Your entire house, every single piece of furniture, every piece of clothing you have ever loved, is covered in this toxic drool that physically—yes, I mean physically—burns when it touches your skin. Oh, and the loud snores? Having a British bulldog is like living with a malfunctioning motorcycle. And then there are the grunts. Grunts mean I love you, I hate this, I refuse, let's go. They don't bark, they grunt. Kind of like the grunts made by old uncles wearing joggers in Mumbai parks, making their way around the track. British bulldogs don't really lick to show affection, they just kind of shove their face into your face and grunt in your ear or your eyeball and melt away every single problem you've ever had.

It's hard to explain that sound. It sounds like home. All I can tell you is I still hear it when I'm asleep sometimes. I hear Watson grunting in my ear, and I wake up, and look at a photo of him that I take everywhere I go in the world. This photo has been on four world tours; it's been in the background of every single Netflix special I've ever done. I'll usually wake up after hearing a grunt and see the photo right by my bed. Four years since he passed, and it's like he's still here. That sound is as familiar to me as an AC compressor kicking in at Baba's house, the sound of a Lagos beach, the sound of a mic check in any venue in the world, one of the songs my band plays at a festival, Shivani's gentle "Viiiiir" from another room, the buzz of a film set. Sounds that, when you close your eyes, you instantly know where you are and your body drums up all the emotions that you're supposed to feel in that place. I hear a grunt, and it resets me, reminds me to be someone simpler, someone more joyful. It reminds me that I am not alone.

Here's how Watson and his grunts came into our lives.

When Shivani and I moved in together in 2009, we went to the mountains for a few weeks so I could write *History of India*. We stayed in a guesthouse that had a dog, so we got a taste of what it might be like to live with a dog full-time. Soon I thought, "Okay, maybe we *should* get that dog." This practice dog was so easy! But what we didn't figure into the decision was the fact that we'd been spending time with a fully trained adult dog, which is nothing like living with a puppy. Ignorance is bliss, and it also led us to Watson.

I spent six months researching where to find English bulldogs in India. I found a few places, and then I went off to shoot a movie. While I was gone, Shivani began the search for some bulldog puppies. Most were cute, but there was one that caught her attention. He looked malnourished and disheveled. He was the runt, and she fell in love with him. In India there are agents that sell dogs, and multiple agents can "represent" one puppy. Three different agents had shown her photos of this one sad little puppy, so he kept showing up to her throughout the day.

She went and met the puppy, and as soon as she held him, she *knew*. He was THE ONE. When I spoke to her, and she sent me a photo of this malnourished dog, I said . . . no. Yep. Smart move. Have you ever told a girl you love that you don't want the puppy she wants? There is no corner of Russia colder than the look I got when I saw her face in Mumbai—a look that said, *What kind of monster does such a thing?*

When I got back home, I took one look at her face and booked a flight to Bengaluru to get the dog. He was about five weeks old and still looked like shit. I took him to the vet to make sure he was healthy, and when it was time to bring him home, I was told that you couldn't fly with a bulldog. This was before there were twenty-five emotional support animals on every flight, so I was screwed. I don't typically take advantage of the perks of fame, but I made some calls and was able to carry Watson onto the plane and hold him in my lap. I booked the very last row of economy on Air India. Thank god for Air India. I boarded with this bulldog in my arms. He was only slightly bigger than my palm. It was like walking on with something the size of one of those cylindrical Bluetooth speakers, but one that only grunts.

I took my seat and laid Watson against my belly. He looked up at me and gently fell asleep, as if he had found something he had been searching for forever, even though he'd only been on the planet for five weeks. Like two Lego pieces that click, we just fit. If there's a moment in which you imprint upon a child or a child imprints upon you, ours happened on that plane ride. I'd done some research and read that if you mimic the mother's breathing, a puppy will fall asleep. So there I was, holding this small round ball on my lap, doing rapid breathing to mimic a dog. I looked like a yoga guru having an anxiety attack. Instead of the puppy passing out, *I* passed out.

When I woke up mid-flight, Watson wasn't moving. He was fast asleep and a little too still. I gave him a gentle shake, but nothing. I gave him a heavier shake. Still nothing. I was getting worried, so I started violently shaking him, which made it look like I was choking a puppy in the middle of an Air India flight. I distinctly remember the lady across from me looking at me like I was some puppy murderer who chose venues at thirty thousand feet to slay his victims. The dog still did not wake up. And at thirty thousand feet in the air, I started to cry. God only knows why, because I'd just met this little rat earlier that day. I distinctly remember thinking, "He looked at me like he trusted me and like he was gonna be okay. But now he's not okay."

In the middle of my panic, the in-flight meal showed up. I took a piece of chicken tikka and held it near his nose, and guess what? The fucking dog woke up. Like nothing had ever happened, this fucker smelled the tikka and opened his eyes. This British bulldog was Punjabi. This experience set the tone of our entire relationship. Watson was near death for his entire life, but when food came along, he was fully alive.

After the flight, Watson came to our apartment, his new home. We got a giant stuffed tiger in case he missed his mother (yes, I know English bulldogs and tigers are not the same). I have photos of him snuggling up to this giant tiger on his first night with us. We read articles about creating rules and boundaries with your puppy, and he stayed in his own bed the first night until we told him it was okay to come out.

That was the first and only night he slept in his own bed. The rest of his life, he slept with us, in my armpit cavity, farting in my face. Just like Shivani had the first time she held him, I fell in love with Watson. He changed my approach to everything. Time started being measured in time away from and time with this little guy. He completely reoriented my life. Instead of taking the first flight out in the morning, I'd take the last one, and then the first one home to see him. He was a cranky son of a bitch and bit me about seventeen times, but I was Dad. I think he just gave me a bite once a year to keep me in line and remind me who was truly in charge.

Now here's the thing. Watson was spoiled as hell. He ripped shoes and bags and books owned by every single person who came through the door. He'd give you the greeting of all greetings when you came into the house, but god forbid you try to leave, because he would take your leg. I know there are dog trainers and behaviorists reading this and prescribing about five thousand solutions to "temperament issues," but to us and the people we knew, that was just Watson.

In all honesty, he also kept our marriage together.

A few years after our wedding, Shivani and I started having problems. Just this sort of silence in the house, because there wasn't enough time to have a real conversation. We were drifting apart. I was always traveling or shooting a film or doing shows. It felt like our lives were going in different directions, which is not an easy thing to realize when you love someone, and you stood on a beach and pledged to spend your entire lives together. Being married to a comedian is challenging. You basically sign up to be with someone who works in a traveling circus. There's also no bar to compare it to. The lives of Western comedians don't apply to us, and no other Indian comedian was working the number of markets I was at this point. My logic was that these opportunities were a first for anyone from India, so I had to take all of it, which wasn't always the best mentality for a healthy partnership.

There was a three- or four-year period where Watson was constantly sick, so every time I left and got on a plane to perform or work, I felt like I was abandoning my family. One of the longest stretches that I was away was when I was shooting an ABC show called *Whiskey Cavalier*. Don't remember it? You're not the only one. When I got the audition, though, I had high hopes. This was a show from Bill Lawrence, the guy who created *Scrubs* and co-created *Spin City* and *Ted Lasso*. The thing about American television, though, is that you can go shoot a pilot, the first episode of a series, and that pilot can wind up not getting picked up. *Or* it *can* get picked up . . . and then you have to move far away from your home.

Bill Lawrence told me he was going to create a role for me in this show. I'd play a guy named Jai Datta, a high-tech hardware, CIA weapons specialist, whatever the hell that means. I was also told that the show would be shot in New York. Jai Datta, the Indian spy who is always two steps ahead, would change my life. Listen up, kids: Signing on to do an American network TV show does not always mean your life will change for the better. Playing the fourth lead on *The Good Doctor* is better than *not* playing the fourth lead on *The Good Doctor*, but it also might not turn out to be a career-spiking opportunity. What I'm saying is: Keep it all in perspective.

So I told Shivani that we (including Watson) were moving to New York. I gave her my *When Harry Met Sally* pitch, and added that it would be amazing for Watson, since it was closer to the climate he was destined to live in. They also had bulldog-specific vets! It was going to be romantic and different, and it might even save Watson's life and cure his ills. But then Bill Lawrence told me they'd switched the shoot. To Prague.

Prague may sound romantic and amazing to you, but in my experience there, the city is good for about six days—unless you love chimney cake, prostitutes, and puppet shows. I spent several weeks there shooting the pilot, and instantly I knew I wasn't going to move Shivani and Watson without knowing whether this series was going ahead. So we were apart. And it was tough. And then the show got picked up for a season, so I had to move to Prague. Not for weeks but for six months. I had signed a six-year contract based in New York, so I could have bailed. But I think the learning is what attracted me. To learn comedy from comedy creators at the top of their game.

So for six months I delivered lines like "I'm gonna hack into their systems, and see what I can do." I wore fancy suits with five other amazing actors in the freezing cold climate of Prague, surrounded by the cheerful demeanor of Eastern Europeans. That's not a knock, but the average twenty-five-year-old Prague resident looks forty and possesses the joy of the world's grumpiest eighty-year-old. So yes, maybe it's a knock. I'd watch Shivani and Watson on CCTV cameras in the house I wished I was in, living the life I should not have left behind, telling myself that it was the right decision to not have them freezing in this tiny flat with me. I told myself I'd made the right call.

I left a wife in India who wanted to leave me because I'd abandoned her and left her to care for a needy, increasingly sick bulldog. I was missing Watson and constantly fighting with Shivani, and the doggie cameras were the only things that kept me going. I'd watch Watson sleeping at night, which helped me sleep at night. I started flying home more often, and by the end of the shoot, I'd flown from Prague to Mumbai for eleven weekends, which was not cheap. I would leave Friday evening after filming, fly for over ten hours, stay in Mumbai for Saturday and part of Sunday, fly back to Prague, and report to set on Monday. I'm sure the crew and the ABC executives were like, *What is wrong with this guy?* But Shivani and I were not doing well. And I missed Watson.

When we wrapped filming, I went back to a tense household. The show premiered in early 2019, and it was not great. The show had this massively committed fan base and got great reviews, but it didn't have great ratings. It was just . . . meh. It was average American television. It's one of the first times in my life that I remember thinking, "Would you watch this if you were not in it, Vir?" And I remember not being able to fully say yes. I felt so stupid. I had signed a six-year contract to shoot in a place I didn't want to be in, for a show I wouldn't even watch.

The money was fantastic, my agents and managers were thrilled about the opportunity, but then the minute the first episode aired, I kind of became "this guy on that show." It was more about the paycheck than what this was going to lead to or open up, which I've learned is the biggest career red flag you need to watch out for. The minute people start focusing on the money, be wary. If the first thing that comes up isn't the idea or the feeling, the money won't last. If you hear people saying things like, "Oh, it looks expensive" or "You're gonna get a great bonus next year" or "Man, did you guys really blow up a chopper?" that is all code for "It makes me feel nothing" or "I haven't actually seen it." Every single cast member of that show became like a family member to me, and since then they have all gone on to do shows that I would watch, irrespective of whether I knew them. I sometimes think back to what they must have thought of this lonely Indian man they spent all those months with. I tried to be a professional, I made it through, and when the season ended, I went home.

Shivani told me she wanted to split up. She'd been alone with Watson for months, and even though I was flying home as much as possible, it wasn't enough. And I get that. So in February 2020, the same month the show came out, we started talking to lawyers. We wanted to keep it amicable, be respectful of each other, and go our separate ways. We were two people who lived in the same house but didn't really know each other. Two people who watched each other from across the world on different screens, with only one thing in common—a bulldog.

Watson fell sick that same week. I swear, it's as if he knew these two people were heading away from each other, and he did what he could to prevent that from happening. And then, in March, the world shut down. I remember being on a Zoom call, being new to the phenomenon and struggling to focus, and out of the corner of my eye seeing Watson collapse and stop breathing for a second. I rushed over to revive him, which I was able to do. We got masks on and rushed him to one of the few emergency vet clinics that were open. We were in full PPE kits (us, not him). He had acute pneumonia. It took us so long to get there, to get him seen and get him healthy, that I started to panic. So now this couple that had spent days ignoring each other and looking for apartments online that they could move into—apartments that weren't too far away from each other so we could share custody of the dog—was forced to coexist. We spent our days together, hand-feeding Watson, nebulizing him three times a day, carrying him to the bathroom, singing to him. He became our entire focus. We slept in separate bedrooms. I took Watson for night duty; Shivani took day duty. We were like two strangers in a tough city, sharing one house, with the world shut down outside our doors. We had limited access to vets, since India had a Wuhan-level Covid lockdown. The streets were empty. No one left their homes. Watson was becoming sicker, and something told me that he wouldn't make it if we stayed in Mumbai. So I thought about Goa, more for Watson than for myself.

Goa is on the western coast of India, with about one hundred miles of beach along the Arabian Sea. I figured fresh air and space might help Watson (and maybe help me and Shivani as well). So I went to her and said, "I don't know how long he has left. I know we want to split up, but if you move to Goa with me, I'll get us through this pandemic and hopefully he'll get healthy again. And then we'll see what happens with us. As a man of honor, I will do my duty by both of you and make sure we all get through this safely, I don't expect anything in return." She agreed.

There were no open houses, so we found a house with a garden in Goa via WhatsApp. We just took it, without ever setting foot in the place. We would end up living there for four years, until December 2024. Borders were closed and there was no travel, but I knew a guy who did movie promos for Bollywood stars, and he had access to private jets. Like I said, I don't call in the perks of fame often, but I guess for Watson I made a few exceptions. I knew this guy was just sitting on these jets, so I called and told him the situation, and asked if there was some secret Illuminati pact that enabled people to get on planes and fly during lockdown. He said there was no secret pact, *but* that it would be expensive. It's a thirty-five-minute flight from Mumbai to Goa, so he called the Goa airport to see if they would let us land. I have only ever flown in and paid for one private jet in my life, and it was for my bulldog.

The day we flew to Goa, Watson was very sick, it was hot out, and we were in full PPE. We might as well have been wearing hazmat suits. There were four seats on the jet, so it was me, Shivani, the pilot, and a vet. We had the vet come, in case Watson had a heart attack on the plane. He had pneumonia, so I was taking no chances. The vet was simply flying to Goa and then flying straight back to Mumbai. What I didn't know was that jets are like cars. They have an ignition switch, and when you turn that switch the AC comes on. In an airplane, they can keep the AC running while you get in and wait to take off, but not in a jet. The AC comes on exactly when you take off. It was like a hot box inside, so I took Watson outside and held him as I stood in the shade under a wing of the plane. While we were waiting for the AC (for our dog), they told us we had too much luggage, so we ended up leaving Mumbai with nothing but Watson's medications. The only private jet experience I have ever paid for, for a damn dog.

Then we landed in Goa, and something changed. We weren't magically in love again, Watson wasn't magically better, but we were two hardened, worn-out Mumbaikars sharing a very clueless, vulnerable moment. It made us both a little kinder. We still gave each other space, but it was a space with a garden and nature. We still didn't talk much, but we talked more softly. We focused on our son, who was now walking and pooping on grass instead of concrete. I remember the first time he took a piss in Goa and instinctively did this thing where he backed sand on top of it using his hind legs. In seven years, I had never seen him do it. You would've thought he had won the Tour de France the way I celebrated his basic dog instinct to cover his piss.

Goa was better for Watson than Mumbai had been, but he was still struggling.

Instead of chasing auditions and flying away to film pilots, my days became about caretaking. I would steam Watson and feed him by hand. It was good to focus on the little things. Shivani and I are old babies, in a way. We weren't taught domesticity. We can't even make toast, so responsibilities at home need to be shared if we want to survive. She had been Watson's full-time mom for seven years, so it was my turn to step up. Living in Goa during lockdown ended up being the best eighteen months of my life, and I think Shivani got to see what it was like to have me around again and maybe she was reminded about the person she had married. When that person is just in and out of your life, you can sometimes think of them in terms of their routine instead of their heart. During this time, Shivani and I grew to appreciate each other again. It's like Watson brought us back together. He knew.

I know the world outside our garden house was in turmoil, but inside the house I just wanted to make Watson comfortable. During that time, I got the chance to make up for everything I'd missed. Every day was work with him: I'd massage his legs in the morning and carry him outside to go to the bathroom. We built ramps for him so it would be easier for him to walk around. I put steamers in the shower, and I'd steam with him twice a day. We had to nebulize him to help his lungs. I played classical music during his baths. I got to take care of this old dog. It became my main purpose, and it felt good to care for him, this wrinkly English bulldog who had imprinted upon me years ago on that plane ride.

I started doing shows via Zoom for charity, donating money to Covid relief in India. I was content. And then, eventually, the world opened up. And Judd Apatow called.

I had once auditioned for one of his movies via Zoom and hadn't gotten the part. But then he called out of the blue and said he was creating a role for me in a movie called *The Bubble*, about a group of actors quarantining during a pandemic and making a movie. Write what you know, right? The movie had Fred Armisen, Keegan-Michael Key, Pedro Pascal, and David Duchovny. And they weren't shooting in Prague, they were shooting in London. It's not every day that you're on a Zoom call with one of your idols and he casually goes, "I'm not sure if you know, but sometimes I just put people who I think are funny in movies—and I think you're funny."

That was a tough conversation to have with my wife: "This Judd guy is a big deal, and he thinks I'm funny, and he wants to send me to London!" We'd just gotten over Prague, just come back together. I also knew that if I left, I might never see Watson again. He was so sick. But there are not many times in life that a Judd Apatow calls you. This wasn't the fourth lead in a Navy SEAL show. This was something else. It was also temporary, since it was a movie and not a show that could potentially go on for years.

So I said yes, and Shivani was on board.

We hired a pet sitter named Scott to help Shivani with all of Watson's care. Scott was amazing, but not many people could give Watson the level of care I had been giving him. Classical music and steam showers? It's a lot. I spent as much time as I could with Watson before I left. I remember the day I had to go. He was fast asleep, and I put my face up against his and told him I would be back in eight weeks. I kissed him a lot more than I usually do. He didn't open his eyes. He stayed asleep and, yes, he grunted.

The second I took off to London, his health started to decline even more.

I was staying at a hotel in London, quarantining for two weeks before I could go on set. On the third day of lockdown, Shivani called. Watson's breathing was deteriorating.

"He's going," she said.

My heart was crushed. Destroyed.

About five hours into his suffering I said, "Tell him not to stay for me," even though the thought of him dying felt like it would actually kill me. I'd made it back from Prague to India eleven times for this dog. Nothing would have stopped me from flying back again. It was mid-second wave, though, and against the law to leave. I stood on a freezing balcony in London, talking to a framed photo of my dog (the one I take with me everywhere), saying, "You don't have to stay," while weeping. If that sounds pathetic to you, you've probably never loved a dog.

An hour later, Shivani called again.

"He's gone."

We sobbed as she held him.

I watched my dog, my son, being buried via a WhatsApp video, which is an experience I would not wish upon anybody in the world. I shot that entire Judd Apatow movie heartbroken. It's not an easy thing to try to improvise and be funny in that state of mind. I felt like I fucked up on that movie because I was around all these people who were my idols, and I was just broken inside. I still grapple with the fact that I wasn't there with Watson. Did he look for me in his final moments? Was he peaceful? Did he feel let down? I'll never know.

It's very hard to lose someone who loves you with that kind of unconditional innocence. To this day, at this very second, as I type these words, I carry the guilt of feeling like I failed as a father.

It's a tough contract to sign with the universe. But it's worth it. You're signing up to be there for an entire life. From training them to walk, to their first everything, to their calming down, to their eating, to their losing their faculties, to caring for them as they pass. Think about that. You're in charge of a whole life journey. I remember this tiny puppy taking his first nap on my chest, when he was no bigger than a papaya, and how our breath just synced up. I remember sitting in a bathroom, drenched in sweat with him, with two steamers pointed at us because it was hard for him to breathe as an old dog. The day you get a dog, you make a commitment to the universe that you will watch them pass; you will be there. When we lost him, I failed that contract.

I always say: Find yourself someone who looks at you the way your pet looks at you. But then you'd have to be sixteen bloody feet tall, which is kind of what you are to pets. No matter how tired you are, you'll dance around the room, make silly noises, sing songs, run around like a fool . . . for them. If we did that with each other, maybe this whole place would be a little better. If you can go through life remembering someone is waiting for you with the love you deserve, that you're never too silly for them, that your accomplishments or failures mean nothing to them, all they care about is your heart, maybe you'll be okay.

Get a pet. Even better, adopt one. Sign the contract. It hurts, but, man, it's worth it.

Now, whenever I do a show, I write B.W.D. on my wrist: Be Watson's Dad. On the other wrist, I write what I want the show to be about: Focus or Play or Improvising. It reminds me what the vibe should be. B.W.D. is my reminder that this isn't all my life is. I may be a comedian, but at the end of the day, I will always be Watson's dad.

Like I said, that well-traveled photo of Watson is hidden just off camera on every Netflix special I've done. I keep it onstage in my line of sight, like a little easter egg for me. He's gone, but he defines how I hope to make people feel, which is how he made me feel. That feeling is hard to articulate, but I see the best in my audience, and I'm able to do that now because I know what it feels like to have someone see the best in me. Everybody deserves someone that thinks the world of them, and I hope comedy makes you feel that. When you come to a show, I hope you feel that I think the world of you.

I didn't make it back to Goa until late spring. Shivani buried Watson on a friend's property, in a beautiful, sunny spot with statues and Tibetan flags. It's a lovely place to be. The first thing we did when I got home was to go there and see Watson. Now, once a month we visit him and clean and rake and garden the place.

A week after Watson passed, a stray dog named Stupid—whom we didn't name, that's just what they called him on the street; we've changed that to Stooopeee anyway—wandered into the house. Stupid is a street dog, this raggedy black Doberman-looking mix. He wandered in one day when Shivani was heartbroken, and he started spending more and more time with her. By the time I got back, Stupid would spend five hours a day with her. He truly is a stupid dog. It's a "the lights are on but nobody's home" kind of situation. We kept him at a distance for a while because our hearts were not ready to accept a dog so soon after Watson had died. A few months later, a dog named Lucy, who'd been abandoned by a neighbor during the pandemic, started stealing Stupid's dog biscuits, and she moved in with us too. The moment Lucy felt safe with us, she slept in our house for three days straight. I think she was exhausted from living on the streets for two years. Now Stupid and Lucy are part of our family. They're our dogs. They're tough and independent, completely different from Watson. These dogs lived on the streets; they're agile and will eat anything. They kill snakes and go to the bathroom in the jungle. They're ruffians, and they're in no way inconvenient. But what I wouldn't give for the inconvenience of Watson again.

Watson bit me, he was completely dependent, he was flatulent, and he snored like a tractor engine. But he also loved us fiercely. At home with Watson, I wasn't thinking about jokes or selling out shows; I was dancing around the house and throwing bones for him to fetch. I'm very socially awkward in real life, but with Watson, I was completely myself.

I mentioned this before: I'm not afraid of death anymore. Don't get me wrong, I love life, I'm grateful for each day I get to wake up in the morning. But when it's my time to go, I'm going to go happily, because I know he's coming to get me, and I have unfinished business with him.

At the time of writing this, Shivani, Stupid, Lucy, and I have just moved back to Mumbai. After almost four years away. What I love about Goa is that time physically moves more slowly than in the rest of the world. So slowly that if you stay more than ten days, it forces you to confront whatever you're escaping from. It's also full of people escaping, who don't judge. I never imagined myself living there, and now I cannot imagine staying there in a hotel. A rented private residence in the tiny village of Parra was our home. Where Watson, Stupid, and Lucy stood on the terrace and looked out at the paddy fields. Where you could be woken by peacocks singing to each other in the rain. Mumbai is a constant chase. When you stop chasing, when you become okay with slow time, you find out who you really are. And when you truly do, the universe chases you. Goa does that for you; it certainly did for me. I will always be grateful for the people I met there, and for the time, as slow as it was.

We came back to Mumbai because we missed being part of the world. It was time to engage with it again, like people our age do, to climb, to get our hands dirty again. The day before we left, we went to Watson's spot in the sun. We performed our monthly ritual, where we cleaned the place up. Cut the brambles, dusted off the flags; there are crystals and stones, and we rearranged them. We never talked when we did it, we just quietly divided up the labor. Raking, chopping, watering, and then . . . standing. We always just stood there in silence for a bit. Then we drove back in silence. Our house in Goa is about forty-five minutes away from where he is, so about twenty minutes into the drive home, I would put on some music and then we'd both feel ready to talk again.

The last time we went there, it felt different. The nature surrounding Watson had reclaimed the spot more than I had ever seen before. Thicker brambles, more moss, more grass. For a second it felt like he wasn't there anymore. It was like he was telling us to go, that he had moved on.

Now Stupid and Lucy are adjusting to Mumbai. We tried to get them a place with a terrace, so they don't miss their wild gallivants in the streets of Goa. Strangely enough, the day we arrived in Mumbai, it was like they both went, "Oh, we're safe now? We don't have to be on constant watch?" They relaxed. They now know where we go, they go.

They say that love takes your breath away, and so does grief. The only way I can describe grief is an inability to breathe. No matter how hard you try you just can't seem to get enough air in your lungs. It's because there's less space in there now. It's because someone or something that used to live outside of you now lives in you. Watson's not in the spot in the sun anymore, he's underneath my chest bone. To anyone dealing with grief of any kind and reading this, that's all I can say. I know a life was lost, but your heart grew. That's what's pressing up against your lungs, that's what's making you fight for each breath. Your heart, where they now reside. If I'm being honest, I haven't taken a full breath since he passed. I know I will when I see him again. I'm not hard on myself about it, I'm proud of the love he left me with.

Which is why I remind myself: B.W.D.

As I write this, I am on a plane to a gig. In my bag is a note from Shivani. It reads, "Go, be present, go rest, go get inspired. I love you and I'm proud of you." If you told me when we were in Mumbai during lockdown that I would one day be getting handwritten notes like this, I would have told you that you were insane. It's all because of Watson.

A SHORT DOSE OF GROUNDING

I'm dyslexic and I keep a journal every morning. I can't write cursive or understand anything I've written, ever. This is a photo of one of my journals:

So journaling has shown me zero fucking benefit. I still keep doing it, and I have no idea why.

CHAPTER THIRTEEN
I NEED YOU TO KNOW ONE MORE THING

LEFT: *Vir with his Emmy for Best Comedy.* REG TIGERMAN.
RIGHT: *Vir and Kavi directing an actor on the set of* Happy Patel.

It ain't up or down, it's all a circle.

It's 2008. I'm sitting in a tent on the set of *Delhi Belly*, telling my friend Kavi about my idea for a spy comedy about an Indian baby named Happy Patel who is adopted by two gay British MI-5 agents. I love slapstick, over-the-top comedies like *Spy Hard*, *Johnny English*, and *Airplane!*, and I wanted this movie to be like that, even though there were no spy movies, let alone spy comedies, in India at the time.

I spent two years writing the script. In America, you typically send your script to agents or producers and wait for feedback, but in India, you narrate. So, I went around to producers and filmmakers, narrating this story, acting it out, doing voices, and giving stage directions as if I was performing a one-man show. In five years, I did about thirty different narrations of this fucking movie, and every single person stared at me as if I were out of my mind. Their stares were blank, their eyes did not shine with laughter, and their checkbooks did not open up to finance the epic story of Happy Patel. Occasionally, if the listener was up to speed on films like the zombie parody *Shaun of the Dead*, they'd get it and laugh, but not enough to come on board. Eventually I put the script away and went on with my life.

Almost fifteen years after I put that script away, I started having strange dreams.

During about a week-long period, I had three separate dreams about Happy Patel. That's when I know that something is about to shift in my life. When I dream about it multiple times. I pulled the script out and reread it. It's about this character trying desperately to fit in and coming to understand that the only way to belong is to be yourself. And it struck me—the first movie I ever wrote was about being an outsider.

Unlike back in 2008, spy movies had become a thing in India. They weren't comedies, they were action movies about an Indian spy taking on Pakistan or the entire Arab world. They were ultrapatriotic and took themselves very seriously, so it was finally time to parody them. I reworked the old script, put it away for a few months, won an Emmy for my Netflix special, and then thought, *I'm back!* Who can I narrate this story to? Who can I call? I hadn't spoken to Aamir Khan in a decade, but what did I have to lose by calling one of the most powerful people in India? Just my dignity!

"Hey, Aamir sir, it's Vir. Das?"

"Hello, Vir."

"So, I have this movie I want to make, and if you don't produce it, it'll never get made."

"That's a lot of pressure," he said.

And then he asked me to come narrate it to him. So, I did. I don't get intimidated often, but I do get intimidated by him. Every single time he calls and I see his name flash on the screen, I stand up. If I tell my friends that I spoke to Aamir on the phone, their first question is, "Did you stand up?" Fuck yes, I stood up. So, I narrated the movie, and he told me he'd give me some money to shoot a few scenes, as a test.

"Shoot them on an iPhone with no lighting, I don't care," he said.

Off I went. I called a director I knew who had been subjected to this same test by Aamir.

"I'm going to just shoot it on my iPhone with no lights and no locations," I told the director.

"Are you insane?" he said. "You need to produce the shit out of it."

So, I used a comedy club as a location and turned different areas of the club into sets—a bedroom in one corner, a living room in another. We had lights, and a crew. People volunteered their time because they heard that Bollywood powerhouse actor-producer-choreographer Aamir Khan was involved. I had directed my Netflix specials, but this was something different. The minute I walked on set and called "action," I felt the exact same way I did the first time I performed stand-up and got a laugh: *Why haven't I been doing this all along?*

Because life is a series of belonging, not belonging, fucking up, and making things right. It's a long and winding path to something unexpected, or something you dreamed about that felt totally out of reach.

Aamir saw our test scenes and told us to go make the movie. The night I got the news, I went out and got smashed to celebrate, and that was the last time I had a decent night's sleep for a year.

Over the three months of making the movie, I broke a finger, cracked a rib, and injured my cricoid cartilage. I had footprints on my back from being kicked, and I pulled a muscle in my hip. My sciatic nerve was totally out of whack. It was terrible and glorious and amazing. The main character tries so hard to fit in, and horrible things keep happening to him, so by the end enough horrible stuff has happened that people just accept him for who he is. But he has to get the shit beat out of him, literally and metaphorically, to understand that. What that means for the lead actor is A LOT of physical punishment if you're doing your own stunts and fight scenes.

Making a movie is a completely surreal experience. You're living in a bubble where time doesn't exist, with a group of people who become your family for a brief period. There are emotional breakdowns, fights, and utter chaos. In one scene, my character gets a finger chopped off and blood spurts everywhere, so we had to test a prosthetic finger with a tube that shot out blood to make sure it worked. I stood there with an assistant director, a girl from a small town in India, as we threw fake chunks of flesh at each other's faces to see if it would stick, and this was *important work*. At least, it was to us.

After months of night shoots, action sequences, stunts, explosions, and chases, the final shot was an insert of a single teacup. It was the most boring shot you could imagine, and it took forty-five minutes to light. When we finished, the whole crew erupted into applause and brought out a cake that said LET'S MAKE A MOVIE, which was something I said all the time during the shoot. "Okay, people, let's make a fucking movie!" And we did. After we ate the cake and broke down the set and said our goodbyes, I went home and slept for three days.

I'm going to direct and act in three more projects in the next two years. Where the fuck is this sleep going to come from? It's weird to have eyes with bags underneath them because you're making movies, but a bright light in them because you are GETTING TO MAKE MOVIES!!!

I always dreamt cinematically. My dreams always had shots and angles and light changes and even soundtracks. Every single movie I have written has been about a dream I had. I've directed a few shows and a feature film by now and I hand-drew every shot I ever took, filling pages and pages of storyboard books. It never occurred to me that stand-up and direction can give you the same high. Not once, not until I did it.

Kavi Shastri and I, who met on *Love Aaj Kal*, two complete and utter outsiders who were background extras on a movie, just codirected for Aamir Khan Productions. Sink or swim, that's a cool story. I just don't know how it ends.

One thing I know from doing stand-up is that if I sink or swim, it's on me. By the time you read this, we'll know whether I made something amazing and all our lives changed, or I made something terrible and nothing changed. Or maybe I made something in the middle. I can't control the reaction. None of us can. But I do know that on the Friday it comes out, I'll be at Gaiety Galaxy, sitting with the crowd. Part of them, but not. On the outside, taking it all in.

One could argue I'm right back where I started. Like I said . . . it's a circle.

EPILOGUE

Vir at NSCI Dome in Mumbai, shooting Fool Volume *for Netflix.*

OCTOBER 2024, MUMBAI

It's 9:30 p.m. on October 19, 2024, and I'm breathing heavily. My heart is jumping out of my chest. Some sort of music is playing in the darkness. I touch my fingers to my wrist and feel my heart beat faster than it ever has before. I am going to have a fucking heart attack. How do I not have a heart attack? Wasn't there some sort of breathing thing I had heard of on an Andrew Huberman podcast or something?

Five counts in and six counts out?

Was it seven?

There is a stadium screaming all around me. Shivani is five feet away from me in the darkness, and Heeya, our chief AD, comes over and says, "Vir, it's time."

Heeya holds me by the hand and starts to guide me through the utter darkness. There is radium tape on the floor, and she has mapped the route to the stage.

My heart is going to fucking explode.

I wonder if people can see how ridiculous this looks. A man in his forties being led by the hand by some twenty-something, five-foot-nothing kid. Like a child in the parking lot of his school. Not gonna lie, it feels good to have someone helping me. I have spent the last eight weeks of my life feeling weak and sick and every kind of terrible emotion that you can imagine.

I know what the song is now. It's "Twist" from *Love Aaj Kal*, the movie I was a background extra in. Some moron thought it would be a good idea to use it as an entry song for the biggest gig of my life in this city. Some ironic nod to how far we have all come. The audience seems to be buying it.

Oh yeah . . . I'm the moron. Why the fuck is my heart beating so fast?

There are four massive LED screens above the tiny little stage. Facing all around the stadium so that no matter where you are sitting you get to see me in close-up. There is writing on them now . . . blue font on black background.

The screen says LADIES AND GENTLEMEN.

I kneel in the darkness. Heeya leaves me there. My knee is on the ground. The ground starts to shake. I can feel a vibration going through my entire body. People start to scream. There are twelve thousand of them.

I have a single clear thought: "Get your head together or you are going to fuck this up. Calm down. Make this about them. You have a job to do."

It helps. I start to think about how many of these people were stuck in traffic, got a babysitter, bought tickets in the twenty minutes we sold this show out. Some of them are thrilled with their seats, some of them are unhappy with theirs. We opened the doors late, so they've been standing in the heat. Are they pissed? I am told we shut down the Bandra-Worli

Sea Link bridge in Mumbai. That is insane. People sent me screenshots of their Google maps, where there's a clear red line across the bridge with the caption "You did this!" There are videos of people just abandoning their cabs and running toward a stadium. People. That's what this gig is about. People. Not one person.

A person came to Mumbai with basically nothing. A person sold out a stadium. A person who is about to shoot a Netflix special in four seconds. A person who will have fifteen cameras pointed at him. About 180 people are working on this person's show right now. Twelve thousand people have paid to see this person. This person came to this city as a complete outsider. Now people know this person.

People . . . this is about people . . . not a person. The person feels like he can breathe again. The person feels heat between his eyes. That's the only way I know how to describe the flow state. To me, stand-up is warmth. When it's going well, I feel the heat. Like the audience and I have the same body temperature. I feel it between my eyes, and on the back of my neck. My eyes are warming up.

The massive LED screen says VIR DAS.

And then . . .

AUGUST 29, 2024.

I'm sitting in a suite at the Taj St. James' Court hotel in London. I'm in the living room area. It's this uber-luxurious hotel that combines old-world charm with rich carpets, colonial furniture, and good old Indian service and hospitality. Maybe one of my favorite places to stay in the world. They're happy to have me and take great care of me.

I'm crying. Silently. Because a voice will not come out of my body.

I did twenty-six shows at the Edinburgh Festival Fringe, and I woke up on day twenty-seven without a voice. No signs leading up to it. No warnings. No vocal fatigue. I just woke up without a motherfucking voice.

I can make sounds, but it feels like my throat is broken by a massive lump inside it. I sound damaged. I sound old. I sound tired, and I sound like there is not enough air and, more important, not enough soul in my body.

No matter what I do, a voice will NOT FUCKING COME OUT OF MY MOUTH.

I have not lost my voice. That has happened before, so I know what that feels like. This is different. This feels like I will never be okay again.

Oh yeah. I just sold out the NSCI stadium in Mumbai in twenty minutes. A record for an Indian artist. The show is in seven weeks. It's the second part of my new Netflix special; the London concert tomorrow night will be part one.

I have spent the entire Edinburgh Festival Fringe obsessing over this show. I had just won an Emmy for the last one. This one has to be better, tighter, more craft, less sympathy, louder laughs, no fat, all heart. I have spent twenty-six days going to the national library of Scotland and sitting in a room obsessing over every single word of this special. I haven't been drinking, not eating carbs, no smoking, no sugar. The show is ready, I am fit, I am at my fighting weight. I am also ready.

SO WHY WON'T A VOICE COME OUT OF MY USELESS, BROKEN BODY?

I have made a video telling folks that the London show has been pushed. I hit upload. I cry some more. People are amazing about it. They send me thousands of DMs of kindness saying things like, "We will come back for you whenever the new date is announced, just be well!" or "Hey man, it happens to all of us."

NO, IT FUCKING DOESN'T! Because I do not know what is happening. I cannot cancel a stadium in Mumbai that I waited fifteen years to sell out. Netflix is on board, the crew is hired, every seat in the arena is gone. So many people will lose their jobs if I cancel.

Shivani is in the hotel room with me and takes me down to the Chinese restaurant. She orders, the staff want selfies, and they try to talk to me. She has to explain that I have no voice. They all look at me sympathetically.

Then the funniest thing happens. As they talk to me, they start talking softly too. I realize that silence is contagious.

Later, we fly Air India, land in Mumbai. Then the countdown begins. The second part of my new comedy special for Netflix is going to be shot at the NSCI stadium in Mumbai, in the dome, for twelve thousand people, in seven weeks.

Dr. Nupur and Dr. Zainab are sticking a camera down my throat. Telling me I have vocal cysts and I need surgery. I'm grateful I'm not naked on an operating table telling lies while singing the national anthem. This feels very true and very real. I begin vocal therapy and medication. I will spend the next seven weeks largely in silence.

Five weeks to go and I am walking around my office rehearsing stand-up comedy in my mind because I am not allowed to use my throat. Every inch of my jaw aches. I have something called TMJ, where my jaw is locking up and I am told that my jaw is connected to my hips. So if I want to loosen my jaw I have to relax my hips. I am reminded how my jaw is usually the reason for trouble in my hips. Ever since the days of boarding school lashings, my jaw, my mouth, has been the problem.

Four weeks to go, and the team comes to me and asks if we need to cancel the NSCI show. I still do not have a voice. Netflix is paying us a lot of money to do my special. I am supposed to perform this thing and direct it? Both impossible without a voice. Also maybe spare myself the humiliation of looking weak in front of twelve thousand people? I'm on heavy medication and not allowed to work out. Even worse, I sound weak. I remind them that the poster has already been printed.

Two weeks to go and I break. I can barely get a sound out. How the fuck am I going to do two back-to-back hundred-minute shows for a taping? That's three hours and twenty minutes of stand-up comedy in one day, and I haven't been onstage in a month now. I was so fucking tight a month ago; now nothing feels right. I've gone through every joke I've ever written in the last three weeks in my head, and I'm CONVINCED I've been using my voice wrong this whole time. I cry while I pray, silently.

I am not going to be ready. I don't feel ready. I am reminded that I have NEVER felt ready. Not for my first film, not for my first kiss, not for my first date, not for Mumbai, not for Delhi, not for Alabama, not for the wedding I canceled, not for the material at the Kennedy Center, not for *Brown Men Can't Hump*. I just WAS. I was there, unready, and it happened. How is this any different?

Eight days to go, and my voice comes back . . . for an outsider. A food delivery guy hands me a parcel and I say, "Thank you, bhaisaab," without thinking. It just comes out of me. Maybe that's the trick. Not to think about it. Any of it. Just to live it. I try to remind myself to do that from this point on. My whole life has been words. It's the only good I know how to trade. Do not think about the words, but trust I've put in enough time that they now live in me and will find their way out. Can I do that for the next half of my life? What kind of book is that gonna end up being? Will I want to write that book more than I did this one? Probably not.

Three days to go and I can hear my voice fully. In seventy-two hours, I will shoot my new special. I am not ready. The maximum length of stand-up I have done so far is fifty-five minutes. I now have to do only a little less than quadruple that duration magically without running out of voice or breath. I have taken to rehearsing with a sixty-six-pound weighted vest on and leg weights so that hopefully when I do the stadium without them it feels easier.

But I can hear my voice.

I HAVE a voice. And it is different.

It does not sound the same. There is a tiny crack there that you may never notice, but I think may never go away. I'm not mad at it. It's my kintsugi. I've changed.

Kintsugi is an art where you fill the cracks of a plate with gold. And it then becomes something broken, but new. Alchemy. That's what makes comedy truly beautiful to me—at its root it is alchemy. This peninsula of words, breath, and idiocy that turns pain into thoughts, thoughts into words, words into jokes, jokes into laughter, laughter into memory, memories into headlines, happy headlines into bullshit, bullshit into thoughts, thoughts into words, words into jokes, jokes into laughter, laughter into memory . . . on and on. Burnt effigies into love.

Alchemy.

October 2024.

I wait in the dark. On one knee at the stadium.

The massive LED screen says VIR DAS.

And then . . .

I step onto the stage.

The ground is shaking. Mumbai is here. I am . . . afraid. I breathe, and I think of Watson, and then I think of who is in this room. Fellow wanderers, complete vagabonds, utter idiots, committed clowns, and lonely people looking to belong. Always looking, never knowing. Here to see a fool.

I belong to them, as much as this book belongs to you.

And now I have a job to do.

I know because I see golden orbs, and stage dust, and the temperature is just right.

It's warm, so warm, almost like we're outside.

ACKNOWLEDGMENTS

This is in no particular order. To my manager, Reg Tigerman, for convincing me to write this book and that books in general are a good idea. People still read books, right? To my entire team at United Talent Agency for allowing me to have a career while living on a different shore across the world.

To Shivani Mathur, and Watson, Stupid, and Lucy Das for giving a constant traveler the feeling of home. To my parents, Ranu Das and Madhur Das, for always being in my corner. Priyanka Khirmani, of Khirmani and Associates, for keeping me a free man. To every employee who worked at Weirdass Comedy and helped build the Mumbai comedy scene, thanks for making me laugh while we were working to make other people laugh. To Akash Sharma for being my strong, unshakeable right hand. To Rakshita Swami who fearlessly led Weirdass Comedy through a very tough pandemic. To Kavi Shastri for being the amazing other side of my creative brain.

To Delhi Public School Noida for recognizing that I was different and pushing me. To Knox College for giving me the audacity to be something different. To Collective Artists Network for helping build and rebuild this crazy India career that has ended fifteen times. To Trisha Das for being the voice in my head. To Siddharth Singhal for being a consistent cheerleader and manager. To Ivan Davidson for telling me I was good enough.

To Netflix India for creating a place for my comedy to live. To the

Comedy Cellar for giving me a comedy home in New York City that makes me want to do better. To the Habitat Mumbai for being Mumbai comedy's ride or die and the place I try out all my new ideas. To Aamir Khan Productions for *Delhi Belly* and *Happy Patel*, two very different kinds of film schools. To Dennis and Sharon Coehlo for giving us a home in Goa to escape to. To Mrs. Surjeet Khanna for standing up for me more than I ever stood up for myself. To Kaizad Gherda, Sidd Coutto, and all the other members of Alien Chutney for teaching me how to write songs and what it means to be in a band.

To the cinema of Mel Brooks for showing me that silly is best. To George Carlin for telling it like it is, Richard Pryor for turning pain into comedy, Eddie Izzard for making it seem like it was all made up on the spot. To the people at CNBC for allowing a scared-shitless twenty-four-year-old to tell jokes. To Zoom TV and *The Times of India* organization: Sorry, I still don't know what a VJ is.

To Dina Gachman for helping me pull all these ideas and feelings out of my head. To my grandfather B.S. Das, otherwise known as Baba, for teaching me the value of stories. To the city of Mumbai for giving me a quintessentially Mumbai "dream come true" story.

And finally, to anyone anywhere across the world who ever bought a ticket to come see me and gave me the privilege of their laughter. It is absolutely insane to think that somewhere across the world right now sits another person who is interested in the madness in my mind. Thank you for showing up, even if I was occasionally fifteen minutes late. Thank you for Ubering. Thank you for walking. Thank you for taking a train or a flight. Thank you for getting babysitters. Thank you for skipping a college class. Thank you for saving money. Thank you for booking the row that you couldn't afford. Thank you for booking the only row that you could afford. Thank you for always keeping me humble and making me scared to disappoint you.

What a privilege, what a life, what a journey! Thank you so much.

ABOUT THE AUTHOR

Emmy-winning comedian and actor Vir Das has emerged as one of the most beloved voices in comedy worldwide. *The New York Times* says, "No artist embodies the globalization of stand-up like Vir Das." Vir has released five comedy specials on Netflix, and clips online have amassed hundreds of millions of views. He was nominated for his comedy special *Vir Das: For India* in 2021, and in 2023 he won his first International Emmy Award for Best Comedy for *Vir Das: Landing*. In addition to his success on the stand-up comedy stage, Vir has created, produced, and starred in multiple series, including ABC's *Whiskey Cavalier*, Netflix's *Hasmukh*, and Amazon's *Jestination Unknown*. He also starred in Judd Apatow's Netflix feature *The Bubble*, and he is currently developing various film and television projects.